Devotions for Confession

The Prodigal Son, detail from a drawing by Rembrandt

DEVOTIONS
FOR
CONFESSION

Selected and arranged by
Fr. Hubert McEvoy, S.J.

SOPHIA INSTITUTE PRESS
Manchester, New Hampshire

Imprimatur: Mechliniæ, 14 Februarii 1962
P. Theeuws, Vic. Gen.

Sophia Institute Press
Box 5284, Manchester, NH 03108
1-800-888-9344
www.SophiaInstitute.com

Sophia Institute Press is a registered trademark of Sophia Institute.

hardcover ISBN 979-8-88911-274-7
ebook ISBN 979-8-88911-275-4

Library of Congress Control Number: 2024936169

First printing

Contents

Acknowledgments

The compiler is grateful to the following publishers for permission to quote extracts from their publications:

Catholic Truth Society (Jarrett, *Meditations for Layfolk*, and Bellord, *Meditations on Christian Dogma*).

Clonmore & Reynolds (Graef, *The Sacrament of Peace*).

Collins & Co. (Vann, *The Paradise Tree* and *The Seven Swords*).

Geoffrey Chapman, Ltd. (Community of Saint-Severin, *Confession*).

Gill & Son Ltd. (Veuillot, *The Catholic Priesthood*).

Longman Green & Co. (Guardini, *The Living God*, and Hughes, *The Faith in Practice*).

Sands & Co. Ltd. (Van Doornik, *The Triptych of the Kingdom*; Eaton, *The Ministry of Reconciliation*; Meschler, *The Gift of Pentecost*; Marmion, *Christ in His Mysteries*; and Galtier, *Sin and Penance*).

Sheed & Ward Ltd. (Martindale, *Faith of the Roman Church* and *Sweet Singer of Israel*; Prohaszka, *Meditation on the Gospels*; Heenan, *Confession*; Wilson, *Pardon & Peace*; and St. Teresa, *Exclamations*)

Mr. Evelyn Waugh and Sheed & Ward Ltd. (Knox, *Retreat for Lay People*)

Thanks are also due to Fr. Gerald Vann for permission to quote from *The Divine Pity*.

Devotions for Confession

Introduction

Our justified admiration of the benefits of the age of frequent Communion has perhaps overlooked the benefits of what is also the age of frequent confession. Yet this ever-growing use of the Sacrament of Penance has surely immense possibilities for the sanctification of mankind if they are once realized. We cannot forget that both the Eucharist and Penance are Sacraments instituted for the "forgiveness of sins."

There is a special character about frequent confession. The definition of Penance as a Sacrament whereby sins, mortal or venial, are forgiven and the grace of God increased in the soul suggests that we have "confessions of necessity" where mortal sin is concerned, but when venial sin alone is submitted, we have "confessions of devotion" since the Council of Trent declared that "venial sins may, without guilt, be omitted in confession and expiated by a variety of other means." Such means are simple acts of sacrifice, obedience to God's will by devotion to duty, prayer, and so on. So the twelfth-century *Ancren Riwle*: "The Confiteor, holy water, prayers, holy thoughts, blessings, genuflections, every good word and every good work wash away small sins, but confession is always the chief means."

Probably the majority of frequent confessions are in fact "confessions of devotion" having their value largely in the second effect of the Sacrament, the increase of grace in the soul. When confession was infrequent, the routine method of preparation and thanksgiving given in prayer books served its

3

purpose adequately. Now, the frequent penitent, no less than the frequent communicant, welcomes help and even instruction. The Sacrament of Penance especially expects very positive cooperation from the penitent — preparation, examination, sorrow, resolution, satisfaction, thanksgiving.

The purpose of this series of preparations and thanksgivings is to direct the attention to at least some of the benefits which the practice of frequent confession provides besides the one immediately sought, the forgiveness of sins. Indeed, without some such help, it is difficult to see how that enemy of all good, and possibly the only danger of frequent confession, the deadliness of routine can fail to creep in. The book tries to give an atmosphere of freshness to each confession by focusing the attention on one or other of the ways by which the rich and varied graces of this great Sacrament can be recognized and turned to account. This was clearly the desire of Pope Pius XII: "To hasten daily progress along the path of virtue, We wish the pious practice of frequent confession to be earnestly advocated. Not without the inspiration of the Holy Spirit was this practice introduced into the Church. By it, genuine self-knowledge is increased, Christian humility grows, bad habits are corrected, spiritual neglect and tepidity is purified, the will strengthened, and a salutary self-control is attained and grace is increased in virtue of the sacrament itself" (*The Mystical Body*).

Clearly, by this approach, much more is achieved than when confession is allowed to be, as it so often is, merely a routine prelude to the reception of Holy Communion.

The Nobility of Penance

Christ was concerned with sin as a fact in life. He became man "to redeem us from sin and to teach us the way to heaven," calling "not the just but sinners to repentance." To lift souls out of the unhappiness of sin, He worked many of His miracles. Significantly, almost His last act before His death on the Cross was to forgive the repentant thief, and the first act of His risen life was to grant the power of forgiving sins in His name. It was His Easter gift to His Church, the first fruits of His passion, a gift placed in the hands of His apostles before night fell, as it is said, on the first day of the life of the infant Church. Moreover, the gift of the great Sacrament of Penance was made in circumstances which marked it forever as the "Sacrament of Peace." Repeatedly in His risen appearances, He was to give the greeting: "Peace!" It was more than a greeting — it was a command that men should always live as in possession of this "quiet of Christ," the peace of a quiet conscience.

"Once more Jesus said to them, Peace be upon you. I came . . . from my Father, and now I am sending you out in my turn. With that he breathed on them, and said to them, Receive ye the Holy Spirit: when you forgive men's sins, they are forgiven, when you hold them bound, they are held bound" (John 20:21–23). It is taken for granted that, in a world where there is so much to trouble the soul, the way to the restoration of peace must be made obvious and certain.

"Now I am sending you." There is meaning here. Previously He had allowed them to use many of His divine powers but, though a promised power, never that of forgiving sins. Now it is altogether different. Yet we are not surprised that the first result of His redemptive sacrifice should be an effective way of dealing with sin, and this time, through His representatives. He would forgive through them as He would teach and sanctify through them. St. Paul is full of the grandeur of this new way of dealing with sin. There has come into the world at last the possibility of that long-lost peace which Adam knew before the Fall when God, "as he walked in the garden in the cool of the evening," called him when he was hiding from God as the apostles were hiding from men before the Easter gift came to them. Divine forgiveness is now as worldwide as man's sinfulness.

That is the nobility of the Sacrament. Every confession shows us the divine plan worked out. By Baptism, itself the complete amnesty from guilt, each soul enters, fully innocent, into the possession of Christ's kingdom in which it is meant to live henceforward in the atmosphere of Christ's peace. All the same, it is a peace to be guarded; for besides the inheritance of peace, Christ brought also a sword. The need for vigilance is in the warning at Baptism — "Keep the commandments of God and carry thy robe of innocence before the judgment-seat of our Lord Jesus Christ." There are two kingdoms claiming man's allegiance: "Satan also has claimed power over you all that he can sift you like wheat" (Luke 22:31), but you must "make it your first care to find the kingdom of God and his approval" (Matt. 6:33). St. Thomas Aquinas puts it clearly, yet with a certain tenderness: "He is our unfailing source, and to him, more than to any other, we must be bound. It is God whom we spurn and lose when we sin; it is God whom we must regain by believing in him and once more pledging our loyalty to him." We do that through the sacrament of peace. There we find the new forgiveness, the Easter gift, the peace of Christ, and admission to the unity of the Church (if our sin has been sufficiently serious to exclude us) at the banquet which the Father spreads for His wayward child. Our Lord, and we do well to remember it, admitted His apostles to Communion at the Last Supper, in spite of their weaknesses, and certainly because of them.

There we have the difference — we can still sin, but "sin shall no longer have dominion over you" (Rom. 6:14).

On the eve of His passion, Christ dictated His legacy: "Peace I leave with you, my peace I give unto you; not as the world giveth do I give unto you. Let not your heart be troubled, nor let it be afraid." These are phrases as carefully chosen as in a last will and testament. So Christ the King carries on His redemptive work, presenting to His Father a "kingdom of peace" but also a "kingdom of justice." Sin is a "breach of the peace" in the soul as it is in ordinary life. Because justice must also reign, His representatives are in the confessional, not as Justices of the King's Bench administering a penal code, but as Justices of the Peace concerned more with maintaining the decreed atmosphere of peace than with punishment, restoring the peace of the kingdom to such as have lost it by sin, granting the royal pardon in the King's name when guilt is admitted and the "recognizances" of amendment given. Peace and justice meet in the acceptance of the penance, something which our human dignity craves, that we may do something to heal the wound which sin inflicts on the body of Christ, the Church. This is an aspect of our sinning so rarely taken into account, even by the devout, that special emphasis is laid upon it in these devotions.

When in repentance we use this great Sacrament, we feel, as Pope Pius XI said, "that we have not demeaned ourselves in any way." On the contrary, we are, merely by being the object of divine forgiveness, endowed with dignity and nobility. Fr. Vann quotes the words of Péguy: "The sinner stands at the very heart of Christendom," and asks, "Why is the sinner the central figure? Why is he more competent than others to say what Christianity is about?

Because Christianity is the religion of redemption, of rescue, of mercy, of God's tenderness and pity; because Christianity means the coming of light from darkness, of life from death: the dry bones live again. And it is the sorrowing sinner who knows this process, knows it in his heart, far more than the ninety-nine who need not penance; it is the sinner who knows the need of a Savior by more than hearsay.... The sinner then, in this sense of the word, is indeed at the heart of Christendom because it is in him preeminently that the Christian mystery is achieved, the divine alchemy is achieved; the sinner knows better than others what Christianity is about because to him sin and grace, mercy, forgiveness are not words learnt in a catechism but realities known in the immediacy of bitter experience.... It should give us new heart, not only for ourselves but for the world as a whole. For the world as a whole, whether it admits it or not, is the Christian world, is the world for which Christ died, the world in which the redemptive process is being worked out to its fulfilment, the world which travaileth even until now, so that it is wrong for us to despair" (*The Seven Swords*).

The Profitable Confession

Before Confession

Go, not only for the purpose of obtaining absolution, but also to obtain grace and strength as you would from Holy Communion. Go with the conviction that this is a Sacrament which has the power to decrease evil in you and to increase good. Go, indeed, with expectation — What will God show me about myself this time? What suggestions will He make to me if I am alert for them?

If there is a period during the hearing of confessions when there are usually fewer penitents, choose that time if you can; it is a kindness to the priest and to others, as well as better for yourself, especially if you wish to ask for advice.

Read unhurriedly the preparation in the book up to and including the prayer for self-knowledge.

In examining your conscience, have your own method of quietly stimulating your memory about, for instance, the places you have been in since your last confession, the people you have met and dealt with, the duties which are yours both to God and your neighbor, and even to yourself. It is a great help in the examination of conscience for confession to be prepared for it by a brief daily, or fairly frequent, "survey" between your confessions. It is a great source of strength not to wait for our next confession before expressing sorrow for our sins. The lists of sins found in most prayer books have their uses, but we must remember that they are rather like the kitchen shopping lists which don't tell you everything in the shops. All the same, it does no harm to read through one occasionally. We do develop faults of which we are quite unaware.

Decide, after your examination, which of your venial sins you are going to confess, remembering that it is not necessary to mention them all. In deciding which you will mention, recall that the dignity of the Sacrament requires a direct, sincere statement. It does not accord with this dignity to try to "be on the safe side" by mentioning sins because you think you *may* have committed them. The Roman Catechism says: "If a person is not sure of having committed a sin, he is not obliged to confess it, but if he does, he must add that he is not sure." It really is better not to say "I missed Mass" if common sense tells you that you could not help it or you were lawfully excused. This obviously applies to many other faults. Sincerity and directness require that in the case of serious sins, at least the approximate number of times should be stated, also the nature of the sin, whether in thought, word, or deed, whether others were involved or affected by it. Since we are confessing to Our Lord, we should not expect the priest to make our confession for us by having to "worm it out" of us. Also lacking in dignity is the "conversation piece" confession which goes into gossipy detail and is often a process of "excusing" rather than of "accusing."

Equally undesirable is the "standing-order" confession where clearly no serious examination of conscience has been made.

Read the prayers for sorrow and for resolution. These help you to *be* sorry intelligently, even if it happens that you have no *feeling* of sorrow. That you are at the door of the confessional proves that you have sorrow in your will. Emotional sorrow is useless by itself.

Be clear about the purpose of amendment, which is the "will" as well as the wish to avoid sin. My will to avoid sin is best shown in the precautions I mean to take even though I recognize that I may fall again, and perhaps am almost sure to fall again.

In Confession

When you say, "Pray, Father, give me your blessing," have in mind the blessing which the priest gives you in answer to your request, though this blessing may not be very audible. You will find it on page 31.

Any suitable formula for making your confession will do, but it is best to have one, even the simplest, like, "Three weeks, Father: I have been bad-tempered, spoken uncharitably, said my prayers carelessly — nothing more." The formula carries one through.

Speak clearly. One need not be loud in order to be distinct. But if with bent head you speak down to the floor, or with your hands over your face, the priest will need good hearing to catch what you say. By not speaking clearly, you make the priest's work more tiring besides running the risk of being misunderstood.

Say how long it is since your last confession in a way that will tell the priest whether it is one or many weeks or months. This is an indication of the frequency of the faults. "About a month" is accurate enough if it was from three to five weeks.

Saying the *Confiteor* in the confessional, superb act of sorrow though it be, is not expected and is hardly thoughtful when the confessional happens to be thronged. If one has an affection for the *Confiteor*, it could be said before confession. It has also been suggested that the shortened form given in the Ritual might be used: "I confess to Almighty God and to you, Father."

Indicate the end of your self-accusation by some becoming formula so that the priest knows you have nothing more you want to say. Many people say: "For these, and all sins which I cannot now remember, I ask pardon of God, penance, and absolution of you, Father." Or say simply: "That is all I can remember, Father."

Always *listen* to the penance. Some get into the lazy habit of not listening, or the worse habit of asking for the penance to be repeated, just to be on the safe side.

Whilst the priest gives you absolution, say your act of contrition quietly but audibly. It is not strictly necessary, but it does unite you in spirit with what the priest is doing on your behalf. There is a shorter act of contrition, and some will find it better to say this slowly and reverently than to hasten through the longer one which, though comforting to you, is hard on the priest who may have to listen to it so many times. Try to be conscious also of how beautifully he is praying forgiveness for you. You will find the prayers on page 31. When confessions are heavy, the priest may omit one or other of these prayers.

When the priest says "Go in peace" or some similar words, accept the peace of the Sacrament gratefully.

Always say "Thank you, Father" as you leave the confessional.

After Confession

Say your penance at once, after a moment's recollection. Repeating the penance because of distractions, or because some time later you are not sure if it was said, is unwise. Fr. Graef says the penance should never be repeated; others, perhaps more wisely, give the advice: when you have been distracted, recollect yourself, repeat the penance once and leave it at that even though you again feel distracted. After all, Our Lord has been aware of your prayer even if you haven't. Remember that distractions spoil our prayer only if they are willful, as when we said the prayer whilst looking about us or took no trouble to settle our mind; unwished-for distractions are due to human frailty and are not sinful.

That is why it is best to make the saying of the penance the first duty after leaving the confessional. In any case, since the penance is an integral part of the Sacrament, it is fitting that the penance should be linked to it as closely as possible. Reading the brief comment in the book also helps to make the mind recollected. Some make a point of *reading* the penance or going to a special part of the church to say it.

If, after leaving the confessional, you recall some sin which you would have mentioned had you thought of it, remember that such sins are in fact absolved, that the priest, in giving you absolution, said it was to the full extent of your need of absolution. Therefore, never return to the confessional unless it is a question of a forgotten mortal sin or unless you are uncertain about some direction given you by the priest.

Say the rest of the prayers in the book, especially those for thanksgiving and the Church. Try to think of some positive way in which you can show your gratitude by helping the Church and your neighbor.

For Converts

First Confession

This is worrying usually. Try to correct this attitude by remembering that Catholics are *bound* to confession only once a year, yet, without any urging, go to confession, on an average, about every three weeks. This can only mean that, whilst no one enjoys the effort, it still cannot be an ordeal. If it were, they would naturally only do the minimum. Again, they obviously would not go so frequently unless they found the Sacrament a definite help.

In examining your conscience for your first confession, reflect that you have probably learned a great deal about sin during your instructions and now have quite a different, possibly a stricter, view of sin. But God does not judge you, and you must not judge yourself, by what you know now; that is for the future, not for the past. You have, in your first confession, to mention only those faults which at the time you committed them you knew to be displeasing to God.

Converts sometimes tend to look upon all sins as equally grave. If you feel that way, you should mention it to the one who is instructing you.

Quite a lot of the fear of the first confession vanishes when you realize that the average confession takes only a minute or two and that if you wish, you can let the priest make your first confession for you by asking questions, though it is better to begin as you mean to go on.

Regular Confession

Really, your second confession may be the most difficult because you will have to decide yourself when to make it. As soon as possible after your first is best, say, not more than a fortnight so that the ice doesn't get too hard to break. Then go monthly until you find what suits you best. But eventually, be regular; otherwise, one week or month is as good as another and quite quickly you find it's a year! As we said, confession is never easy, but it's easier if you go regularly. Don't be put off if you happen to see a little "scuffling" outside the confessional in the matter of *taking turns*. It's regrettable, but not tragic, rather an indication of the businesslike, somewhat homely, way in which people regard the confessional.

Until you feel quite at home, tell the priest: "I'm a recent convert, Father." Do not mind if he thinks you are apologizing for yourself and tells you not to, perhaps by asking: "What difference does that make?" You know it makes a big difference, and usually you will find that it establishes a sympathetic relationship which can be most helpful. If the priest asks you how the new life is going, then you have your chance to bring out anything that may be worrying you or puzzling you.

The "routine" of confession is usually a convert's main difficulty. Converts throughout their previous life have unconsciously acted on Catholic doctrine — they have done wrong in various ways, felt sorry, perhaps even told God they are sorry, and certainly tried to undo the harm or make some reparation for it, and in that way, they have, without confession, found peace of soul. Naturally, because it is Catholic teaching that our venial sins are forgiven by our other good deeds and desires. That is why to many converts, confession appears not really necessary, especially since they are probably leading better lives than before and the confessional ordeal seems rather tremendous for what it achieves. The thing to do then is to recall the Catechism statement that confession, "besides forgiving sin, increases the grace of God in the soul," as well as doing all the other wonders described in this book. The sense of futility is because the effects of the Sacrament are in the soul, and naturally, you cannot see them.

As a convert, you will be particularly assailed by the "same old story every time" difficulty. Your confession tends to be the same because it's the same you that makes the confession. Admittedly, it is a pity that we say much the same when we want to be better, but the explanation is simple — by the time we are in our late teens, which is the earliest moment when we begin to be really critical of ourselves, our tendencies and weaknesses become rather established. But there is this comfort: though your sins are the same because you are the same person, you really are more sorry for them, more anxious to amend and to make reparation for them.

Above all, be clear that temptations are not sins; also, that it is not necessary to confess all venial sins and the exact number of times even if you know them.

In the Matter of Scruples

The first consideration to be taken seriously in any attempt to ease the burden of scruples must be this — confession, the Sacrament of Penance, instituted by Our Lord to bring forgiveness and consequent peace of soul and mind, must be completely adequate for its purpose, and that for every soul without exception.

The essential effect of Penance takes place within the soul. It is peace with God, "peace of soul." Since it is a sacramental effect, there is joined to this peace of soul the knowledge and certainty of forgiveness, guaranteed by the Sacrament. Thus to "peace of soul" in the purpose of God there is joined "peace of mind" or an awareness of this peace of soul based on faith in the efficacy of the Sacrament. That is, there is a recognition, a judgment, in fact, of the state of tranquility. The Sacrament has done what we expected it to do. We may be conscious of this tranquility, even before absolution, because we have properly disposed ourselves for it; we know what it is we have to regret, and "true contrition is sealed by peace."

Whenever, then, the scrupulous person finds, after confession, no firm conviction of complete forgiveness, and therefore, no real peace of mind, he must reach this conclusion — "It is not the Sacrament which is at fault, but myself; confession is not wrong in relation to me, but somehow I am wrong in my relation to confession." Until this admission is made, there can be no lasting cure for scruples.

Devotions for Confession

Wrongness in Our Relation to Confession

Somehow, we are wrong in our relation to confession. This is where the real task of diagnosing the cause of scruples begins. That "somehow" can be broken down into a great many possible causes. Peace of mind is based on a recognition, a judgment. But the judgment can itself be disturbed; it can also be disturbed by factors outside itself — by the will and by the emotions. Here we have the true cause of scruples — the balance of the intelligence, the will, and the emotions is somehow upset. The three are not working harmoniously to produce the tranquility of conviction.

This section is not a treatment of scruples in general. Some few cases of scrupulosity cannot be helped by reading but only by careful personal guidance. But because the majority of scruples do appear to be traceable to any or all of three controllable causes — faulty knowledge, faulty judgment, or faulty emotional control — there is good reason to suppose that the scrupulous can do a great deal to recognize their condition and help themselves to a cure.

Faulty Knowledge

Faulty knowledge, that is, of the Sacrament itself and of its requirements for valid confession with sure forgiveness, easily leads to the attempt to make confession do what it was never meant to do. St. John tells us: "It is when we confess our sins that he forgives our sins, ever true to his word, ever dealing right with us, and all our wrong-doing is purged away" (1 John 1:9). That is surely straightforward. We are meant in confession to give a simple, sincere statement of our sins. All Our Lord's dealings with sinners — and they are frequent enough — show that He required for full forgiveness nothing more than the simplest, undetailed expression of guilt and regret. The publican struck his breast: "O God, be merciful to me, a sinner!" and went down to his house justified. Mary Magdalen, at His feet, spoke no word, and to the other sinful woman, His only question was: "Hath any man condemned thee?" If generous forgiveness is the measure of repentance that is sufficient, the prodigal son's confession was perfect though he said no more than, "Father, I have sinned."

The scrupulous must, then, first realize that nowhere in the Gospels is there any sign that Our Lord wants the kind of confession they want to make. Moreover, the Church, through which God makes His wishes known, does not expect it either, having said clearly that the only sin one is *bound* to tell in confession is mortal sin, and about which we are certain; this for the simple reason that in mortal sin our eternal salvation is at stake.

The word *bound* is important. We *may*, in confession, speak of details, of the attendant circumstances of a sin, to relieve our minds, to secure guidance, to increase humility (we must, of course, mention them if they notably increase the malice of the sin). But once we insist on doing so with the idea of making forgiveness more certain, we are guilty of devising a special "sacrament of penance" for our own private use which is not that of Our Lord, nor of the Church, and will never bring peace, simply because it is not Our Lord's sacrament.

Fr. Steuart, S.J., helps the scrupulous to recognize themselves: "The little that he wants — only the recognition that I have sinned. Not what have you done or how often you have done it, but are you sorry that you did it? . . . The devil tries to throw a veil over the face of Christ, by making us dwell on the enormity of our sin and nothing else. God wants of us the approach of confidence, not of fear (except in the sense of reverence), and that we should know that there is no limit to the forbearance of God. He is longing only that His own should come to Him, or if they have strayed, come back. Fear is lack of confidence, of trust, it even amounts to doubt. We fear we have exhausted the mercy of God; we must call up in front of our vision the figure of Christ" (*Spiritual Teaching*).

When scrupulosity centers upon venial sins, mental anxiety is a pure waste of energy since their confession is optional because they do not separate us from God. If we confess them, it should be with the knowledge that the simple statement of the sin, or of any doubt attaching to it, is understood by the Church *to embrace all those uncertainties and half-apprehended motives and hesitations which accompany most of our human activity.*

Faulty Judgment

Faulty judgment is a cause of scruples in the sense that intelligence is not allowed to play its due part in the judgments made about our actions so that dissatisfaction inevitably follows because our own conclusions do not then present themselves to us as reasonable. In a certain and true sense, the confessor is a judge, but the Sacrament supposes that the penitent presents his case intelligently after a considered, even if brief, judgment of his actions. St. Paul, always a severe critic of himself, makes insistent appeal for this use of intelligence. His direction before acting, "Scrutinize it all carefully, retaining all that is good, and rejecting all that has a look of evil about it," is what we should be able to do *after* acting. In other words, "retaining the good" is simply recognizing what we can honestly say in our defense; "rejecting the evil" is recognizing where we willfully did wrong. The scrupulous, if they will face up to it, are as able to decide for themselves whether an action was sinful, that is, whether they deliberately intended to offend God, as they are to decide whether a particular remark was thoughtlessly made or was deliberately intended to wound another.

The dignity of the Sacrament demands that we make use of our intelligence. Its neglect is the besetting fault of the scrupulous. They often think they have, or are trying to have, and sometimes are thought to have, a delicate conscience. It is not so. Examining one's conscience is exactly the same process as recalling what it was that I did which happened to give pleasure to someone. This must be so because conscience is not a separate operation of my intelligence but an ordinary process of reasoning. A delicate conscience is like a fine balance; it weighs accurately and in a normal way judges an action to be sinful, mortally or venially, or not sinful at all but merely foolish, careless, indiscreet, and so on. "A delicate conscience confesses personal failings simply, calmly, directly; the scrupulous conscience confesses in a confused, meandering, doubtful and repetitious sort of way. The delicate conscience is immediately relieved and at peace after absolution; the scrupulous conscience finds in frequent and compulsive confession only temporary relief or none at all. The delicate conscience evokes a healthy and proportionate sorrow for human failings but remains unanxious and untroubled in its hopeful relationship to Almighty God; the scrupulous conscience is persistently uneasy, fearful, distrusting not only self but the confessor, and even Almighty God" (Hagmaier and Gleason, *Moral Problems Now*).

This is how the scrupulous person should reason with self when mortal sin is in question:

"The Church tells me clearly that there are no doubtful mortal sins — and for this reason: mortal sin is a matter of my eternal salvation, which God so earnestly desires, even more than myself, that He will surely make it clear to me if my sin is really mortal that I may duly repent of it as such. For me to persist, then, in trying to decide for a mortal sin when I am honestly in doubt is nothing less than trifling in a matter of serious import, namely, my eternal salvation. This must be so since I could not with full knowledge commit a mortal sin and afterwards become uncertain of such a momentous decision of the will. Therefore, that I am in the least degree uncertain is clear proof that my sin, however serious, was still not mortal."

If it happens that later knowledge shows me that a past sin could have been mortal had I realized its gravity, my rule must be that I judge it by what

I knew at the time, not by what I now know. My present knowledge is for the future. "Here, as in other matters, it is the truth that brings freedom. Truth may be despotic, but in the estimation a man forms of his personal guilt, it demands no more than that he should be frank with himself in answering the question, How far did my knowledge go, and what was my intention?" (Galtier, *Sin and Penance*).

Uncertainty may also arise as to whether a past mortal sin was confessed, or fully confessed. This is how I must reason: "If there is now mortal sin on my soul, God is to be counted upon, as we said, to make it clear. In any case, I know that I could not omit, or play down, a sin known to be mortal without remembering the fact."

Therefore, certainty as to the manner of confessing mortal sin can always be had. Scrupulosity, however, so far as confession is concerned, centers upon the simplest human actions and their possible sinfulness. It is usually not just a fear of sinning, which is desirable in all of us, but an uncertainty about having sinned. Strictly, in this diagnosis, the remedy also appears — to say, "I am afraid that I have sinned" or "I am afraid lest I sinned" is the same as saying, "I am uncertain whether I sinned." All I have to do is think quietly until I reach *reasonable* certainty, the kind of certainty that I have when I say, "I honestly think so and so is a genuine friend."

Faulty judgment is particularly evident when the penitent wants more than this reasonable certainty. He is then not merely trying to make *confession* do what it is not meant to do but is also trying to make his *mind* do what it is not made to do; namely, to reach *absolute* certainty about all past actions. Many human limitations make this difficult, even impossible, but there is one human limitation in particular which the scrupulous should note. It is this — the mind, besides its function of remembering, has also a function of "forgetting," of clearing itself, as it were, as one cleans the slate or the magnetic tape for a fresh recording. To prove how effectively this works, ask yourself,

"Just what was it that I did a fortnight ago today?" You will be surprised to find that you have completely forgotten almost everything about which you were perfectly clear at the time. It should be obvious then this must be even more so in the case of spiritual affairs, and that to try and recapture accurately the state of mind in which an action was done, sometimes even but a few hours previously, is to do violence to the mechanism of the mind, and at best to induce a recollection which cannot be trustworthy since it is forced.

It is best to say: "I will confess this sin now according to the memory of it which God has seen fit to leave in my mind." The same decision should be made about that notoriously difficult question, the degree of consent given to unworthy or impure desires in thought or action.

It is important to see that all this is but ordinary common sense. We all admit that there have to be in our day-to-day living what we call varying degrees of certainty. We say: "I feel sure, absolutely sure, tolerably certain, I am inclined to think, it is my considered opinion," and we are prepared to act accordingly. Scrupulosity is nothing more than the refusal to accept and live with this human limitation in spiritual matters as well. What sensible, even saintly, people do is not good enough. The scrupulous are not content to say in confession, "I gave bad example" or "I may have given bad example." Is there pride here? Again, sensible people will confess a doubtful sin "as God sees it"; the scrupulous person, and it is really unconscious arrogance, wants himself to see it as God sees it; he will not make the surrender, which is really a virtuous act of humility and trust, of being content with his finite intelligence. He persists in making yet another inspection of the doubtful sin, only to find it different yet again and, as the mind becomes more and more exhausted, even more doubtful. This, too, when all the time God, whom the scrupulous person is presumably trying to tell, sees the sin exactly as it is. The scrupulous person should say firmly: "God knows my sin; He doesn't want me to tell it to myself, which is what I'm really trying to do. He only wants me to be sorry for what it was. Even if God did let me see my guilt as He sees it, would I then have God's view of myself? Would I have any real conception of His pity for my weakness, of the gladness with which He pardons me, of the generous grace He wants to give me? Yet these are the things it would profit me most to know. Why cannot I trust Him and tell Him simply?"

It is faulty judgment again to chase after the ripples of consequences which widen out after so many human actions — bad temper and a quarrel between parents; the children overheard and were troubled; neighbors perhaps listened and were scandalized; the relatives got to know; the quarrel spoiled a child's birthday. There's no end to it! It is true, of course, that circumstances can increase the malice of a sin, but only if they are foreseen. Otherwise, we are certainly not *bound* to mention them. We *may* do so, but they are better kept as silent motives for deeper sorrow. In no sense need they be painfully recollected or ferreted out as evidence required for full forgiveness. Doing so only diverts the attention from the real fault, which is want of control. Far better to concentrate on the stone which caused the rippling circle of consequences. The scrupulous would cure themselves if, instead of this detective inquiry, which only deepens their worry without increasing their sorrow, they would ask simply: "What made me do this?"

St. Paul asks: "What man knoweth the things of a man?" (1 Cor. 2:11). Even the clearest and most unprejudiced thinker is never a safe judge in his own cause, and certainly the scrupulous person is not. That is why Our Lord instituted a divine sacrament which would supply for all this human uncertainty. Who can fully know what sin really is — his own or anyone's? Will any amount of scrupulous searching find that out? That is why, "never, and certainly not in confession, does Christ demand from us perfect acts. He does not even demand the utmost possible, or confession would really be a perpetual torture, the source of ever-new worry and anxiety" (R. Graef, *The Sacrament of Peace*).

24

The scrupulous must accept the task which they shirk — they must acknowledge the duty which is theirs of using their gift of intelligence, after simple prayer for light and guidance, just as they do in their ordinary human affairs.

"The chief difficulty of the scrupulous person is precisely his over-dependence, his need to have others make decisions for him.... What he needs more than anything else is somehow, in some way, to learn to stand on his own two feet and make decisions for himself" (Hagmaier and Gleason, *Moral Problems Now*).

Faulty Use of the Emotions

Faulty use of the emotions, of fear, sorrow, anger, and the rest, but particularly of the emotion of fear is probably the commonest cause of scruples. Here again there is misuse of God's gifts; the emotions are an important part of our human makeup. If intelligence is necessary for full and fruitful living, so is a correct use of the emotions. They are meant to stimulate the intelligence, and for that purpose, we use them constantly. Faced unexpectedly with an onrushing car, it is the emotion of fear which dictates the dash to safety, as it is fear of ignorance which makes us learn, fear of poverty which makes us work. Our Lord experienced the whole range of human emotions and shows us the correct use of them, even of the emotion of anger. "In most cases, the intellect of the scrupulous is in no way impaired; he is usually able to judge the moral actions of others and to give them correct advice, though he may be helpless in evaluating the simplest of his own activities. The impairment lies in the emotions, not in the intellect" (Hagmaier and Gleason, *Moral Problems Now*).

We all know misuse of our emotions, how hatred and anger drive us to make unfair judgments, how fear, particularly of failure, can destroy initiative. So can the unreasonable fear of sin prevent correct judgment by intelligence of our actions. We should learn to look dispassionately at our temperament when assailed by scruples. We may be through fear "perfectionists," chafing at all human limitations or because we cannot put the examiner's mark of 100 percent on all we do. We may be habitually anxious, fearful about every task; we may be of too reserved a disposition, living too much with ourselves and, therefore, seldom checking our judgment of a situation, or for that matter, of a sin, with that of ordinary people. We may be naturally timid, afraid to take decisions. Whether these defects are due to physical weakness, faulty religious training or outlook, or simply to a laziness of will, which is only another form of mental or physical laziness, these temperamental defects will hamper our judgment in spiritual matters as in all others.

"Whatever leads to discouragement, to despair, to trouble, is contrary to charity, which teaches us to make every effort, even with fear and trembling, but never to distrust the goodness of God, who wills all men to be saved and to repent. We serve a Master who is rich in mercy to those who invoke him; he cancels a debt of ten thousand talents on a very brief petition. We must have sentiments worthy of his goodness" (St. Francis de Sales).

So, whilst fully recognizing the torture that scruples can cause, it must be admitted that compared with the trouble the scrupulous take to get others to understand them and the trouble they undoubtedly give to others, they take singularly little trouble to understand themselves, with whom the problems originate. It does seem that, after initial help from the confessor, the quickest and the most lasting cure of scruples is self-cure. It seems inevitable that the patient, if we may so style him, must sooner or later learn to diagnose himself, observe himself, catch himself out in his attitudes of indecisiveness, fear, and depression and, as St. Thomas More says, "with reasoning thereat" discuss his attitude with himself until he sees how emotion is interfering with calm judgment. Training oneself to manage one's emotions in ordinary affairs is the first, and necessary, step to calm and reasonable assessment of one's spiritual state, and so to an intelligent, and therefore tranquil, examination of conscience.

Just as we learn in ordinary life to do a certain amount of simple doctoring of ourselves by the recognition of obvious symptoms and their known causes and remedies, the scrupulous should make themselves familiar with, and be convinced by, the simple distinctions of moral theology so ably presented in simple books on confession. We say, *be convinced by them*. "Is it likely that God, having created us as we are and given us the nature that we have, would call upon us to do things which are too difficult for that nature, which war against it? That is nonsense; He has made us to harmonize, and it is only we who have distorted it.... God doesn't ask me to play the game and not tell me the rules" (Fr. Steuart, S.J., *Spiritual Teaching*).

St. Teresa of Avila made the prayer: "Well knowest thou, my God, that in the midst of all my miseries I have never ceased to recognize thy great power and mercy. May it prove of avail to me that I have never offended thee in this."

In the end, it comes to this: "Turn back to the Lord and let thy sins be" (Ecclus. [Sir.] 17:21) and to remembering that God, through the Sacrament of Penance, gives peace of soul; it is for us to translate that into peace of mind.

St. Francis de Sales on the Scrupulous

Our first misery is that we esteem ourselves; if we fall into any sin or imperfection, we are astonished, troubled, impatient simply because we thought there was something good, resolute, solid within us, and, therefore, when we find there was no such thing, we are grieved and offended at having deceived ourselves. If we knew ourselves as we really are, instead of being amazed to see ourselves prostrate on the ground, we should be surprised to see ourselves stand for a single day, or even for one hour.

Endeavour to perform your actions perfectly, and having done this, think no more about them, but think of what you have yet to do, advancing with simplicity in the way of God without tormenting your mind. It is necessary to detest your defects, not with the detestation of trouble and vexation, but with a tranquil detestation, to behold them with patience, and to make them serve to lower you in your own esteem. Regard your faults with more compassion than indignation, more humility than severity, and preserve your heart full of a sweet, calm, peaceful love.

Live entirely to God, and for the love He has borne to you, endure yourself with all your miseries. I do not mean to say by this that you should be continually tying up your mind in order to hold it in peace; for you must do everything with the simplicity of a loving heart, keeping near Our Lord as a little child near its father, and when you happen to fall into some faults, whatever they may be, ask pardon meekly, saying to Him that you are certain

He loves you well and will forgive you, and this always simply and joyfully.... It is only the too great care we have of ourselves that makes us lose our tranquility of mind and leads us to odd fantastic notions, for when we meet with some contradiction and perceive a little of our want of mortification, or when we commit some fault, however trifling it may be, we immediately imagine that all is lost. Is it so great a wonder then to see you stumble occasionally? "But I am so miserable, so full of imperfections!" Bless God for having given you this knowledge, and do not lament it so much; you are very lucky in knowing that you are only misery itself. After having blessed God for the knowledge He has given you, remove that useless tenderness which makes you mourn over your infirmities.

In a word, be not vexed because you have been vexed, nor troubled because you have been troubled, nor disquieted because you have been disquieted by those annoying passions, but resume control over your heart and place it lovingly in the hands of Our Lord, begging of Him to heal it.... It is necessary to be sorry for faults committed, with a repentance, strong, calm, peaceful, and constant, not turbulent, not disheartened. Are you certain that delay on the highway of virtue is your own fault? If so, humble yourself before God, implore His mercy, entreat His forgiveness, confess your fault and cry to Him for mercy, even in the ear of your confessor, to obtain absolution for it. But having done this, remain in peace, and having detested the offence, embrace lovingly the disquiet that is left to you.... It is good to have confusion when we have a knowledge and feeling of our misery and imperfection, but we must not rest there, or fall therefrom into discouragement, but lift our heart to God by a holy confidence, the foundation of which should be in Him and not in ourselves, for we change, but He never changes, always remaining the same and as good and merciful when we are weak and imperfect as when we are strong and perfect.... To be a good servant of God is not always to be consoled, always in sweetness, always without aversion or repugnance for virtue. If it were, then neither St. Paul, nor St. Angela, nor St. Catherine of Siena would have properly served God.... Timid and cautious souls who always wish to see where they put their foot, who turn aside every moment for fear of making a false step, who cannot bear to have their shoes soiled, never advance so quickly as others who are less punctilious but more daring. It is not those who commit the least number of faults that are the most holy but those who have the greatest courage, the greatest generosity, the greatest love, who make the boldest efforts to overcome themselves and are not immoderately apprehensive of tripping, or even of falling and being dirtied a little, provided they advance.

God is a great master; let us allow Him to act. He will not fail at His work. Let us propose to ourselves to avoid carefully the least thing in the world that could displease Him. But when we have fallen into some faults, let us be sorry on His account, not on our own.

Live joyful: Our Lord looks upon you, and looks upon you with love and with tenderness in proportion to your weakness. Never let your mind entertain thoughts to the contrary, and when they come, regard them not, turn your eyes away from their unworthiness and turn them towards God with a courageous humility to speak to Him of His ineffable goodness by which He loves our poor, abject, fallen nature, notwithstanding all its misery. Our imperfections need not please us; we must say with the great apostle: *Miserable man that I am, who will deliver me from the body of this death?* But they need not astonish us or take away our courage. We should rather draw submission, humility, and diffidence in ourselves from them, but not discouragement, nor affliction of heart, much less doubt of the love of God towards us. Thus God does not love our imperfections and venial sins, but He loves us much in spite of them.

The Confession Prayers

The Priest's Blessing

May the Lord be in your heart and on your lips, that you may truly and humbly confess your sins in the name of the Father, and of the Son, and of the Holy Ghost. Amen.

The Absolution

May almighty God have mercy on you and, having forgiven your sins, lead you to life everlasting. Amen.

May the almighty and merciful Lord grant you pardon, absolution, and forgiveness of your sins. Amen.

May Our Lord Jesus Christ absolve you, and I by His authority do now absolve you from every bond of excommunication (suspension), and interdict as far as I am able and you have need of it. Therefore do I absolve you from your sins in the name of the Father, and of the Son, and of the Holy Ghost. Amen.

May the passion of Our Lord Jesus Christ, the merits of the Blessed Virgin Mary, and of all the saints, whatever good you have done, or whatever evil you have suffered, win for you forgiveness of your sins, an increase of grace, and the reward of eternal life. Amen.

Devotions for Confession

Preparations and Thanksgivings

Preparation 1

God and the Sinner

"He had entered Jericho, and was passing through it; and here a rich man named Zacchaeus, the chief publican, was trying to distinguish which was Jesus, but could not do so because of the multitude, being a man of small stature. So he ran on in front, and climbed up into a sycamore tree, to catch sight of him, since he must needs pass that way. Jesus, when he reached the place, looked up and saw him; Zacchaeus, he said, make haste and come down; I am to lodge today at thy house. And he came down with all haste, and gladly made him welcome. When they saw it, all took it amiss; he has gone in to lodge, they said, with one who is a sinner. But Zacchaeus stood upright and said to the Lord, Here and now, Lord, I give half of what I have to the poor; and if I have wronged anyone in any way, I make restitution of it fourfold. Jesus turned to him and said, Today, salvation has been brought to this house; he too is a son of Abraham. That is what the Son of Man has come for, to search out and to save what was lost" (Luke 19:1–10).

"My heart thrills with joy in the Lord; pride in the God I worship lifts my head" (1 Kings [1 Sam.] 2:1).

Devotions for Confession

The Value of the Sacrament

"Jesus looks upon him; Zacchaeus catches the bountiful glance which penetrates his soul, pervades it, and gilds it. Who could describe this glimpse? It is the in-pouring of God and the imparting of strength. By such a glance the soul is transfigured. We do not recognize him if he himself does not look at us; therefore we beg and implore him to glance at us, to come, to call us, he the warm strong life which fills us and loves.... Only let me possess thee, thy love and appreciation. When bounty, beauty, strength, and life knock at our door, do not let us lock them out but receive them with joy and give way to their power. God gives immeasurably more than he takes. He demands money, flesh, and blood and gives in their stead soul, strength, and joy. It will be our salvation when Jesus enters and we are able to humiliate ourselves, to be enthusiastic, to become purer, to rejoice, and make sacrifices; when our soul throbs with joy and our thoughts soar.... Let no one say that he cannot do it. We are able to love, let us love therefore and make sacrifices. Let us wash and burn out the ignoble and let us believe in the good and in its strength. The friendship of Jesus reforms and saves us" (Prohaszka, *Meditations on the Gospels*).

"Humility goes first, and honour comes in her train" (Prov. 15:33).

In Humility

"We must not take up any attitude we like towards God. We have not to decide what God shall be allowed to command us; nor pick and choose among his undoubted commands. Our attitude must be, from the very outset, one of *awe*. Even though, under the light of the Christian revelation, we know that God loves us, we have to beware of off-handedness, familiarity, frivolity, indolence. May God, from time to time, *overwhelm* us with a sense of his majesty and holiness.

"It is when we become quite 'small' in the presence of God, that we can advance with complete serenity and simplicity" (C. C. Martindale, S.J., *The Sweet Singer of Israel*).

"Seeing before our eyes, O Lord, our own acknowledged sinfulness, there is little pride in our hearts; but do thou lift heavenwards, O Lord, the eyes that are humbled before thee, for our hope is, and forever must be, in thee" (African Collect, fifth century).

"What are we, but folk of his pasturing, sheep that follow his beckoning hand?" (Ps. 94:7).

For Confidence

"Seven times the just may stumble, and rise to their feet again" (Prov. 24:16).

"Let us remember what Christ himself has said: 'I am not come to call the just, but sinners.' And indeed did he not call Matthew the publican to the rank of an Apostle? And whom did he place at the head of his Church that he willed to be without 'spot or wrinkle, or any such thing, but that it should be holy and without blemish,' and for the sanctification of which he came to give all his precious Blood? Whom did he choose? Was it John the Baptist, sanctified from his mother's womb, confirmed in grace and of such eminent perfection that he was taken for Christ himself? No. Was it John the Evangelist, the virgin disciple, he whom Christ loved with a special love, who alone remained faithful to him, even to the foot of the cross? Again no. Whom then did he choose? Knowingly, deliberately, our Lord chose a man who was to forsake him. Is it not remarkable?... Why was this? Because his Church would be composed of sinners. Except the most pure Virgin Mary, we are all sinners; we have all need of divine mercy.... Our miseries, our failings, our sins, we know them well enough; but what we do not know — souls of little faith — is the value of the Blood of Jesus and the power of his grace.

"Our confidence has its source in God's infinite mercy towards us, and increases in proportion to our sorrow for sin" (Marmion, *Christ in His Mysteries*).

"Blessed Lord, grant that I may obtain thy mercy shortly when I call for it with true penance and hope of forgiveness. For why? Because I have ever trusted in thee" (St. John Fisher).

"Fear him? Ay, and trust him; you shall not miss your reward. Fear him? Ay, and fix your hope in him; his mercy you shall find, to your great comfort. Fear him? Ay, and love him; your hearts shall be enlightened" (Ecclus. [Sir.] 2:8).

For Self-Knowledge

"So gracious the Lord is, so merciful; turn back to him, and his face shall be hidden from you no more" (2 Par. [2 Chron.] 30:9).

"There is nothing brighter than the eyes of God. Nor is there anything more comforting. They are inexorable but they are the source of hope.

"To be seen by him does not mean being exposed to a merciless gaze but to be enfolded in the deepest care. Human seeing often destroys the mystery of the other. God's seeing creates it.

"We can do nothing better than press on into the sight of God. The more deeply we understand what God is, the more fervently we shall want to be seen by him. We are seen by him whether we want to be or not. The difference is whether we try to elude his sight, or strive to enter into it, understanding the meaning of his gaze, coming to terms with it and desiring that his will be done" (R. Guardini, *The Living God*).

"My God, thou knowest me through and through; all my present, past and future are before thee as one whole. Thou seest all those delicate and evanescent motions of my thought which altogether escape myself. Thou canst trace every act, whether deed or thought, to its origin, and canst follow it into its whole growth and consequences. Thou knowest how it will be with me at the end; thou hast before thee that hour when I shall come to be judged. . . . Yet, O Lord, I would not that thou shouldst not know me. It is my greatest stay to know that thou readest my heart. O give me more of that open-handed sincerity which I have desired. Keep me ever from being afraid of thy eye, from the inward consciousness that I am not honestly trying to please thee. Teach me to love thee more, and then I shall be at peace, without any fear of thee at all" (Newman, *Meditations and Devotions*).

"Let me listen, now, to the voice of the Lord God within me; it is a message of peace he sends to . . . his loyal servants that come back now to take counsel of their hearts" (Ps. 84:9).

For Greater Sorrow

"A blessed man is he who fears the Lord, bearing great love to his commandments" (Ps. 111:1).

"True contrition is something very great. Perfect contrition, that is, repentance from love borne to God, already brings about complete reconciliation with God, even without the sacrament of penance. 'Many sins are forgiven her who loveth much.' After such perfect contrition there remains only the obligation to confess these sins at the next opportunity. For the sacrament of penance, imperfect contrition, that is, repentance from fear of punishment, suffices. In conjunction with the sacrament of penance, imperfect contrition brings about what perfect contrition has wrought by itself. In the sacrament of penance, Christ, as it were, takes upon himself part of our contrition, to make confession as easy as possible for us.... The more frequent our confessions, the more frequent are such acts of contrition and resolutions in our soul. In conjunction with the sacrament of penance, even imperfect contrition works in our soul the miracle of raising from the dead, of healing, nourishing and strengthening" (R. Graef, *The Sacrament of Peace*).

"Have mercy on me, O God, according to thy great mercy; not according to my wretchedness but according to thy great mercy which is far greater than my extreme need.... I crave great mercy from thee, for it is not the way of such generosity as thine to give but little, and scarce would my prayer deserve thy hearing did I ask but little mercy from thee" (attributed to St. Anselm of Canterbury, twelfth century).

"Well for us that he at least is patient, repent we, and with flowing tears ask his pardon! He will not overwhelm us with reproaches, as men do; not his the human anger that bursts into flame. Abate we our pride, and wait on him with chastened spirits; entreat him with tears to grant us relief at a time of his own choosing" (Jth. 8:14).

Resolution

"Take courage; never slacken your resolve; still for your loyal service you shall have reward" (2 Par. [2 Chron.] 15:7).

"The inner life must have a master-motive. What is it to be? There is another question that must first be answered. What was the divine purpose in giving me life and placing me in this world? The answer is simple yet mysterious. We all know it — and we all forget it. He made us for his own glory. And we know that each human being's contribution to that glory is first and foremost the saving of his own soul. Now there is only one master-motive worthy of such a life with such an end and purpose — the will of God. That was the master-motive of the life of Christ our Lord. 'My food,' he said, 'is to do the will of him that sent me that I may perfect his work' " (Stephen J. Brown, S.J., *From God to God*).

"If, O my soul, thou wouldst have God love thee, renew his likeness in thy-self, and his love will come to thee; be once more his counterpart, and his love will pursue thee. Reflect on the nobility he has given thee — for as God is everywhere in life, ruling all things, so to thy bodily frame does thy soul give life, moving and ordering in all its parts. God lives and loves and so dost thou. O noble creature that thou art, recognize thy dignity, for not only is his nature clearly marked in thee, but in thy likeness to him lies thy beauty. As thy Creator, who made thee to his image, is charity, goodness, is humble, meek, patient and merciful, and all else that is noble, as we are told of him, so thou, too, hast been created that thou mayest be instinct with charity, purity and holiness in all their nobility and beauty, yet with humility and gentleness. The stronger these virtues are in thee, the nearer to God thou art and the deeper will grow thy likeness to him" (Anon., twelfth century).

"We are his design; God has created us in Christ Jesus, pledged to such good actions as he has prepared beforehand to be the employment of our lives" (Eph. 2:10).

Thanksgiving 1

A Thought Before Saying One's Penance

"It is but just, after God's exceeding mercy in remitting our sin … that we should in some way atone for our guilt. But the sacrament does lessen the amount of punishment due to us. It applies Christ's merits to our souls, and therefore the performance of satisfactory acts, as part of the sacrament, has a greater effect than the same acts would have independently thereof. But even as these could lessen the temporal punishment due to us, clearly the sacramental satisfaction can lessen this punishment even more effectively" (H. Harrington, *The Sacrament of Penance*).

For Perseverance

"One who gazes into that perfect law, which is the law of freedom, and dwells on the sight of it, does not forget its message; he finds something to do, and does it, and his doing of it wins him a blessing" (James 1:25).

"We may reckon up our failures, and ask whether, with such a record, success can ever be hoped for. In a hundred ways we may plead to be dismissed, and suffered to remain second- or third-rate. But human nature pleads against itself. It answers that the power that has made can also unmake; that the creature which has voluntarily accepted the yoke can also set itself free. It is true we cannot all be heroes, if by heroism is meant something that depends upon accidental gifts, something that must shine conspicuously before the eyes of other men. But if it means a constant aspiration for the right; if it means a steady march towards it, no matter what may tempt us to look elsewhere; if it means an unflinching refusal to be beaten, however often the enemy may have us down; if it means a strong determination that the right thing shall be done in us and by us, at whatever cost to ourselves — then yes, even we can be heroes, even we can never be conquered, and not to be conquered is to win" (Abp. Goodier, S.J., *The Meaning of Life*).

"My God, thou knowest infinitely better than I, how little I love thee. I should not love thee at all, except for thy grace. It is thy grace which has opened the eyes of my mind and enabled them to see thy glory. It is thy grace which has touched my heart, and brought upon it the influence of what is so wonderfully beautiful and fair. How can I help loving thee, O my Lord, except by some dreadful perversion, which hinders me from looking at thee? O my God, whatever is nearer to me than thou, things of this earth, and things more naturally pleasing to me, will be sure to interrupt the sight of thee, unless thy grace interfere. Keep thou my eyes, my ears, my heart, from any such miserable tyranny. Break my bonds — raise my heart. Keep my whole being fixed on thee. Let me never lose sight of thee, and while I gaze on thee, let my love of thee grow more and more every day" (Newman, *Meditations and Devotions*).

"Fear the Lord, and doubt his promises? Love him, and not keep true to the way he shews us? Fear the Lord, and not study to know his will? Love him, and not find contentment in his law? Fear God, and not keep the will alert, the soul set apart for him? Be this our thought, that it is God's power we have to reckon with, not man's" (Ecclus. [Sir.] 2:18–22).

Devotions for Confession

In Gratitude

"Home-coming at last, consolation at last ... The harvest of men's thanks, it is I that bring it to the birth. Peace, the Lord says, peace" (Isa. 57:18).

"Let our gratitude be ardent and inspired by love, let it be humble, and from the knowledge of our sinfulness and undeservingness, and from the knowledge of the sublimity of God, let it be practical. Our life should be a *Deo gratias*" (Prohaszka, *Meditations on the Gospels*).

"In thy mercy, O Lord, save us. We suffer, as thou well knowest, from our own foolishness, and our hearts are often troubled, knowing the just judgment we deserve; but let the glad memory of this our pardon give peace to our hearts" (Gothic Breviary, seventh century).

"All so transitory; and what men you ought to be! How unworldly your life, how reverent towards God!" (2 Pet. 3:11–15).

In Forgiveness of Others, as We Have Been Forgiven

"So may the peace of Christ, the very condition of your calling as members of a single body, reign in your hearts" (Col. 5:15).

"O God, thou didst so richly endow blessed Stephen with thy own gift of forgiveness, that he not only followed thy example in his passion, but so learnt thy lesson of patience as to plead for his persecutors.... Courageously he bowed his head to the hail of stones from impious hands, and with yet greater courage prayed for those who stoned him. Surely he who, forgetful of any thought of revenge, so prayed for his enemies, will, mindful of the law of charity, be not found wanting by those who beseech him" (Gothic Breviary, seventh century).

For the Work of the Church, Christ's Body, Hindered by Our Sins

"Experience shows us that, like Christ, we have to cast our satisfactions into the great store of human merits and satisfactions in union with his, and then we draw forth, as our share of the total, infinitely more than we contributed. Each one has to bear his own burden proportionately; but his contribution is infinitesimally small, on account of the great proportion taken by Christ. Imitate St. Paul who said: 'I rejoice in my sufferings … and fill up those things that are wanting of the sufferings of Christ, in my flesh.' … As you have contributed to the sum of sin which Jesus bore, contribute as much as you can to the sum of satisfaction which he, in union with humanity, offers to the Father" (Bellord, *Meditations on Christian Dogma*).

"Let us now pray thee in humbleness, O Christ the Saviour. … Show mercy to thy servants and forget not our sufferings, how we stumble with feeble heart and miserably go astray. But come now, King of men, and linger not, for we have need of thy mercies, that thou deliver us, and in righteousness grant us salvation, so that henceforth we may ever do better things among thy people" (Anglo-Saxon Prayer).

Preparation 2

God and the Sinner

"There is no sound tree that will yield withered fruit, no withered tree that will yield sound fruit. Each tree is known by its proper fruit; figs are not plucked from thorns, nor grapes gathered from brier bushes. A good man utters what is good from his heart's store of goodness; the wicked man, from his heart's store of wickedness, can utter nothing but what is evil; it is from the heart's overflow that the mouth speaks.

"How is that you call me, Master, Master, and will not do what I bid you? If anyone comes to me and listens to my commandments and carries them out, I will tell you what he is like; he is like a man that would build a house, who dug, dug deep, and laid his foundation on rock. Then a flood came, and the river broke upon that house, but could not stir it; it was founded upon rock. But the man who listens to what I say and does not carry it out is like a man who built his house in the earth without foundation; when the river broke upon it, it fell at once, and great was that house's ruin" (Luke 6:43–49).

The Value of the Sacrament

"What means it that you so transgress the Lord's command, to your peril, forsaking him, and by him forsaken?" (2 Par. [2 Chron.] 24:20).

"Penance is that moral virtue by which we turn our minds from sin to God, regretting the evil we have done, endeavouring to make reparation, and purposing to sin no more.... Nature itself dictates this sentiment to upright and generous minds when conscious of offences against parents, rulers, benefactors, and God most of all. We have examples of penance in Adam, Noah, David, the Israelites, the Ninevites. Penance was the burden of the prophet's continual exhortations; it was the cry of our Lord's precursor, 'Do penance for the kingdom of heaven is at hand.' St. Augustine says that no one, however blameless, should dare to appear before God without having done penance. The virtue of penance is an essential condition of validity for the sacrament of penance; without it the sacrament is an empty form and a mockery of God. The virtue alone is of so great efficacy that it supplies for the absence of the sacrament when there are obstacles to its reception....

"Penance has a further signification. It is a sacrament in which God gives efficacy to our sentiments of penance, and gives us assurance of pardon. One of our greatest requirements is repeated forgiveness for our daily sins, and the assurance of it.... These graces are given to us by God through certain outward observances, which remind us of our needs, indicate the nature of the grace accorded, compel us to make a definite effort, suggest the habits of mind that are required, impress our memory, and give us a certain moral assurance that the divine action and our action have been duly exercised. The sacrament of penance, like the other sacraments, has this further advantage, that it acts not merely in proportion to our dispositions, but with an additional efficacy implanted in it by the goodness of God. It gives us more definite and efficacious graces of forgiveness than could be gained by the Jews of old in virtue of their repentance, or by those outside the Church, who do not know of the divine ordinance that supplements our imperfect dispositions, and gives a new value to our inadequate sorrow for sin.... Such is the sacrament of reconciliation, of peace, of comfort to troubled souls. Few words are of more happy augury than those of Jesus to his Church: 'Whose sins you shall forgive, they are forgiven'" (Bellord, *Meditations on Christian Dogma*).

In Humility

"He that was once brought low shall be high in renown; the downcast eye shall win deliverance" (Job 22:29).

"Our self-accusation should be open and honest. Some of us seem to be contented with establishing in our examination of conscience a harmless formula in which sins can be covered up. Nice words are chosen which aim at deceiving the confessor. Thus, in many cases, we have regular concealment rather than disclosure of the conscience. We should accuse ourselves in meek humility rather than adding an excuse to every sin. The plain facts should be stated rather than long stories recited. This applies in particular to the sins against the sixth commandment" (R. Graef, *The Sacrament of Peace*).

"And that, Father, is thy desire that we should aye reckon that we had need of thy help, and that we should not trust on ourself and fully put our trust in thee. And then, Father, for to make a full end, we ask, *sed libera nos a malo* — Deliver us from evil" (Hilton, *The Goad of Love*).

"Human pride must be abated; no room for any greatness but the Lord's" (Isa. 2:11).

For Confidence

"It is he that rescues me from every treacherous snare, from every whisper of harm. Sheltered under his arms, under his wings nestling, thou art safe; his

faithfulness will throw a shield about thee. Nothing shalt thou have to fear"
(Ps. 90:3–4).

> "He stood to be baptized with sinners
> As one of them he fasted in the desert
> As one of them he was tempted
> He was a friend to the timid Nicodemus
> He was a friend to the Samaritan woman
> Telling her of her own sins
> Making her confession for her
> He was a friend to her friends
> He was a friend to the publican, Levi
> He dined with him and his friends
> Till self-respecting men were scandalised
> Saying: Why doth he dine
> With publicans and sinners?
> He was a friend to the woman who was a sinner
> Saying: Many sins are forgiven her
> Because she hath loved much
> And to her: Go in peace
> Thy faith hath made thee safe"
> (Abp. Goodier, S.J., *The Life That Is Light*).

"Graciously hear us, we who long for thee, O Lord, and in thy kindness teach us to be confident and happy in the thought of thee. Thou art ever near to those who suffer; pay heed, then, to our repentant prayer and fill our hearts with the peace which is thy own, surpassing all human understanding" (Gothic Breviary, seventh century).

"He has given charge to his angels concerning thee, and they will hold thee up with their hands, lest thou shouldst chance to trip" (Matt. 4:6).

For Self-Knowledge

"The Lord is God; his light shines out to welcome us" (Ps. 117:27).

"May the Lord Almighty bless us. In the fullness of his mercy, may he give strength to our hearts, sanctify our minds, widen our hearts, ennoble us with chastity, and continually increase our worthwhileness by the doing of good works. May he give us quiet of mind in the fulfilling of our hopes, and grant us final perseverance and the strengthening of our charity. Let his powerful protection be our defence against the deceits of the world and of Satan. May our petitions always seem good in his sight that he may graciously and generously grant our desires, bring to nought the evil we have done and give us the graces we need" (Bobbio Missal, seventh century).

"Behold my heart, O my God, behold it within, search it, because I remember, O my hope, that thou dost cleanse me from all unworthy affections, drawing my gaze to thyself, plucking my feet from the snare" (St. Augustine, *Confessions*).

"Thy kindly influence, Lord, thy gracious influence is all about us. At the first false step, none is so ready to rebuke us, to remind and warn us of our error, bidding us come back and renew our loyalty to thee" (Wisd. 12:1–2).

For Greater Sorrow

"You will be distressed, but your distress shall be turned into joy" (John 16:20).

"It is the teaching of the Catholic Church that imperfect contrition, or attrition, as it is called, is sufficient when we go to confession. . . . It is important to understand that attrition is without value for the purposes of the sacrament of penance unless it be built upon the right motives. Sorrow for natural reasons is not enough. Humanly speaking, with no formal reference to God, sin can be seen as something repulsive. But it must be regarded as repulsive because it deprives the soul of its final end. . . . Not only is the soul made to God's image and likeness, but God himself dwells in the soul by grace. But for sin, God would remain united to the soul" (J. C. Heenan, *Confession*).

"What shall I do, O Lord my God, about those evils by which, through thy just decision, thou dost allow thy servant to be tried, and even at times overthrown? Indeed, my Lord, they are past numbering, these evils by which my sinful soul is troubled. Nor is there always that urgent sorrow, that care to avoid them that I would desire. . . . I can but own all this to thee, my Jesus, for I know thee as my Saviour, my hope and my comfort" (St. Aelred of Rievaulx, *Pastoral Prayer*).

"I will turn all their sorrow into joy, comfort and cheer their sad hearts" (Jer. 31:13).

Resolution

"Beloved, choose the right pattern, not the wrong, to imitate. He who does right is a child of God; the wrongdoer has caught no glimpse of him" (3 John 11).

"The wind breathes where it will, and thou canst hear the sound of it, but knowest nothing of the way it came or the way it goes"; the Holy Spirit is not like some egotistic genius, determined that his interference should be recognized and acknowledged wherever it is brought to bear. He is quite content that his inspirations should seem, to us, bright ideas of our own; that his shaping of our characters should be unaccompanied by any glow of feeling, such as might indicate the source whence it comes. The pattern he weaves in us is something contained in, not super-added to, the common fabric of our lives.

"But because he will work thus imperceptibly, that is no reason why we should pretend that he is not there, behave as if we were the masters of our own destiny, and needed no impulse from without. We shall be happier about the decisions we make, and gain from that a sense of confidence which will help us to justify our decisions, if we make a practice of appealing for his unseen, unfelt influence at every cross-roads of our lives, even the most insignificant" (R. A. Knox, *Pastoral Sermons*).

"O God, Sanctifier of the faithful, their guide and their safeguard, forgiver of sinners and restorer of innocence, consoler of the sorrowful, O gracious and kindly Paraclete, the true support of the faint-hearted, change my evil impulses to good, and give increase to my worthier desires. Change my sadness to cheerfulness, my insincerity to uprightness, my half-heartedness to earnestness, my fears into love and my desire of earthly good to heavenly, my love of passing things to eternal" (Thomas à Kempis, *Meditations*).

"And now ... all that rings true, all that commands reverence, and all that makes for right; all that is pure, all that is lovely, all that is gracious in the telling; virtue and merit ... let this be your rule of conduct. Then, the God of peace will be with you" (Phil. 4:8–9).

Thanksgiving 2

A Thought Before Saying One's Penance

"We must say once again that it is useless to try to understand the acts of the penitent except in terms of love. It is out of the question to make 'satisfaction' apart from love, and if our sins call for reparation … this very act of penance should be one of justice activated by love; it will be supernatural only if it comes from the heart" (Community of St. Sévérin, *Confession*).

For Perseverance

"You must hold what is evil in abomination, fix all your desire upon what is good … buoyed up by hope, patient in affliction, persevering in prayer" (Rom. 12:9–12).

"Once more, do not let us be surprised; never let us forget that Christ, our model in all things, was tempted before us, and not only tempted, but touched by the spirit of darkness; he permitted the devil to lay a hand upon his most holy Humanity.

"Above all, do not let us forget that it was not only as the Son of God that Jesus overcame the devil, but likewise as the Head of the Church; in him, and by him, we have triumphed and we still triumph over the suggestions of the rebel spirit. This is in fact the grace that our Saviour wins for us by this mystery; herein is to be found the source of our confidence in trials and temptations; and it only remains for us to see how unshaken this confidence ought to be, and how, by our faith in Christ, we shall ever find the secret of victory" (Marmion, *Christ in His Mysteries*).

"O God, Lover of all that is good, guide of our wills, do not suffer me to follow blindly my emotions, but do thou ever be my Leader that I may walk according to thy good pleasure. O heavenly King, grant me the freedom of the kingdom which thou hast promised to the loyal of heart; strengthen me that I may avoid sin, help me to love thee alone and to obey thee, thou who art the support of every creature. Save me, then, by the sign of thy cross, in soul and body from enticements to sin ... and from all dangers, both those I know and those which I do not suspect" (Prayer of Nerses, eleventh century).

"Pray, so that you may not enter into temptation" (Luke 22:46).

In Gratitude

"My Lord, my Master, my strong Deliverer, it is thou that shieldest my head in the day of battle" (Ps. 139:8).

"Confession, then, there must be, for confession alone gives stability to any conversion to the cause of God. If men were constituted differently, something more purely interior *might* suffice to restore relations of love between themselves and God; but we must take men as we find them, as our Lord did, and by his great sacrament of mercy, which is expressed by confession and the sincere acknowledgment of guilt, the hunger of the human heart is alone fully satisfied.... The sincere penitent, the soul that is truly sorrowful for the evil it has done, desires some sign and assurance that his return to

God and a better life is real. He wants to *hear* words of pardon. He wants to *see* his sins handled by someone who has power to cast them aside for ever. He wants to be nursed and tended; he would have his wounds washed by some experienced hand, he longs to face the future with courage. And so, in the conversion to grace, in the forgiveness of the past, there is speech, there is intercourse: the sins are specified and handled, words of power and truth are spoken. All is above-board, and the work is complete and permanent. On these lines it was that our Lord founded the sacrament of his love for penitents" (R. Eaton, *The Ministry of Reconciliation*).

"O my dear Lord, how merciful thou hast been to me! When I was young, thou didst put into my heart a special devotion to thee. Thou hast taken me up in my youth, and in my age thou wilt not forsake me. Not for my merit, but from thy free and bountiful love, thou didst put good resolutions into me when I was young, and didst turn me to thee. Thou wilt never forsake me" (Newman, *Meditations and Devotions*).

"His promises are like metal tried in the fire; he is the sure defence of all who trust in him" (2 Kings [2 Sam.] 22:31).

In Forgiveness of Others, as We Have Been Forgiven

"How is that thou canst see the speck of dust which is in thy brother's eye, and art not aware of the beam that is in thy own?" (Matt. 1:3).

"May God, who for our sin's healing willed to be crucified, destroy in us by the power of the cross all urgings to sin that we may die to our former unworthy selves, walking henceforth in the new life which Christ our Lord has taught us. So learning the generosity of true justice, we shall not only refrain from ever returning evil for evil, but rather seek to give comfort where we may. This will, indeed, be an offering acceptable to God" (Benedictional of John Longlonde, sixteenth century).

For the Work of the Church, Christ's Body, Hindered by Our Sins

"It was through him that all things came into being, and without him came nothing that has come to be. In him there was life, and that life was the light of men.... He, through whom the world was made was in the world, and the world treated him as a stranger. He came to what was his own, and they who were his own gave him no welcome. But all those who did welcome him he empowered to become the children of God, all those who believe in his name; their birth came, not from human stock, not from nature's will, or man's, but from God" (John 1:3–13).

"For all we are Christ's creatures, and of his coffers rich, And brethren as of one blood, as well beggars as earls,

For on Calvary of Christ's Blood Christendom 'gan spring,
And blood-brethren we became there, of one Body won"
(Langland, *Piers Plowman*).

"O God, who fashionest all things, but the crown of whose work is man, made in thy likeness and gifted with intelligence, to whom, when thou hadst made him and brought to what thou wouldst have him be, thou didst further adorn with divine gifts, giving him particularly the gift of charity, that so all might be one, even as thou and thy only-begotten Son, our Lord and God, Jesus Christ, are one. Do thou, then, free us from all insincerity and unite us all in the unity and joy of the Holy Spirit. Grant us to appreciate the wonder of this fraternal union that we may live together, even as we are called, in the one hope of our vocation in Christ Jesus our Lord" (Liturgy of St. Severus of Antioch).

Preparation 3

God and the Sinner

"Two others, who were criminals, were led off with him to be put to death. And when they reached the place which is named after a skull, they crucified him there; and also the two criminals, one on his right and the other on his left. Jesus meanwhile was saying, Father, forgive them; they do not know what it is they are doing.... And one of the two thieves who hung there fell to blaspheming against him: Save thyself, he said, and us too, if thou art the Christ. But the other rebuked him: What, he said, hast thou no fear of God, when thou art undergoing the same sentence? And we justly enough; we receive no more than the due reward of our deeds; but this man has done nothing amiss. Then he said to Jesus, Lord, remember me when thou comest into thy kingdom. And Jesus said to him, I promise thee, this day thou shalt be with me in Paradise" (Luke 23:32–43).

The Value of the Sacrament

"If any of us does fall into sin, we have an advocate to plead our cause before the Father in the Just One, Jesus Christ" (1 John 2:1).

"I once did a great injury to a very dear friend. Something he had done tried me, something he had said had roused me. I was bitter at the moment, reckless of consequences; at the same time I knew within my heart that his friendship would bear the strain. I let myself go; I spoke the stinging word, did the wounding deed, turned on my heel and slighted him. He took the insult and said nothing; he was older, greater than I, and could afford to forgo an apology. When we met again, it was as if nothing cruel had been done. Since then we have gone on as before: our friendship has never diminished. But I know him too well to suppose that the memory of that day can ever fade from his mind.... Though all is past and done with, yet the sorrow abides; though love has increased, yet the pain is always there; though friendship has restored me to equality, yet the craving is greater now than ever it was before to make atonement and to show him that I am true. I know now of what I am capable; I know how much his friendship can be trusted; and the fact that we both love each other the more because of what has happened, does but make me remember without ceasing the injury that I once did him.

"If this is true of a friend among men, what shall I say of the Friend of friends? *'Peccatum meum contra me est semper'* — 'My sin is always before me.' I have done him an injustice. I have resented the strain of his friendship, sacrificed him in the face of a trying circumstance, exchanged him for others, whom I had neither the courage nor the character to despise. He has taken the insult and has said nothing; it was not his dignity that was lowered, but mine that was annihilated, by the condescension. He has forgiven, and has told me so, giving me his word as guarantee. He has said that, so far as he is concerned, the past shall be as if it had never happened. But am I on that account freed from the burthen of the consciousness of shame? The fact of the insult still remains — the fact of the wound, and the scar that marks its place, still stands. If I ever forgot that, the agony that I have caused, the creature in me that could sink so low, I should be a presuming, an arrogant knave.... All the more can I never forget — no, not even though he has died, and has risen, and is in his glory. That does not alter me; it does not alter my action; it does but bring home to me the more who it is whom I have offended, what it is that I have done.

"This is abiding sorrow, that everlasting element of true contrition. It is consistent with great joy of heart, for it is the outcome of perfect forgiveness. It is consistent with a burning love; indeed, it is its necessary companion. None the less it is an agony, otherwise it would not be sorrow. 'Lord, that I had never offended thee!' Rightly understood, this is a strong heart's cry, and its note is combined of sorrow and gladness, of contrition and love, of the certainty of hope that has routed despair" (Abp. Goodier, S.J., *The Meaning of Life*).

In Humility

"Should I defend myself, in phrases of studied eloquence, being what I am? Nay, though I had right on my side, I would not plead against him as an adversary, I would sue to him for mercy as a judge" (Job 9:14).

"True humility sees everything in its place, self included, and therefore gives the first place to God in everything. Forthwith I can live in peace, and profit by my chance of orderly action. The more I stand in loving awe of God, the less I shall risk *not* working for him, with him, and through him" (C. C. Martindale, S.J., *The Sweet Singer of Israel*).

"O my Lord, how can one ask thee for favours, who has served thee so ill and has hardly been able to keep what thou hast already given? How canst thou have any confidence in one who has so often betrayed thee? What, then, shall I do, Comfort of the comfortless, and Help of all who seek help from thee? … Bid us pray to thee, and say that thou wilt not fail to give" (St. Teresa, *Exclamations*).

"None of us lives as his own master, and none of us dies his own master. While we live, we live as the Lord's servants, when we die, we die as the Lord's servants; in life and death we belong to the Lord" (Rom. 14:7–8).

For Confidence

"Draw near to me, the Lord said, and I will draw thee to myself" (Jer. 15:19).

"The sacrament is the source of the consolations of the Holy Ghost, and retains the sweetness which marked the circumstances of its institution. On the evening of Easter Day the risen Lord appeared for the first time in the midst of his disciples, and his paschal greeting was the institution of the sacrament of penance.... This paschal peace, this paschal joy, are still to be found in the sacrament of penance, and this peace and joy are none other than the Holy Ghost.... In this sacrament the Holy Ghost unceasingly plays the part of the compassionate father of the parable. He goes forth to meet the poor wanderer, he kisses him, he makes good his losses, he clothes him with a new garment" (Meschler, *The Gift of Pentecost*).

"All our well-being lies, O Lord, in cleaving to thee. Even to stray from thee is hurtful to us; to turn from thee is death. But to seek union with thee is to know the fullness of life. Grant, then, to us, O Lord, whose trust in thee is absolute, that we may find in thee true happiness" (Gothic Breviary, seventh century).

"As a shepherd, who finds his flock scattered about him, goes looking for his sheep, so I will go looking for these sheep of mine, rescue them from all the nooks into which they have strayed.... I will bring them back to their own country" (Ezek. 34:12–13).

For Self-Knowledge

"God so loved the world, that he gave up his only-begotten Son, so that those who believe in him may not perish, but have eternal life. When God sent his Son into the world, it was not to reject the world, but so that the world might find salvation through him. . . . Rejection lies in this, that when the light came into the world, men preferred darkness to light; preferred it because their doings were evil. Anyone who acts shamefully hates the light, will not come into the light, for fear that his doings will be found out. Whereas the man whose life is true comes to the light, so that his deeds may be seen for what they are, deeds done to God" (John 3:16–21).

"One may study all the sciences and branches of knowledge, all the arts and occupations, scanning the heavens, sounding the deep secrets of nature and its different kingdoms; but man, who is endowed with an immortal soul, must learn, too, to plumb the depths of his own heart, to feel the first impulse which thrusts him forward towards God, to distinguish eternal values from temporary and ephemeral, virtue from vice, and merit from fault before the tribunal of God, and to reflect on the offence and the compunction and sorrow that wipe it away" (St. Pius X).

"O Jesus most patient, who for my salvation wast dragged from one judgment-seat to another, grant me, I earnestly ask, the full light of sincerity to the right ordering of my actions. Form my understanding of things according to thy will. Enlighten my will, that it may rightly make progress in thy royal road of holiness, going in strength from virtue to virtue" (attributed to Tauler, fourteenth century).

"Where your treasure-house is, there your heart is, too. The eye is the light of the whole body, so that if thy eye is clear, the whole of thy body will be lit up;

whereas if thy eye is diseased, the whole of thy body will be in darkness. And if the light which thou hast in thee is itself darkness, what of thy darkness? How deep that will be! A man cannot be the slave of two masters at once; either he will hate the one and love the other, or he will devote himself to the one and despise the other.... Make it your first care to find the kingdom of God and his approval" (Matt. 6:21–33).

Resolution

"Each day, while the word, Today, has still a meaning, strengthen your resolution, to make sure that none of you grows hardened; sin has such power to cheat us" (Heb. 3:13).

"Men and women are his children. He has called them to life. He wants them to grow, one through the other, so that they may 'praise him in greater fullness.' He presses in on our consciences. Holiness can find room to grow only in freedom. When man fails, he is judged by God in his conscience. But the purpose of God's judgment is his desire that man should live. In his sin man feels that the deepest nerve of real life has been damaged, the nerve of goodness and union with the eternal holiness. God makes him feel this. But 'he desireth not the death of the sinner, but rather that he may turn from his wickedness and live.' God does not cut him off. He says: 'Thou hast sinned, but there is still a way. The way is different because of sin but there is still a way. Take thy sin upon thee. Overcome it and proceed.' When man acts rightly, God gives his consent and there is the bliss of his holy life in this assent, God lives therein, and God's free creatures live and grow in this affirmation" (R. Guardini, *The Living God*).

"Thou art just, O Lord, and lovest justice, and thou dost require of men sincere dealing. Deliver us, who trust in thee, from all insincerity with ourselves or others. Grant that we may always do what is pleasing in thy sight, and see to it that all our actions are marked by that uprightness and justice which alone makes them worthy of thee" (Spanish Collect, seventh century).

"Go on, then, ordering your lives in Christ Jesus" (Col. 2:6).

Thanksgiving 3

A Thought Before Saying One's Penance

"Doing penance is intrinsically a rebuilding of the damaged walls of the spiritual Jerusalem. The *Christianus poenitens* is a most hopeful person as a result of such a conviction. He is not like the Jews who sat by the river of the land of captivity, shedding inconsolable tears and feeling desolate at the thought of the distant Jerusalem; he is like the Jews after their return from captivity, busily engaged in the work of reconstructing the walls of the Holy City which their enemies had razed to the ground. But man, left to himself, is unequal to so great an enterprise. For this reason, Christian penance is to be regarded as a portion of the adorable mystery of Christ, in whom God re-establishes all things that are in heaven and earth" (Vonier, *Christianus*).

For Perseverance

"The Lord's perfect law, how it brings the soul back to life; the Lord's unchallengeable decrees, how they make the simple learned! How plain are the duties which the Lord enjoins, the treasure of man's heart; how clear is the commandment the Lord gives, the enlightenment of man's eyes! How sacred a thing is the fear of the Lord, which is binding for ever!… By these, I, thy servant, live; none ever lived by them that was not richly rewarded. And yet, who knows his own frailties? If I have sinned unwittingly, do thou absolve me. Keep me ever thy own servant.... Every word on my lips, every thought in my heart, what thou wouldst have it be" (Ps. 18:8–15).

"Let us remind ourselves again that when we talk of a second conversion, we are talking, not of something we want to do for our Lord, but of something we want our Lord to do in us. Let us ask him to effect this alteration in our lives, gradually, if he will, imperceptibly, if he will, leaving us, if he will, a prey to all the old scruples, all the old despairs; but just that touch of his artistry which will turn our cold blue-print into a masterpiece" (R. A. Knox, *A Retreat for Lay People*).

"Lord, sweet Jesus, this life is full of temptations and enemies, and help there is none, save in thee, dear Jesus. Take me, then, sweet Jesus, to be under thy rule and thy shepherding, and let thy handiwork never be undone. Take me, therefore, wholly to thy heart, that all my desiring be for thee, who wholly ransomed me, so that my heart may never turn from thee for any temptation, but ever cleave fast to thee" (Richard Rolle, fourteenth century).

"Wilt thou not choose life, long life, for thyself, and for those that come after thee? Wilt thou not learn to love the Lord thy God, and obey him, and keep close to his side? Thou hast no life, no hope of long continuance, but in him" (Deut. 30:19–20).

In Gratitude

"Bless the Lord, O my soul, unite all my powers to bless that holy name. Bless the Lord, my soul, remembering all he has done for thee, how he pardons all thy sins, heals all thy mortal ills, rescues thy life from deadly peril, crowns thee with the gifts of his kindness and compassion; how he contents all thy desire for good" (Ps. 102:1–6).

Devotions for Confession

"A good prayer of thanksgiving, from the bottom of our heart, must never be forgotten, even though it may be short. He who gives thanks will receive further gifts.... It is appropriate that sometimes we should give thanks also on behalf of the other nine who forgot to return. We should give thanks in general for the institution of the sacrament of penance and for the innumerable graces showered upon us and the whole world through this sacrament" (R. Graef, *The Sacrament of Peace*).

"Behold, O Lord, I have laid before thee the heartfelt confession of my many sins. Thy kindness has seen good to lift them from my unhappy soul. Heart and soul and all that is in me would now praise and thank thee for so great a benefit. Yet am I as deeply in thy debt also in this, that if there be evil that I have not done, it is surely because thy hand has guided me away from it, by refusing me the power to do it, or correcting my desire, or granting me strength to resist.... Indeed, my Jesus, thou art my Saviour, my hope, my comfort" (St. Aelred of Rievaulx, twelfth century).

"The Lord's mercy that is so abundant, the pardon that is ever theirs who come back to him!" (Ecclus. [Sir.] 17:28).

In Forgiveness of Others, as We Have Been Forgiven

"Father, forgive them; they do not know what it is they do" (Luke 23:34).

"O Sweet Jesus, who didst not shun the company of publicans and sinners, but showed kindly friendliness and a ready forgiveness of past sins to Matthew, to Zacchaeus, to Mary Magdalen and to the woman taken in adultery, grant that I likewise may gladly welcome all with simple charity and affection.

May I easily and quickly forgive all those who injure me" (Nakatenus, *Cæleste Palmetum*).

For the Work of the Church, Christ's Body, Hindered by Our Sins

"Here as elsewhere, the life and power of God in us have more than a merely private purpose: they are given primarily to restore *this* man, *this* woman, to oneness with God, but the oneness has its social responsibility; the healing and strengthening are intended not least to empower them to help in the redemptive activity of Christ in healing and restoring the world. 'Go, and now sin no more' is not only a negative command and encouragement: it means, too, 'Go now, and by being yourself thus filled with the light and life, help others to come to the light and the life, for that is your vocation as a Christian reclaimed' " (G. Vann, O.P., *The Divine Pity*).

"We call upon thee, O Lord Jesus Christ, and with praise beseech thee. Be with us, and in mercy grant us pardon and forgiveness. Inspire us also with holy desires such as thou mayest fulfil through us; place on our lips such conversation as thou wilt delight to hear, and let all our works deserve thy blessing. We do not ask thee to make us other than we are, but that thou wouldst make us, even as we are, one with thee. Be thou in truth Emmanuel, our God with us. Deign to stay with us, to fight the good fight with us, for with thee standing by us we shall surely prevail" (*Missale Mixturn*, seventh century).

Preparation 4

God and the Sinner

"There were some who had confidence in themselves, thinking they had won acceptance with God, and despised the rest of the world; to them he addressed this other parable: Two men went up into the temple to pray; one was a Pharisee, the other a publican. The Pharisee stood upright, and made this prayer in his heart, I thank thee, God, that I am not like the rest of men, who steal and cheat and commit adultery, or like this publican here; for myself, I fast twice in the week, I give tithes of all that I possess. And the publican stood far off; he would not even lift up his eyes towards heaven; he only beat his breast, and said, God, be merciful to me; I am a sinner. I tell you, this man went back home higher in God's favour than the other" (Luke 18:9–14).

The Value of the Sacrament

"Kindly be thy judgement of my sin, Lord, for thy own honour's sake, my grievous sin" (Ps. 24:11).

"They went to pray, that is they wanted to sink into the depths of their consciousness, to beg God for the forgiveness of their sins, to rise to his love and grace, so that they might be filled with sunshine and strength, and going back amidst men they might spread good-will and self-sacrificing love amongst their fellow-men. The Pharisee did not achieve this, haughtiness and conceit filled him with blindness instead of sunshine and led him away from God. He forgot his sins and forgot prudent fear. The publican achieved the regeneration of his soul in spite of his sins, for his repentance was humble. He who looked at himself so as to despise others, did not see God; he who for shame of seeing himself cast down his eyes, saw the Lord and found his grace. Behold we are near to the Lord in our humility; but we divest grace and prayer of its strength if we are filled with self-conceit.... The publican teaches us humility. He stands afar off, he casts his eyes down, and smites his breast. His soul is filled with the knowledge and feeling of his own misery and he seeks the grace of God.... He saw the final danger which threatened his hope and repentance and he cried out: God, be merciful to me a sinner. Behold how deeply the soul ploughs with the grace of God; how the dignity of serious thoughts comes to the surface and teaches him reverence, repentance, self-forgetfulness without lessening his trust in God. Those who act in this way will be justified" (Prohaszka, *Meditations on the Gospels*).

In Humility

"And what harvest were you then reaping from acts which now make you blush? Their reward is death. Now that you are free from the chains of sin, and have become God's slaves instead, you have a harvest in your sanctification, and your reward is eternal life" (Rom. 6:21–22).

"The desire that God's name should be something hallowed, something kept apart and rescued from all unworthy associations is not so much a favour we would ask of him as an act of benevolence towards him on our part. It is a protestation from us, that the God to whom we pray is a God of such infinite holiness, that the very name by which he is known among men should be a word not spoken lightly, but full of mystery and awe ... a hush must fall upon our hearts, a pause must be made in our tumultuous thoughts, before the right atmosphere can be established in which we, creatures of a day, can approach him who dwells in inaccessible light, the sovereign Ruler of Creation" (R. A. Knox, *Pastoral Sermons*).

"Alas for me, have pity on me.... I do not hide my wounds. Thou art the Healer, and I am weak. Thou art the merciful and I am wretched" (St. Augustine, *Confessions*).

"Know for certain, the Lord has not abandoned thee. Kind welcome the outcast shall have, from one so rich in kindness" (Lam. 3:31–32).

For Confidence

"Boldly and carefully set about your task, and the Lord will be with you" (2 Par. [2 Chron.] 19:11).

"What is repentance? It not only means that a person realizes he has done wrong, wishes it had not happened, is prepared to bear the consequences, and is determined to make amends. Repentance is more than that. Repentance is an appeal to the living God. He is the Holy One, unapproachable and intolerant of all wrongdoing. At the same time, however, he is Love and he is the Creator who has the power not only to bring man to life but to bring him to something inconceivably higher still: he has the power to re-create and purify the personality burdened and defiled by sin" (R. Guardini, *The Living God*).

"Thou, O God, canst do all things; change me into being wholly thine. Give me real life; enlighten my understanding, sanctify my soul, make me stronger in body and soul that I may depend on thee alone, reverence thee, love thee, before all else, and earnestly serve thee. From this day forward, let all my desires be in harmony with thy will and thy desire.... For to this end thou gavest me being, that I might use it in thy service" (Fr. Augustine Baker, *Holy Wisdom*).

"To the task, then, the Lord will be at thy side" (1 Par. [1 Chron.] 22:16).

For Self-Knowledge

"Listen, Lord, to my prayer; give my plea a hearing, as thou art ever faithful; listen, thou, who lovest the right. Do not call thy servant to account; what man is there living that can stand guiltless in thy presence?... Do not turn thy face away from me, and leave me like one sunk in the abyss. Speedily let me win thy mercy, my hope is in thee, to thee I lift up my heart, shew me the path I must follow; to thee I fly for refuge.... Thou art my God, teach me to do thy will; let thy gracious spirit lead me on, till I find sure ground under my feet. For the honour of thy name, Lord, thou wilt grant me life" (Ps. 142:7–11).

"But do, sometimes, take stock of your position; make sure that other interests do not wholly engross and absorb your spiritual energies, cutting down unreasonably the time, interfering unseasonably with the attention, which you owe to the things of God; make sure that your pleasures are not becoming an idol, to be schemed for, looked forward to, lived for, instead of recreations that you simply take, and take with gratitude, as they come. Examine yourself to find, not the sin you most often commit, but the thing in your life which counts for most next to your religion, the thing which is more likely than anything else to count for even more than your religion. And then imagine to yourself what would happen if a strong temptation came across your path in that very matter" (R. A. Knox, *Pastoral Sermons*).

"I beseech thee, loving Jesus, King of everlasting glory, to remember me, poor as I am, in the kingdom of thy Father, and to send now from heaven the Paraclete, the Holy Spirit, to be my true comfort, bringing me greater earnestness and even greater wealth of the gifts of the Spirit" (Thomas à Kempis, *Meditations*).

"Thanks to thee, O Lord my God, for coming to me and making me aware of my sinfulness. As if it were, for the first time, I have, through thy inspiration, seen once more into my heart and know myself as I really am. I will seek, now, one of thy friends and will make known to him my faults, as thou hast bidden me do, that his counsel and help may free me from my sins and restore me to thy friendship" (Anon., twelfth century).

"Then, sudden as the dawn, the welcome light shall break on thee, in a moment thy health shall find a new spring; divine favour shall lead thee on thy journey" (Isa. 58:8).

For Greater Sorrow

"Make thy peace with him, as thou lovest thy own wellbeing; so shall fair hopes attend thee. Let his lips be thy oracle, his words written in thy heart. Turn back to the Almighty for thy healing, and rid thy dwelling-place of guilt. Firm rock shalt thou have" (Job 22:21–24).

"It is the peculiar spirit of Christian repentance to live with the conviction that things can be made right again in the most complete manner, however great the havoc that may have been wrought. There might be true sorrow without any such persuasion. Man could be profoundly contrite, but also deeply convinced that the wrong done will be eternally an incurable wound in the spiritual world. Now such is not the grace of Christian penitence. It is, on the contrary, a sorrow full of faith in a power that builds up everything that has been pulled down" (Vonier, *Christianus*).

"O kind and sweet Lord Jesus Christ, Saviour of the world, I, an unworthy sinner, yet redeemed by thy precious Blood, do now humbly yet gladly have recourse to thee, my God and my Saviour. I beseech thee, Lord, to direct me in soul and body, even to my very thoughts and words; and so to rule me that I avoid all occasions of sin lest I fall into some snare of evil. My God and my Redeemer, make me ever cling to thee, make me ever loyal to thee, that none of life's chances may ever part me from thee" (*Libellus Precum*, eighteenth century).

"Lord, I have sinned greatly in what I have done; give my sin quittance" (1 Par. [1 Chron.] 21:8).

Resolution

"It is for thee, servant of God … to aim at right living, holiness and faith, and love, and endurance. Fight the good fight, lay thy grasp on eternal life, that life thou wert called to" (1 Tim. 6:11–12).

"If you conquer yourself, you shall more easily subdue all other things. The perfect victory is to triumph over oneself. For whosoever keeps himself in subjection, so that sensuality obeys reason, and reason is in all things obedient to me, he is truly conqueror of himself and lord of the world. If you desire to attain this height, you must begin manfully by laying the axe to the root, in order to remove and destroy your secret inordinate attachment to yourself or to any private and material good. This vice of inordinate self-love is the source of almost everything that has to be radically destroyed. If this evil be vanquished and subdued, there will at once follow great peace and tranquillity" (Thomas à Kempis, *The Imitation of Christ*, bk. 3, 53).

"O my soul, ponder earnestly the nobility of thy first innocence, and acknowledge the image of the Trinity, so worthy of reverence, in thyself and the honour due to the divine likeness in which thou art made. Aim at a fitting nobility in thy bearing and behaviour, for the grandeur of the reward merits such a pursuit. Then, at the last, when He shall appear, thou wilt truly have a likeness to him who seeks identity with thee. In so far as thou seekest here to make thyself ready for the vision of God, even so will he seem to thee. If thou dost renew thy first beauty, thy King will love thee, for he is thy God, thy Friend, thy Spouse" (Anon., twelfth century).

"And now, after so much wrong-doing, such punishment for lives ill-lived, such pardon for our sins, and the deliverance that is with us this day, should we turn back?" (1 Ezra 9:13).

Thanksgiving 4

A Thought Before Saying One's Penance

"Prayers recited by the command of the confessor have a special efficacy as being part of the sacrament itself.... The performance of a sacramental penance is the outward sign of goodwill. It shows that we are anxious to make good" (J. C. Heenan, *Confession*).

For Perseverance

"It is for thee to live by his commandments, by the decrees and observances he has enjoined on thee, to obey the Lord's good pleasure. So shalt thou prosper" (Deut. 6:17–18).

"We are to think of today as the beginning of a new series. I mean, O my God, to hear your voice today, not to neglect it as yesterday and the day before. There are, perhaps, words of yours which I have hitherto neglected or set aside, but not quite managed to forget; they still echo in my ears, like some human utterance which comes back to me after a little, although at the time I was not attending to it. Your voice has been suggesting to me that in this or that matter I might reform my habits; that I might serve you better by making this or that small sacrifice. And I heard the suggestion, and said to myself, 'Oh well, I can do that any day.' Yes, but any day is no day; the solution of the difficulty is Today. This is the day which the Lord hath made — it was today you meant me to start. The long-refused invitation shall be accepted at last" (R. A. Knox, *A Retreat for Lay People*).

"Let our steps now be unfaltering along thy ways, O Lord. As we walk in them, grant that we may have the continual help of thy mercy, and be safeguarded against all temptation. So when we come into the presence of thy holiness, we shall, without sense of unworthiness, enjoy the fullness of thy glory" (Gothic Breviary, seventh century).

"Courage and a man's part, that is what I ask of thee; no room for fear and shrinking back, when the Lord thy God is at thy side wherever thou goest" (Josh. 1:9).

In Gratitude

"Tell me this, if a man has a hundred sheep, and one of them has gone astray, does he not leave those ninety-nine others on the mountain side, and go out to look for the one that is straying? And if, by good fortune, he finds it, he rejoices more, believe me, over that one, than over the ninety-nine which never strayed from him" (Matt. 18:12–13).

"It does not follow that we shall *feel inclined* to do what we see we ought to do, and even what we are resolved, God helping us, to do. But the 'fixed heart' will do its work despite all shyness, reluctance, or indolence. The bravest man is often he who feels most frightened. It remains that, however deep be my awe of God, however appalled I be at the thought that I have rebelled against him, and that the world rebels, and that much of it is a continual affront to him, yet I know that I can repent, nay, in Christ, I can atone even for sins that are not mine: that my life can be one of gratitude for the past — trust for the future — and joy in God even here and now" (C. C. Martindale, S.J., *The Sweet Singer of Israel*).

"O my dear Lord, how merciful thou hast been to me.... Thou wilt never forsake me. I do earnestly trust so — never certainly without fearful provocation on my part. Yet I trust and pray that thou wilt keep me from that provocation. O keep me from the provocation of lukewarmness and sloth. O my dear Lord, lead me forward from strength to strength, gently, sweetly, tenderly, lovingly, powerfully, effectually, remembering my fretfulness and feebleness, till thou bringest me into thy heaven" (Newman, *Meditations and Devotions*).

"Was there ever such a God, so ready to forgive sins, to overlook faults?... He loves to pardon" (Mic. 7:18).

In Forgiveness of Others, as We Have Forgiven

"Was it not thy duty to have mercy on thy fellow servant, as I had mercy on thee?" (Matt. 18:33).

"Thy command it is, O God, that, before every other command, we should observe the sacred covenant of charity. Give us grace, then, to guide our keeping of every commandment by the law of charity. Grant us the strength to keep in check all inordinate desires, all sad and irritable moods, that by the power of thy will working in us we may be able to quell in ourselves all their storms and surges" (Benedictional of John Longlonde, sixteenth century).

For the Work of the Church, Christ's Body, Hindered by Our Sins

"The kings of this earth have power over earthly life, the priest over eternal life, by his power of absolution; before him they who bear the golden crown and sceptre must kneel to be judged, and the King of kings ratifies his just judgement. So, too, he has the privilege of being able to lay the first robe of innocence renewed upon the prodigal sinner and kill for him the fatted calf by admitting him to the banquet of the Father in Holy Communion, of making him once more a member of the Mystical Body, making whole the seamless robe of Christ" (Père Petit, *Templum Spirituale*).

"Do thou, almighty Father, protect all, keep all safe, sanctify, govern, correct and console them. Since thou didst gather them together and give them thy name, let them be so filled with love of thee that their sense of their Christian vocation and their sharing in thy work of redemption may never weaken" (Alcuin, *Sacramentary*, ninth century).

Preparation 5

God and the Sinner

"When a great multitude had gathered, and more came flocking to him out of the cities, he spoke to them in a parable. Here is the sower gone out to sow his seed. And as he sowed, there were some grains that fell beside the path, so that they were trodden under foot, and the birds flew down and ate them. And others fell on the rocks, where they withered as soon as they were up, because they had no moisture. And some fell among briers, and the briers grew up with them and smothered them. But others fell where the soil was good, and when these grew up they yielded a hundredfold. So saying, he cried aloud, Listen, you that have ears to listen with.... Those by the wayside hear the word, and then the devil comes and takes it away from their hearts, so that they cannot find faith and be saved. Those on the rock, are those who entertain the word with joy as soon as they hear it, and yet have no roots; they last for a while, but in time of temptation they fall away. And the grain that fell among the briers stands for those who hear it, and then, going on their way, are stifled by the cares, the riches, and the pleasures of life, and never reach maturity. And the grain that fell in good soil stands for those who hear the word, and hold by it with a noble and generous heart, and endure, and yield a harvest" (Luke 8:4–15).

Devotions for Confession

The Value of the Sacrament

"The spirit yields a harvest of love, joy, peace, patience, kindness, generosity, forbearance, gentleness, faith, courtesy, temperateness, purity. No law can touch such lives as these; those who belong to Christ have crucified nature with all its passions, with all its impulses. Since we live by the spirit, let the spirit be our rule of life" (Gal. 5:22–26).

"The gravity of sin comes from its being an offence against God, but its effect on the soul is to be measured neither by the guilt nor by the temporal punishment inexorably affixed, but by that deep sense of loneliness it brings with it. Scripture is full of the comparison between the soul and a waterless desert; in one place comes the phrase, "the desolation of the wicked." Now this represents a quite apparent effect that sin has upon the soul. It makes a man realize as nothing else does the terrible loneliness of life. It is possible that after a while this perception wears off, and the soul becomes in this way, as in others, hardened to the sense of sin; but at first, when the conscience is still delicate and refined, after an offence against God, human nature feels itself to shrivel up and become cut off from the rest of the world.... The great effect produced in the soul by sin is an intense feeling of loneliness brought about by the very offence against God, for by the fact of sin the deep consciousness of the intimate union between him and ourselves can no longer be experienced....

"Sin's loneliness is evident, and the cause of it no less clear; for by sin the presence of God, made perfect by sanctifying grace, is removed. After all, God is the most intimate neighbour of the soul; no other power can creep so close to the heart and tangle itself so cunningly with the roots of our desire. The will is at his mercy alone, so as to be moved by him without in any sense destroying its freedom. Every movement of goodness is effected by the special impulse of his virtue, and every thought that turns to the things that are more excellent must have been inspired by his illumination. For him, then, was my soul wholly formed, and without him it is baulked of its purpose and reduced to a hungry longing for what it cannot achieve. Thence it is restless till it finds its peace in him; thus it is lonely, deprived of all that is most required by its several faculties. Man, in other words, was made for love, the diviner part of him for divine love. By sin is all this love dried up; the parched and thirsty soul feels, therefore, the need of the dew of God.... The soul by sin is thus made solitary; I have therefore in my heart to see that the grace of God is not removed and the life of my soul destroyed. When I am feeling particularly the loneliness of life, perhaps the cause is that I lean too little upon God; perhaps it is that my sins will not let me feel that inward presence that is the sole real source of peace here below. I was created by Love for love, and when by sin I act contrary to Love, my heart must necessarily feel his absence" (Bede Jarrett, O.P., *Meditations for Layfolk*).

In Humility

"Lord, do not withhold thy pity from me; thy mercy and faithfulness that have ever been my shield. I am beset with evils past numbering, overtaken by my sins.... Deign, Lord, to set me free; Lord, give heed and help.... I, so helpless, so destitute, and the Lord is concerned for me! Thou art my champion and my refuge; do not linger, my God, do not linger on the way" (Ps. 39:12–18).

"There is nothing very creative about not loving evil, there is a great deal that is creative about hating evil and being aglow with love. And in fact we shall be most likely to succeed in the essential business of avoiding evil-doing if our motive is a positive love of what is good. The Christian life is not to be expressed in the chilly ideal of duty for duty's sake, but in the heartwarming ideal of duty for love's sake. Jacob's laborious years were as but a few days because of the greatness of his love: anyone can be good and do good for a little while, but for most of us the attempt to serve God is a matter of many laborious years, probably at best plodding and pedestrian; and only love will save us from one of two alternative disasters: either becoming disheartened and giving up the struggle, or, on the other hand, by driving ourselves ruthlessly and unlovingly to do our duty, becoming in the end inhuman, cold and arid. Law or duty will always seem burdensome to us, something imposed upon us, bearing down on us against our will and inclination, unless we 'internalize' it, make it part of ourselves, part of the inner pattern of our personalities, by falling in love either with the law itself or with the lawgiver or both" (G. Vann, O.P., *The Paradise Tree*).

"With what wisdom does God free us from pride if we are tainted by it, or defend us against it if we are unspoilt by it! How mercifully he destroys love of this world in us, making us long after our true home! How faithfully he works our salvation in us, we all unknowing!... Nay, never could he desert those whom he finds to be humble and men of good will" (Blosius, *Spiritual Life*).

"Fear God, and keep his commandments; this is the whole meaning of man" (Eccles. 12:13).

For Confidence

"To the Lord betake you, and in him find strength" (Ps. 104:4).

"The Prodigal Son, the Samaritan woman, Magdalen — all these examples of the kindness of the Heart of Jesus are but the manifestations of a higher love: the infinite love of the Father towards poor sinners. Never let us forget that we are to see in what Jesus does as man, a revelation of what he does as God, with the Father and their common Spirit. Jesus receives sinners and forgives them: it is God himself, who, under a human form, stoops towards them, and welcomes them" (Marmion, *Christ in His Mysteries*).

"O good Lord, we be sinners in like manner as thou earnest into the world to call unto thee; we labour and be laden with the multitude of our sins, we also be made weary by the means of our wickedness. Therefore, blessed Lord, say unto us: 'Come ye unto me,' and anon we come, we humble and meek ourselves before the throne of thy mercy. Other hope and trust have we none, in any condition, but only in thee.... Have in mind the promise thou made to every penitent sinner coming unto thee, which is, thou shalt not cast them away, and, also, thou shalt refresh them. We come, therefore, unto thee, good Lord, cast us not away, but refresh us with thy grace and thy mercy" (St. John Fisher).

"It is my God that brings me aid, and gives me confidence; he is my shield, my weapon of deliverance, my protector, my stronghold! It is he that preserves me from wrong. Praised be the Lord! When I invoke him I am secure" (2 Kings 22:3–4).

For Self-Knowledge

"Share with the Lord the burden of all thy doings, if thou wouldst be sincere in thy intent" (Prov. 16:3).

"The glory of a good man is the testimony of a good conscience. Have a good conscience and you shall always have joy. A good conscience can bear very much, and is very joyful in the midst of adversity. But an evil conscience is always fearful and uneasy. Sweetly shall you rest, if your heart do not blame you" (Thomas à Kempis, *The Imitation of Christ*, bk. 2, 6).

"To thy faithful people, O Lord, graciously grant the gift of safe judgement, proved patience, and the power of self-control. So all will feel the touch of thy guiding hand, and know the joy of the Holy Spirit" (Cornish Pontifical, tenth century).

"Hold out, we beseech thee, O Lord, the right hand of thy mercy to those who seek thee, that they may abandon merely human values and so secure for themselves the real consolations of this life and the eternal joys to come" (Gregorian Sacramentary, ninth century).

"If we claim fellowship with him, when all the while we live and move in darkness, it is a lie; our whole life is an untruth.... Sin is with us; if we deny that, we are cheating ourselves; it means that truth does not dwell in us. No, it is when we confess our sins that he forgives us our sins, ever true to his word, ever dealing right with us, and all our wrong-doing is purged away" (1 John 1:6–9).

For Greater Sorrow

"If thou wilt have recourse to the Lord thy God, if thou wilt but have recourse to him with all thy heart, in the bitterness of thy tribulation thou wilt find him again" (Deut. 4:29).

"Real sorrow for sin, contrition, is essentially a question not of feelings but of will: a real awareness of one's own sinfulness and then a determination to repent, to change what needs changing. The goodness of a confession is not measured by the extent to which we feel sorrow: we cannot turn on appropriate emotions at any given moment as one turns on a tap. But emotions are important because they so strongly help or hinder the will: it is much easier to be sorry if one feels sorry. And if we think often and deeply about the two things, closeness to God and separation from God, love and sin, if we gradually steep mind and heart in these realities, they are likely to become for us, at least at times, a deeply felt as well as a deeply known and deeply lived experience" (G. Vann, O.P., *The Paradise Tree*).

"In union with thy bitter sufferings, O Lord Jesus Christ, which were truly my own deserving, and which, for the sake of my freedom from sin, thou didst accept, I, along with all those who suffer with thee, who are sincere in their penitence, and seek to follow thee in truth, now acknowledge before thee all my sins wilfully committed, and all the good deeds neglected, or carelessly done, or done for wrong motives. I confess them, even as thou dost know them, their number and their seriousness. I lay before thee all those wasted days of my life, the days when I sinned, the days when I gave thee no praise.... These days, alas, are gone; I may not have them again, but let me at least in sorrow recall them" (attributed to St. Bernard of Clairvaux).

"Pity thy own servant, and teach him thy decrees. Perfect in thy own servant's heart the knowledge of thy will. Put off the hour, Lord, no more; too long thy commandment stands defied. Precious beyond gold or jewel I hold thy law. Prized be every decree of thine; forsworn be every path of evil-doing. Right wonderful thy decrees are, and well my heart heeds them. Revelation and light thy words disclose to the simple.... Rule thou my path as thou hast promised; never let wrongdoing be my master" (Ps. 118:125–133).

Devotions for Confession

Resolution

"Who is it, Lord, that will make his home in thy tabernacle, rest on the mountain where thy sanctuary is? One that guides his steps without fault, and gives to all their due; one that tells the truth in his own heart" (Ps. 14:1–3).

"The will, to be sure, has been given us for the maintenance of order within ourselves. Sense, memory and imagination must be subordinated to it, and it does wrong in abdicating its position before their caprices. That it experiences violent repulsions and attractions is no evidence of its inability to resist them.... This moral struggle is the natural condition of man. For the maintenance of interior order and to permit the will of God to reign within him, he must win a victory over self. In this warfare, which goes on daily, he must expect to be daunted by its menace" (Galtier, *Sin and Penance*).

"Do thou, O Lord Jesus Christ, and our longed-for Lord, as a searching fire purge out the dross of our sinfulness and make us to be as pure gold and as silver fire-refined. Kindle in our hearts the desire ever to seek after thee with such earnestness that all our desiring be eagerly set on thee in our haste to be wholly thine" (Gothic Breviary, seventh century).

"No lamp like thy word to guide my feet, to shed light on my path. Never will I retract my oath to give thy just commands observance.... Nay, Lord, accept these vows of mine, teach me to do thy bidding. Needs must I carry my life in my hands; yet I am ever mindful of thy law" (Ps. 118:105–109).

Thanksgiving 5

A Thought Before Saying One's Penance

"Since therefore the penitential prayers are of such importance we should make every possible effort to say them with great devotion and attention.... Yet they should be said once only, even if we were distracted. It is better to have said a prayer under distraction than to train oneself by repetition into excessive timidity" (R. Graef, *The Sacrament of Peace*).

For Perseverance

"Let them find in all thou doest the model of a life nobly lived" (Titus 2:7).

"The Psalmist says: *Trust in the Lord, and do good, and dwell in the land, and you shall be fed with the riches thereof.* There is one thing that keeps many back from spiritual progress and from fervent amendment, namely, dread of the difficulty and the stress of the conflict. Yet assuredly they especially do advance beyond others in virtue who strive manfully to overcome those things which are hardest and most contrary to them. For there does a man profit more, and merit more abundant grace, where he more overcomes himself and mortifies his spirit. All have not, indeed, equal difficulties to overcome and mortify. Yet a diligent and zealous person, though he have more passions, will make greater progress than another who is more docile but less fervent in the pursuit of virtues. Two things especially conduce to great amendment, namely, forcibly to withdraw oneself from nature's vicious inclinations, and fervently to pursue the good that one most needs" (Thomas à Kempis, *The Imitation of Christ*, bk. 1, 25).

"Almighty, eternal God, whose ways are ever mercy and truth, grant, we beseech thee, that we whom thou dost so tenderly care for, may continually grow in goodness" (Leonine Sacramentary, seventh century).

"Man's feet the Lord must guide, if he would be sped on his journey; stumble he may, but fall never, with the Lord's hand to uphold him.... Offend no more, rather do good, and be at rest continually" (Ps. 36:23–27).

In Gratitude

"Be these thy study, the mercies of the Lord" (Ps. 106:43).

"The more the soul reflects on the charity wherewith God has pursued it, the deeper must be the regret it experiences at having fled before it, and thus is born the desire to inflict upon self some sort of punishment. It is a protection against sin, but still more it is love's revenge. And the soul realises that this is so in God's estimation also; that since he looks to the heart, he sees in this eagerness to chastise self for offences committed in the past a profession of justice, respect and love" (Galtier, *Sin and Penance*).

"My God, what hast thou done for me!... Again and again thou dost help me. I fall, yet thou dost not cast me off. In spite of all my sins, thou dost still love me, prosper me, comfort me, surround me with blessings, sustain me and further me. I grieve thy good grace, yet thou dost give me more. I insult thee, yet thou never dost take offence, but art as kind as if I had nothing to explain, to repent of, to amend — as if I were thy best, most faithful, most steady and loyal friend. Nay, alas! I am even led to presume upon thy love, it is so like easiness and indulgence, though I ought to fear thee. I confess it, O my true Saviour, every day is but a fresh memorial of thy unwearied, unconquerable love" (Newman, *Meditations and Devotions*).

"Yes, Lord, thou art my hope; my soul, thou hast found a stronghold in the most High.... He has given charge to his angels concerning thee, to watch over thee wheresoever thou goest" (Ps. 90:9–11).

In Forgiveness of Others, as We Have Been Forgiven

"Never be quick to take offence; it is a fool's heart that harbours grudges" (Eccles. 7:10).

"O Lord, all merciful, have mercy on all who believe in thee, on all who belong to me, as even on all who are strangers to me.... Forgive my enemies, those who hate me. Forgive them the wrongs they may have done me, and take away all malice in their hearts against me" (Prayer of Nerses, twelfth century).

For the Work of the Church, Christ's Body, Hindered by Our Sins

"It does matter for the individual, in which period and in what surroundings his life and work take place. In the vicinity of chemical factories, trees often die. Bad air affects the health of both the evil and the good. Every one of us is responsible for the atmosphere in which we live. The evil poison it, the good purify it.... Thus every one of us bears his share of responsibility in the atmosphere of his time" (R. Graef, *The Sacrament of Peace*).

"O admirable mystery, O wonder beyond praise, O interchange beyond our telling, O marvel of divine condescension open to our unceasing praise! Servants of little worth; and behold, we are made sons of God, heirs of God and coheirs with Christ! How can we deserve this, how be worthy of it? I beseech thee, tender God and Father, through the great High-Priest who offered himself in sacrifice to thee for his flock, through him I beseech thee that we be not ungrateful for such great benefits, unworthy of such mercies. Send thy Holy Spirit from heaven that he may help us to appreciate and reverence, as we should, so great a wonder, that he may make the loyalty of our service and the quality of our lives to be in harmony with the fullness of such nobility" (attributed to Alcuin, ninth century).

Preparation 6

God and the Sinner

"In those days John the Baptist appeared, preaching in the wilderness of Judea; Repent, he said, the kingdom of heaven is at hand. It was of him that the prophet Isaias spoke, when he said, There is a voice of one crying in the wilderness. Prepare the way of the Lord, straighten out his paths. And he, John, wore a garment of camel's hair, and a leather girdle about his loins, and locusts and wild honey were his food. Thereupon Jerusalem and all Judea, and all those who dwelt round Jordan, went out to see him, and he baptised them in the Jordan, while they confessed their sins. Many of the Pharisees and the Sadducees came to his baptizing; and, when he saw these he asked them, who was it that taught you, brood of vipers, to flee from the vengeance that draws near? Come, then, yield the acceptable fruit of repentance; do not presume to say in your hearts, We have Abraham for our father; I tell you God has power to raise up children to Abraham out of these very stones. Already the axe has been put to the root of the trees, so that every tree which does not shew good fruit will be hewn down and cast into the fire. As for me, I am baptizing you with water; but one is to come after me who is mightier than I, so that I am not worthy even to carry his shoes for him; he will baptize you with the Holy Ghost, and with fire. He holds his winnowing-fan ready to sweep his threshing-floor clean; he will gather the wheat into his barn, but the chaff he will consume with fire that can never be quenched.

Devotions for Confession

"Then Jesus came from Galilee and stood before John at the Jordan, to be baptized by him.... So Jesus was baptized, and as he came straight up out of the water, suddenly heaven was opened, and he saw the Spirit of God coming down like a dove and resting upon him. And with that, a voice came from heaven, which said, This is my beloved Son, in whom I am well pleased.

"And now Jesus was led by the Spirit away into the wilderness to be tempted there by the devil" (Matt. 3:1–4:1).

The Value of the Sacrament

"We entreat you not to offer God's grace an ineffectual welcome. (I have answered thy prayer, he says, in a time of pardon, I have brought thee help in a day of salvation. And here is the time of pardon; the day of salvation has come already)" (2 Cor. 6:1–2).

"Sin and penance are two corresponding notions in Christianity. From the beginning they are in the foreground of the Gospel preaching. 'Do penance,' cries John the Baptist, 'for the kingdom of heaven is at hand;' 'behold him who taketh away the sin of the world.' And the Lamb of God, who came to carry out his work of purification, himself began by preaching penance. Was it not for sinners he had come? If a soul refused to cleave to him, was it not condemned to die in sin? Thereafter, the personal work of Christ completed, the Apostles received from him the mission to 'preach penance and the remission of sins.' They too were to remit and retain sins on conditions of which they would be the judges; upon the Church, instituted for the salvation of all mankind, would devolve the task of leading men to God by wresting them from sin through penance.

And so it has been fulfilled. As often as individuals, peoples or kings have applied to the Church to make their peace with God, the same answer has been given to them as was given by St Peter to the Jews on the day of Pentecost.

"From the days of the Baptist, then, the way of approach to the kingdom of heaven remains the same: sin, the obstacle to be overcome; penance, the means to surmount it. Essential as the starting point from which to take the road, penance is equally so, if there is to be no check or turning aside. Where one has fallen or gone astray, it alone will raise up and bring back to the straight path; and they alone stride towards the goal where God awaits them, who guard against every fault by maintaining in their souls the spirit of penance....

"Thus, the preaching of the kingdom of God remains the same as in ancient days. The Church addresses the faithful as Christ addressed his disciples, 'Unless you do penance, you also shall perish.' To renounce this doctrine, to allow it even to fall into oblivion, would be equivalent on her part to a rejection of Christ and his work.

"So also, refusal on the part of Christians to give ear to this lesson and to apply it to themselves is to turn their back on Christ. The centuries may pass, but his word remains, it is unchangeable; and just as Christianity cannot be separated from the Crucified, so the teaching of the Crucified cannot be separated from this fundamental lesson of his, that in order to be saved it is necessary to do penance" (Galtier, *Sin and Penance*).

In Humility

"Do not undervalue the correction the Lord sends thee; do not be unmanned when he reproves thy faults. It is where he loves that he bestows correction, like a father whose son is dear to him" (Prov. 3:11–12).

"In submitting the aspirations of our souls to the control of those who have the grace and the mission to direct us in our seeking after divine union, we run no risk of going astray, whatever be the personal merits of those who guide us. At the time when the Magi arrived in Jerusalem, the assembly of those who had

Devotions for Confession

authority to interpret the Holy Scriptures was composed in great part of unworthy members; and yet God willed that it should be by their ministry and teaching that the Magi learnt officially where Christ was born. Indeed, God cannot permit a soul to be deceived when, with humility and confidence, she has recourse to the legitimate representatives of his sovereign authority. On the contrary, the soul will again find light and peace. Like the Magi going out from Jerusalem, she will again see the star, radiant and splendid, and, also like them, full of gladness, she will go forward on her way" (Marmion, *Christ in His Mysteries*).

"At thy gate, O Lord, do I knock, from thy treasury I ask for mercies. I, these many years a sinner, have often turned away from thy paths. Grant me grace to confess my sins, to forsake them, and for the future to live by thy grace. At what gate shall we come to knock, save at thine? O gracious Lord, what have we to plead for our offences if thy mercy plead not with thyself, who art a King whose glory earthly kings do worship?" (Liturgy of the Syrian Jacobites).

"God ... dwells also among chastened and humbled souls, bidding the humble spirit, the chastened soul, rise and live" (Isa. 57:15).

For Confidence

"Yet, such is his mercy, he would still pardon their faults, and spare them from destruction; again and again he turned his vengeance aside, let his anger die down. He would not forget they were flesh and blood" (Ps. 77:38–39).

"Even though, after you have been accepted by him, you should have gone astray, even though you return to him naked, yet God will receive you again as his son because you have returned to him" (Tertullian, *Concerning Penance*).

"Jesus, Lord of my life ... why have I joy in anything but thee? Why love I aught but thee? Would that I might see how gladly thou didst lay thyself on the cross for me! O that I could cast myself between those very arms, wide-opened, as they are, to me, invitingly, as a mother to embrace her child. Truly, indeed, O dear Lord, thou didst come to thy loved ones with the same open welcome as the mother gives to her children. Each is loved, each precious to her.... Would, sweet Jesus, it might be that with loving arms I could so closely embrace thee that nothing more could draw my heart away from thee" (An Orison of our Lord, ca. twelfth century).

"Sin we, still we are thy worshippers; have we not proof of thy power?" (Wisd. 15:2).

For Self-Knowledge

"When a man has hope in view, like a jewel it shines before him; look where he will, his way lies clear" (Prov. 17:8).

"Because the little catalogue goes on and on unchanged through the years, it does not mean that the sacrament is ineffective: its purpose is not only to cleanse us from sin but also to strengthen and deepen the love of God, and whether this second purpose is in fact being achieved in us is something that we cannot know but must leave, humbly and hopefully to God.... 'Who knows his own frailties?' asks the Psalmist, and goes on, 'If I have sinned unwittingly, do thou absolve me'" (G. Vann, O.P., *The Paradise Tree*).

"Almighty, eternal God, thou dost indeed penetrate the depths of our secret thoughts, and in thy far-seeing gaze every desire of our hearts lies open. Enable us to search, then, the hidden places of our minds. Cleanse with the dew of the Holy Spirit all our thoughts. So will our thinking and our acting alike be worthy of thy Majesty" (Anon.).

"Do but open my heart wide, and easy lies the path thou hast decreed" (Ps. 118:32).

For Greater Sorrow

"While health serves thee, do penance for thy sins" (Ecclus. [Sir.] 18:21).

"Now Christian penitence, duly considered, is something as original, something as fresh and independent of man's general religiosity, as is Christian prayer, Christian sacrifice or Christian charity. The *Christianus poenitens* is behaving in a way which cannot be defined in terms of ordinary sorrow for sin. Christian penitence does not exist outside Christianity, any more than the Eucharistic sacrifice exists outside Christianity.... It is only after his baptism, after his incorporation into Christ, that man can be the *Christianus poenitens*. The sins of the baptised are not dealt with by God in the manner in which he deals with sin generally. In Christ, through baptism, we are given a penitence, as we are enriched with a sacrifice; we receive a true sacrament and a heavenly mystery of spiritual cleansing.

"The *Christianus poenitens* is essentially one who has to bewail his lack of fidelity to Christ, to whom he has already sworn fealty by baptism. The sins of Christians are offences against a state, the state of the redeemed. By committing sin we walk unworthy of our calling" (Vonier, *Christianus*).

"O God, who dost not wish that sinners should be lost, but that they should sin no more, in thy kindness soften thy anger which we have deserved, and give us the full forgiveness for which we pray, that our sadness may be turned to joy" (Gregorian Sacramentary, ninth century).

"Forget the long record of our sins, and haste in mercy to our side" (Ps. 78:8).

Resolution

"Let everyone who names the Lord's name keep far from iniquity.... It is by keeping himself separate from these that a man will prove the object of his Lord's regard, hallowed and serviceable, and fit for all honourable employment" (2 Tim. 2:19–21).

"The fact is that the more profoundly a man has become a Christian, the more alive will be his concern to do the will of God, and the more aware he will be that this will is the most precious and the most gentle and the most powerful thing in the world. And the more he realizes his own wretchedness and untrustworthiness, the more he will turn to the Lord of the world and pray that he may cherish and fulfil that high purpose on which the meaning of everything depends. At the same time he will grow the more confident that his will will be done and will triumph over the powers of evil" (R. Guardini, *The Living God*).

"Be mindful of thy mercies, O Lord; give help to this, thy creature, in his strivings, strengthen the hesitant steps he makes towards thee. Draw him to thyself who by his own power cannot reach thee unless thy love encourages him. Make me, thy servant, to be pleasing and acceptable to thee, for well thou knowest that only so can I hope to please thee. Grant me the virtues which are thy delight, thou who givest every graceful gift to those who seek thee. I would that thou wouldst be my only love, even my only fear, the only love I fear to lose" (William of Auvergne, thirteenth century).

"To be master of myself was a thing I could not hope to come by, except of God's bounty; I was wise enough already to know whence the gift came. So to the Lord I turned, and made my request of him" (Wisd. 8:21).

Thanksgiving 6

A Thought Before Saying One's Penance

"When the Church tells me: For your penance say ... it is not alluding to a scale in an ecclesiastical penal code, but is requiring me to acknowledge my unjustness and to accept a punishment. It summons me to confess that I have deprived God of his glory, that I have been disloyal in my friendship with him, that I have been not only ungrateful but unjust. If I am truly penitent, I must necessarily acknowledge this. How is it, then, that the penalty enjoined on me by the Church serves the purpose of bearing witness, and bears so little relation to my degree of guilt?... Because these prayers will constitute for me, a sinner, an act which of itself will bind me once again to my Redeemer" (Community of St. Séverin, *Confession*).

For Perseverance

"Freely shall my feet tread, if thy will is all my quest" (Ps. 118:45).

"In times of moral defeat, when the consciousness of sin and of the consequent separation from God makes prayer impossible, we must try not to be too sensitive with ourselves. If we were able to do wrong in the sight of God, we must be able to bear this wrong before him. A consciousness of guilt and hurt pride should not be allowed to become a barrier between us and God.

Not only can such a barrier become permanent, but the inner disinclination to pray may use it as a convenient excuse to avoid the toil of prayer. Anyone who has reason for self-reproach should admit his guilt and start afresh without allowing it to interfere with his normal life of prayer. If in doing so he experiences remorse or shame, this is as it should be and he must bear it" (R. Guardini, *Prayer in Practice*).

"Free us, O Lord, from the hidden causes of our sins, and enlighten our hearts with the light of thy Word in his twofold nature. Put on us the armour of courage and show us the way of blameless life. By thy grace purify us from our secret weaknesses and strengthen in us the desire of what thy will would accomplish in us" (African Collect, fifth century).

"You still need endurance, if you are to attain the prize God has promised to those who do his will" (Heb. 10:36).

In Gratitude

"He shall find in me a father, and I in him a son, I will not cancel my merciful promises to him" (2 Kings 7:13–15).

"From first to last, it is a gift freely bestowed. It is Christ who has merited it and made it possible, who has put within easy reach the means of obtaining it. But, from first to last, too, a real co-operation is required on the part of those who are to benefit; they, too, must entertain a hatred of sin, must make self-accusation and must be ready to make satisfaction to God. Nothing, no one, can dispense them from this personal contribution. But once they are restored to grace, the mystical union between them and Christ that, as a result, is now re-established, permits them to share in the satisfaction of others. Thereafter, if they have a little generosity, if they entertain in their hearts some little love for God and men, it only remains for them to take their share in the general work of reparation and redemption" (Galtier, *Sin and Penance*).

"In thee, almighty, eternal God, we live, move, and are, and there is no time of our lives, no single moment even, which sees us empty-handed of the benefits of thy loving kindness. But to-day we would acknowledge our renewed happiness … and, therefore, we the more greatly rejoice, since in our new-found gladness we live again the memory of thy past graces" (Gothic Missal, seventh century).

"No greater proof could we have of thy consideration, of that abundant mercy which is thine" (Bar. 2:27).

In Forgiveness of Others, as We Have Been Forgiven

"Have done with it all, resentment, anger, spite" (Col. 3:8).

"O Christ our God, thou dost inspire reverence, for thy divine power surpasses all our understanding. It was that wondrous kindness of thine which would not let thee spurn Judas in his approach to thee. Giving him thy accustomed affectionate welcome, thou didst awaken in his heart the full knowledge of his guilt and the need of repentance. Grant, O Lord, that, after this opportunity for our own reconciliation, we may give each other welcome without deceit and without resentment" (Liturgy of St. Gregory).

For the Work of the Church, Christ's Body, Hindered by Our Sins

"The absolution of the sinner in the sacrament of penance is not merely a private affair of the individual Christian but is very much the affair of the whole community. It is necessary for the repentant sinner to return to God and be re-united with him through the mediation of the Church.... It is in a sense implied in the fact of our having normally to go to a church and take our place publicly among the penitents for the reception of the sacrament. It is very forcibly impressed on us if we realise that the priest who absolves us can only do so by the authority of the bishop of the diocese who is the head of the local Christian community. And it is also expressed in the sentence of absolution: before he absolves the penitent, the confessor still leads him back into the community of the Church: 'May our Lord Jesus Christ absolve you, and I by his authority absolve you from every bond of excommunication'" (J. Cunnane, in *The Furrow*).

"May God, who has cleansed us with the water flowing from his wounded side and redeemed us by shedding his own precious Blood, strengthen our appreciation of the redemption he won for us. Once more renewed in life, as we formerly were by the waters of baptism and the Holy Ghost, may he grant us again the full fellowship of his heavenly kingdom. Having restored to us the beginning of our faith, may he now give his own completion to all our good works in the fullness of charity" (Pontifical of Magdalen, twelfth century).

Preparation 7

God and the Sinner

"If some woman has ten silver pieces by her, and has lost one of them, does she not light a lamp, and sweep the house, and search carefully until she finds it? And when she does find it, she calls her friends and her neighbours together; rejoice with me, she says, I have found the silver piece which I lost. So it is, I tell you, with the angels of God; there is joy among them over one sinner that repents" (Luke 15:8–10).

The Value of the Sacrament

"Learn to prize what is of value" (Phil. 1:10).

"In reality the lost groat was part of the wife's dowry. Anyone who has been in the East must have noticed the strings of different coins worn by the women.... Even the peasant women may sometimes feel proud and hold their heads high, so great is the number of coins with which their foreheads are adorned.

"It is impossible for us not to realize the intense tenderness which our divine Lord has for the souls ransomed with his precious Blood: the pursuit of the lost sheep; the groat sought for until found where it lay concealed in dust and darkness; trifles these, mere trifles in the eyes of the world. What was one less in a large flock? What mattered a groat, the loss of which could be so easily concealed? Were these worth so much sadness, uneasiness, fatigue, even suffering? To argue thus is indeed to misunderstand his love and the value which he sets on what he loves. The value of things depends on the esteem we have for them, and this in turn depends both on the pleasure we find in their possession, and on the difficulty with which they are acquired and retained. Hence it follows that nothing would be equivalent, in the heart of our divine Lord, to the soul of the smallest child, because it reminds him of the Blood which he shed for it on the cross, and of the delight which he takes in its innocence, which will one day be in such danger, exposed to the temptations of the world. If that soul should grow weak and yield to the tempter, how he will grieve until he can raise it up and strengthen it against fresh temptations. The tried fidelity of the angels and the elect does not cause him to forget the lost sheep; and one would say that heaven is empty because of this sole absent one, just as to the Prodigal's father the house seemed deserted from the day that his ungrateful son quitted it" (M. J. Ollivier, O.P., *The Parables of Our Lord*).

In Humility

"From a humble soul, an obedient will, the prayer must come that wins thee" (Judith 9:16).

"Become *as little children, learn of me.*... Such is the judgment of God upon our sojourn here below: these are the principles he praises, and lays down for the salvation of the world. They are clothed in words of power, yet the message is so wrapped around with love, that it comes to us as an entreaty rather than as mere advice or a cold command. Our Lord himself lived the life thus framed; and then he preached it; he suffered in order to prove its truth, and to convince men that he loved them and had their welfare at heart. He declared that so great was the malice and attractiveness of sin that no code short of his would ever be a match for it.... He throws a light on the forces that govern the world; he bids us walk in love and obedience to law; he tells us we belong to God and are to go back to him. By his incarnate life begun at Bethlehem, continued in Galilee, consummated on the cross of Calvary, where he remains fixed by the very force of his love for men, he assures us that we are responsible beings endowed with a true sense of sin, and that in the light of his judgment which frees us from all doubt and uncertainty, we can walk secure to our true home in God" (R. Eaton, *The Ministry of Reconciliation*).

"Rouse up in my heart, O Lord my God, such a longing for thee that I feel I must needs go in search of thee. Grant also that I may find thee, and, having found thee, love thee and in that love find pardon for my every sin and, being once pardoned, sin no more. Give me now a repentant heart, O Lord my God; give me a lasting regret, even to tears, for my sins.... O my Redeemer, drive all pride from my heart and grant me thy own humble spirit. My Saviour, free me from the unrestraint of anger and put on me the buckler of patience. Root out from me all resentment that I may be amiable to all men. Give me, O tender Father, firm faith, prudent hope and enduring charity" (Anon., twelfth century).

"If I am to be healed, Lord, it is thou must heal me; if I am to find deliverance, it is thou must deliver me" (Jer. 17:14).

For Confidence

"It is the Lord, watching over those that fear and trust in his mercy, that will protect their lives.... Patiently we wait for the Lord's help; he is our strength and our shield; in him our hearts will find contentment, in his holy name we trust. Lord, let thy mercy rest upon us, who put all our confidence in thee" (Ps. 32:18–22).

"Help thou my soul, mighty Lord; support it, O Father of mankind. Heal it yet again, eternal God, our Judge, strong and powerful, in all its distress. Sin-stained it is, and times there are when I fear for my soul, despite the kindness thou hast shown me in my life here. Thanks be to thee for all things, for all those undeserved gifts and mercies. From the memory of these will I take heart, look forward with cheerful trust and gird myself for the way to come" (Exeter Book, tenth century).

"It is he that has scourged us for our sins; he it is that will deliver us in his mercy" (Tob. 13:5).

For Self-Knowledge

"God lives and looks on me" (Gen. 25:11).

"The vital element of every movement towards God is its supernatural character.... The first movement of repentance comes not from the sinner but from God: 'If anyone says that without the previous inspiration of the Holy Ghost, and without his help ... man can repent as he ought, let him be anathema.' The mercy of God anticipates our human action in returning to him: 'Convert us, O Lord, to thee, and we shall be converted.' Illuminated by this divine action, we make an act of faith in God.... Then, realising that we are sinners and hoping to obtain the divine mercy, we begin to have some initial love of God as the fountain of all justice, and because our sins have offended God, we hate and detest them" (E. J. Mahoney, *Sin and Repentance*).

"Grant to the minds of thy people, almighty God, the light of thy own intelligence and the clarity of thy own thoughts. So the perplexity and uncertainty of evil will not trouble those minds which have been illumined by thy grace" (Spanish Collect, seventh century).

"He has fashioned each man's nature, and weighs the actions of each" (Ps. 32:14).

For Greater Sorrow

"Ah, if thou too couldst understand, above all in this day that is granted to thee, the ways that can bring thee peace!" (Luke 19:42).

"When we think of our attitude to created things, we have need of sorrow and repentance: not because we have loved excessively, but because we have not loved sufficiently, we have been selfish, and so have not loved aright. And it is so natural for us to go on thinking of the healing sacrament which can redeem the past and give us hope and renewal of strength for the future. All is not lost because hitherto we have failed; and if we want to see the mercy of God in the fullness of its patience, we can see it here and be humbled and glad. It is never too late to call upon the gentle forgiveness of God: there is more joy in heaven over one sinner doing penance than over the ninety-nine just who need not penance. It is never too late; but the mercy goes further even than that: we can never turn again too often. We are to be forgiven, not seven times, but till seventy times seven — as often as we repent" (G. Vann, O.P., *The Divine Pity*).

"Of a surety I am thy servant, O Lord, in desire always and resolve, even if not in word and deed. Deep is my regret that knowing myself as thy servant, I do not pay thee the reverence I ought. O my Lord, since thou art in truth my Lord, can I not live as a servant of thine should? . . . Thou hast given me grace,

Devotions for Confession

O my all-wise Creator to contemplate and realise thy beauty, yet I daily seem to grow less worthy of thee. All the same I know that I shall never become a stranger to the happiness of thy friendship if only I do not weary in my desire of thee" (St. Anselm of Canterbury, twelfth century).

Resolution

"Rid your minds, then, of every encumbrance, keep full mastery of your senses, and set your hopes on the generous gift that is offered you.... Obedience should be native to you now; you must not retain the mould of your former untutored appetites. No, it is a holy God who has called you, and you too must be holy in all the ordering of your lives" (1 Pet. 1:13–15).

"Sincere and genuine contrition, however real and true, does not automatically prevent all further sin. With many sins, especially against the sixth commandment, when they have become inveterate and grown into a second nature, relapses must be expected. It will take some time to break the evil habit. These relapses will be confessed and we must not be discouraged if in the beginning progress is slow. We need not doubt the sincerity of contrition and the honesty of resolution even though a relapse seems certain. Contrition and resolution again are mainly a question of the will and of reasonable knowledge. If I ask a house-owner: 'Can you promise that your house will never go on fire?' he will reply: 'Sorry, I cannot promise; there are a number of fire risks which are quite beyond my control.' ... What we can promise and what we can firmly resolve is that we will do with all our might everything that will prevent us from committing grievous sin" (R. Graef, *The Sacrament of Peace*).

"O God of justice, I beseech thee to give me a heart which fears thee, a mind which has understanding of thee; grant me with the eyes of the soul to know thee, and a hearing alert for thy word. Grant me some tiny spark of wisdom to show me the ways of just living.... Free my heart from all disloyalty; stir me out of my lazy ways and root out my evil impulses. Cleanse my tongue from its habit of disparaging others, from the habit of lying, from the foolishness of gossip, and from all those actions which spring from my vanity" (Book of Cerne, tenth century).

"Bless thee he will, as he has promised, if only thou wilt listen to his voice and observe all the commandments" (Deut. 15:5).

Thanksgiving 7

A Thought Before Saying One's Penance

"Satisfaction is necessarily something other than a way of compensating for offences committed. It is a collaboration between two persons who have become reconciled, a collaboration which on the part of the penitent is one of obedience and docility" (The Community of St. Séverin, *Confession*).

For Perseverance

"Take your standard from him, from his endurance, from the enmity the wicked bore him, and you will not grow faint, you will not find your souls unmanned" (Heb. 12:3).

"When I confront a duty and fail to fulfil it, the will of God has not been done. Does that imply the end of the will of God? Does God thereby cease to have a will for me? No — for at once he says again: Do this. Admittedly a change has come over his will. The wrong has been done. It was not in accordance with his will, but once it has been done, the eternally one, eternally the same, but living and ever creative will of God, surrounds me as the doer of the wrong that leaves its mark within and its trail of consequences without. It is sin in the sight of God. But he now says: Do this!... When an officer is given an order and carries it out wrongly, the matter is finished. The order was what it

110

was and has been wasted because it was not carried out properly. There is no way out. But there is always a way in the sight of God. Whatever may happen, good or evil, God passes judgment on it, but at the same time he takes up what has happened and calls me to take the next step. It may be a way oppressed with a sense of guilt and loss; but it is a way all the same. Not a way marked out in advance but a way which God prepares under every man's feet, which he creates anew from every step we take" (R. Guardini, *The Living God*).

"My God, I have had experience enough what a dreadful bondage sin is. If thou art away, I find I cannot keep myself, however I wish it — and am in the hands of my own self-will, pride, sensuality and selfishness. And they prevail with me more and more every day, till they are irresistible. In time the old Adam within me gets so strong, that I become a mere slave. I confess things to be wrong which nevertheless I do. I bitterly lament over my bondage, but I cannot undo it. O what a tyranny is sin! It is a heavy weight which cripples me — and what will be the end of it? By thy all-precious merits, by thy almighty power, I entreat thee, O my Lord, to give me life and sanctity and strength! *Deus sanctus*, give me holiness; *Deus fortis*, give me strength; *Deus immortalis*, give me perseverance" (Newman, *Meditations and Devotions*).

"Let us rid ourselves of all that weighs us down, of the sinful habit that clings so closely, and run, with all endurance, the race for which we are entered" (Heb. 12:1).

In Gratitude

"See where mercy and faithfulness meet in one; how justice and peace are united in one embrace! Faithfulness grows up out of the earth, and from heaven, justice looks down" (Ps. 84:11–12).

"Our gratitude, however, must be expressed in deeds rather than in words. Full use must be made of this sacrament, and we must profit by all the graces it conveys to us. We must grow in trust in the power of the precious Blood and we must adhere to the words of our divine Lord: 'Whose sins you shall forgive, they are forgiven them.' We must have the courage to write off the past after each confession and to take a new foothold in the life of grace. We must not waste any energy on worries about the past, whatever has happened, but we must give ourselves completely to the present moment, the will of God, the only reality in life.

"Our gratitude must also show itself in putting into practice our sincere and genuine contrition" (R. Graef, *The Sacrament of Peace*).

"O good Jesus, true Shepherd, kindly Master, King of everlasting glory. Thee I adore, bless, and thank who hast held me so dear, who hast wrought such wonders for me, suffered such indignities for my sake. Be merciful to me, a sinner, cleanse me, heal and strengthen me. Guide me, teach and enlighten me. Would that I had not, even to this hour, ever been ungrateful to thee; would that I could to some degree please thee, would that passion and evil desires were deadened in me; would that I were really humble and teachable. Then, indeed, would I stand in freedom of heart and quiet of mind before thee" (Blosius, *Spiritual Life*).

"Then the kindness of God our Saviour dawned on us; his great love for man.... In accordance with his own merciful design he saved us, with the cleansing power which gives us new birth, and restores our nature through the Holy Ghost" (Titus 3:4–5).

In Forgiveness of Others, as We Have Been Forgiven

"Reproach comes amiss where all stand in need of correction" (Ecclus. [Sir.] 8:6).

"O Holy Lord, Father almighty, eternal God, give to thy servants the perfection of charity that they may be moved by thy own example to return good for evil. Rather than rejoice in revenge, may they earnestly desire friendship with those who do them wrong" (Leonine Sacramentary, seventh century).

For the Work of the Church, Christ's Body, Hindered by Our Sins

"Those in the Church who have penetrated most deeply into the mind of Christ realize that it is their duty to associate themselves with him in the work of reconciliation and reparation. They are transported with admiration at the thought of the solidarity it has pleased God to establish between us and his incarnate Son, at the thought of the Communion of Saints, which is the effect of that solidarity, and the pooling of reparation it has made possible. The same love for God and men actuates them, impelling them to confront sin and to take the offensive against it. They gradually acquire a sensitiveness to sin that amounts to pain; as they think on the offence it has given to God and the chastisement it has drawn upon men, they feel such a degree of loathing that it lies like a weight on their souls. With Christ, and for the sake of Christ, they experience the necessity almost of offering themselves as mediators, as victims, that God's honour may be avenged and his justice satisfied, and that, on the other hand, the sinner, the real sinner, may be spared and find forgiveness. This, in their minds, is to continue and complete in themselves what was wanting in the cross of Christ — that cross which was to weigh equally upon the members of his mystical body and imprint upon them its seal" (Galtier, *Sin and Penance*).

"May God who inspires us to repentance, and consoles us when repentant by healing us, all deformed as we are by sin, make us fit once more for acceptable work in the service of his Majesty. May he grant us to be truly ashamed of the evil we have done, and fully, and for all time shun the same" (Benedictional of John Longlonde, sixteenth century).

Preparation 8

God and the Sinner

"When they found all the publicans and sinners coming to listen to him, the Pharisees and scribes were indignant; Here is a man, they said, that entertains sinners, and eats with them. Whereupon he told them this parable: If any of you owns a hundred sheep, and has lost one of them, does he not leave the other ninety-nine in the wilderness, and go after the one which is lost until he finds it? And when he does find it, he sets it on his shoulders, rejoicing, and so he goes home, and calls his friends and his neighbours together; rejoice with me, he says to them, I have found my sheep that was lost. So it is, I tell you, in heaven; there will be more rejoicing over one sinner who repents, than over ninety-nine souls that are justified, and have no need of repentance" (Luke 15:1–7).

The Value of the Sacrament

"This is what the Lord God says.... The lost sheep I will find, the strayed sheep I will bring home again" (Ezek. 34:11–16).

"This sacrament has no connection with either vengeance or punishment, but it is, on the contrary, an undiluted grace. It is the continuation of those words of Christ echoing down the ages and bringing redemption to mankind: 'Thy sins are forgiven thee — go in peace.' — By virtue of baptism and confirmation, we already have a share in our Lord's life of grace. Experience, however, teaches us how fragile is this divine life in us, and how easily it is affected by the vicissitudes, the unrest and the unceasing change of our existence. God leaves us our freedom; he does not take away all our temptations. He offers us his grace and his help, but does not forcibly intrude himself upon us. We know that man sins. But even as far back as the Old Testament, we can hear the words of the prophet Ezechiel, telling us that God does not desire the death of the sinner, but rather that he should be converted and live.

"Christ, the incarnate revelation of God's love for us, came down to save sinners and to convert them; the Good Shepherd seeks for the lost sheep along the mountain paths and the valleys, and every morning the father goes out to see if the prodigal son has returned. It was Jesus who defended Mary Magdalen from the scorn of the Pharisees as she wept at his feet, and saved the woman taken in adultery from a purely human justice. We are told, and it is true, that in heaven there will be more joy over one sinner who repents than over the ninety-nine just who are in no need of repentance. Christ knows what man is really worth; he values him at his just value. The high ideal which he puts before us, and the sanctity which he attaches to the hunger and thirst for such an ideal, do not make him forget that nevertheless sin and man are in truth but one. He knows that man stands in constant need of the great Physician. He does not desire to refuse forgiveness, even after the rejection of a proferred grace, and so he has instituted a sacrament which goes far beyond the remembrance of his mercy and is a token of his enduring solicitude that the smoking flax shall not be quenched, nor the bruised reed broken, but repaired and healed" (Van Doornik, *The Triptych of the Kingdom*).

In Humility

"Merciful the Lord is, and just, and full of pity; he cares for simple hearts, and to me, when I lay humbled, he brought deliverance. Return, my soul, where thy peace lies; the Lord has dealt kindly with thee; he has saved my life from peril, banished my tears, kept my feet from falling. I will be the Lord's servant henceforward in the land of the living" (Ps. 114:5–9).

"My son, walk before me in truth; and seek me always in the simplicity of your heart. He that walks before me in truth shall be secure from the assaults of evil....

"True, O Lord; and as thou sayest, I beseech thee, so let it be done to me. Let thy truth teach me, let it guard me and preserve me to final salvation. Let it deliver me from all evil affection and inordinate love, and I shall walk with thee in great liberty of heart.

"I will teach you (says the Truth) those things that are right and pleasing in my sight. Think on your sins with great displeasure and sorrow; and never esteem yourself to be anything on account of your good works.

"Of a truth you are a sinner, subject to, and entangled with, many passions. Of yourself you always tend to nothing, speedily do you fail, speedily are you overcome, speedily disturbed, speedily dissipated. You have nothing in which you can glory, but many things for which you ought to abase yourself; for you are much weaker than you can comprehend" (Thomas à Kempis, *The Imitation of Christ*, bk. 3, 4).

"O King of kings and Lord of lords, it is only he who becomes as a little child in your sight who is great before you. Behold us at your feet.... Grant to us that humility of spirit which, however contemptible and unworthy it may make us seem to the world, will yet make us known and loved by you. Teach us to rise from the depths of our own nothingness and to fix our hopes on the high realities of everlasting life. Grant that our souls may ardently long for the things that never pass away; grant that we may gain them by your grace. Endow us with strength of will, that we may be steadfast in true and faithful devotion to duty. Give us courage in the face of weariness and adversity, in times of joy and sorrow, courage which will repel evil, which will be constant in resignation, which will transform crowns of thorns into diadems of merit" (Pius XII).

"Happy, Lord, is the man whom thou dost chasten, reading him the lesson of thy law! For him thou wilt lighten the time of adversity" (Ps. 93:12–13).

For Confidence

"If it be thy will, thou hast power to make me clean. Jesus was moved with pity; he held out his hand and touched him, and said, It is my will; be thou made clean" (Mark 1:40–41).

"How difficult it is, sometimes, to feel certain that there is anything important in being sorry for our sins — in a world where God is so openly defied, where his laws are so frequently and so deliberately broken, can it really make much difference whether I, this one, undistinguished creature of his, am sorry to have taken part in a world-wide conspiracy against him? Can it really interest him to be told, week after week or month after month, that I have been guilty of backbiting, of ill-temper, of telling small lies? If we would be honest with ourselves, I think that many of us would admit that what really disheartens us about our sins is not the greatness of them but the littleness of them: they are so mean, so petty: we are almost ashamed to admit that our lives, even when they are lived amiss, are lived on so unheroic a level. . . . Unimportant people, sinning dull sins and repenting of them, month after month so ineffectually — we are dogged by a sense of unreality which threatens to spoil all our freshness in our approach to Almighty God. Yes, but remember those words, the most comforting, I sometimes think, which ever fell from the lips of the world's Comforter: 'She (Mary Magdalen) hath done what she could'" (R. A. Knox, *Retreat for Lay People*).

"Give me grace, O Lord, to be in all things strong, prudent and just, with a wise restraint at need. Grant me an exact faith, unshakeable trust in thee, perfect charity. Fill me with the spirit of intelligence and wisdom. Let me be always thoughtful for others and in all things courageous, with loyalty and reverence. O Light, perfect and eternal, enlighten me!" (Alcuin, *De Usn Psalmorum*, ninth century).

"Let thy silent teaching of us, and our own spirit of reverence, join us to thyself in holy familiarity. Draw us to thyself, though we approach in awe; draw us into such an experience of joy in thy nearness, holding us therein, that our trust in thee may be the real source of our happiness" (Gothic Breviary, seventh century).

"Thy reproof, Lord, not thy vengeance; thy chastisement, not thy condemnation!... My own wrongdoing towers high above me, hangs on me like a heavy burden.... On thee, Lord, my hopes are set; thou, O Lord my God, wilt listen to me" (Ps. 37:2–16).

For Self-Knowledge

"No heart but is open to the Lord's scrutiny, no thought in our hearts but he can read it" (1 Par. [1 Chron.] 28:9).

"The scrutiny of God must not alarm me. He reaches to the very truth of things and need not, like a human judge, sift evidence, or listen to partisan speeches or, himself, possibly be confused and mistaken. I would prefer that God should see me thoroughly, my sins included. Even among our fellow-men there are those who seem to look deep into you, and read the 'back of your mind,' I may fear, or resent that: 'but not the gaze of God'" (C. C. Martindale, S.J., *The Sweet Singer of Israel*).

"Who, with all his intelligence, could appreciate fully such a work of mercy, or fail to marvel at it or see it with reverence? What words of praise could do it justice? O willing, overwhelming love, a wonder for our unceasing admiration is this miracle of divine condescension. Overawed, I yet rejoice with gratitude.... It is because we are the adopted sons of Christ. How came such a privilege to be ours? How shall we measure our due return? Happy indeed is the soul which, blameless in its living, knows the glory of such a dignity, supported as it is unceasingly by divine assistance. I beseech thee, then, my Lord, surpassingly kind, grant me grace in all things to bless and glorify thee" (attributed to Alcuin, ninth century).

"And Jesus said to them, the light is among you still, but only for a short time. Finish your journey while you still have the light, for fear darkness should overtake you; he who journeys in darkness cannot tell which way he is going. While you still have the light, have faith in the light, that so you may become children of the light" (John 12:35–36).

For Greater Sorrow

"Come back, sinners, and do his will; doubt not that he will show you mercy" (Tob. 13:8).

"Repentance is man's lasting portion. It accompanies him like a shadow. All attempts at ridding him of his dark fellow-traveller, and at robbing repentance of the place which it has held in religion from times immemorial ... are doomed to failure. He who has once lifted his eyes to heaven and there perceived the glory of infinite strength and beauty, finds that his tears will flow easily enough at the spectacle of himself and his sinfulness. This perception arouses both the impulse to repent of sin which takes its rise in the functioning of the free and noble will, and the realisation of the duty of repentance. The tears of sorrow are a sweet obligation upon us" (Prohaszka, *Meditations on the Gospels*).

"My dear Lord and Saviour, how can I make light of that which has had such consequences! Henceforth I will, through thy grace, have deeper views of sin than before. Fools make jest of sin, but I will view things in their true light. My suffering Lord, I have made thee suffer. Thou art most beautiful in thy eternal nature, O my Lord; thou art most beautiful in thy sufferings! Thy adorable attributes are not dimmed, but increased to us as we gaze on thy humiliation. Thou art more beautiful to us than before. But still I will never forget that it was man's sin, my sin, which made that humiliation necessary. *Amor meus crucifixus est* — 'my Love is crucified,' but by none other than me. I have crucified thee, my sin has crucified thee.... All I can do is to hate that which made thee suffer. Shall I not do that at least? Shall I not love my Lord so much as to hate that which is so great an enemy of his, and break off all terms with it? Shall I not put off sin altogether? By thy great love of me, teach me and enable me to do this. O Lord, give me a deep-rooted, intense hatred of sin" (Newman, *Meditations and Devotions*).

"We have defied the will of the Lord our God; trust and loyalty we had none to give him, nor ever shewed him submission, by listening to his divine voice and following the commands he gave us … straying ever further from the sound of his voice" (Bar. 1:17–19).

Resolution

"It is my decrees you will execute, my commands you will obey, following them closely; am I not the Lord your God?… They give life to the man who lives by them" (Lev. 18:4–5).

"In order to pardon us God does not require that we should be sure of not falling again. (Such a certainty would be something very like presumption.) He asks us to have the intention of doing what is in our power with the promised help of his grace in order to avoid sinning again. Have we this intention? In this case we have no need to fear hypocrisy and insincerity. Our gloomy forebodings in no wise modify our intention, especially since they are based on a blameworthy distrust regarding the grace of the sacrament. The sacrament of penance is a means of progress, but it is not so principally because of the psychological effort that it requires of us; it is so because to our ailing soul it applies its remedy, the expiatory and meritorious Blood of Jesus Christ. Not only does Jesus bestow on us the pardon that he obtained on our behalf by his passion, but he gives us healing and strengthening graces for fresh struggles in the future.… Don't worry yourself, then, about 'to-morrow.' To-morrow's grace will suffice for to-morrow so long as you continue in prayer and trust in God. To-day you have to-day's grace, a grace of contrition. The desire to bear in imagination to-morrow's temptation is a desire to bear a burden for which you have not received help; it is hardly surprising that it seems too heavy and, in advance, overwhelming" (Henri Charles Chéry, O.P., *Frequent Confession*).

"Thou, almighty, eternal God, hast decreed that mankind should exist in a society that is just and sincere. Therefore thou hast taught us to reject all that is contrary to justice since such things disturb harmony. Thou hast also bidden us to avoid all unjust dealings, that there may be peace with all and injury to none. We ourselves, then, must the more earnestly reject whatever displeases thee, and seek always those things which we know make us approved in thy sight" (Leonine Sacramentary, seventh century).

"To the task! Never doubting, never daunted; the Lord thy God will be at thy side, never failing thee, never forsaking thee, and see thou hast strength to do all that must be done" (1 Par. [1 Chron.] 28:20).

Thanksgiving 8

A Thought Before Saying One's Penance

"Sacramental penance has a special significance with regard to atonement. The penitential prayers belong to the sacrament; therefore they have a sacramental character, conveying special blessings to us" (Graef, *The Sacrament of Penance*).

For Perseverance

"I have bestowed my love upon you.... Live on, then, in my love" (John 15:9).

"God does not give marching orders. He is a living power ruling within me. The will of God is not merely a claim on me, it is also an active force. It is the special way in which he admonishes, urges, helps, sustains, acts and moulds, struggles, overcomes and perfects inside me. The will of God is the power with which he helps me to fulfil his demands. Seen in this light, it has another name: it is the power we call Grace when the will of God is done, it is the gift and achievement of this will itself.... It is my work but mine only through his, his will acting in me; the whole process being a mysterious unity.... It is his loving will for the individual child of God, a living force which encourages and sustains" (R. Guardini, *The Living God*).

"It is the thought of our human frailty, O Lord, that moves thee to show mercy towards us; for thou knowest well what we are and for what purpose thou didst give us life on earth. Have care, then, for me, the work of thy hands, that thy fashioning of me be not in vain, the blood thou hast shed for me be to no purpose. Do thou, who seekest saints among sinners, grant this grace — free me from sin and give new light to my mind that I may see thee, and know thee, as thou art, that, seeing thy guiding hand everywhere, I may follow thee closely. So shall the happy ending of my life be my coming unto thee, Jesus Christ, my Lord and my God" (attributed to St. Bernard of Clairvaux, twelfth century).

"O my dear Lord, lead me forward from strength to strength, gently, sweetly, tenderly, lovingly, powerfully, effectually, remembering my fretfulness and feebleness till thou bringest me into thy heaven" (Newman, *Meditations and Devotions*).

"I know no other content but clinging to my God, putting my trust in the Lord, my Master" (Ps. 72:28).

In Gratitude

"Thanks while yet thou livest, thanks while health and strength are still with thee, to praise God and to take pride in all his mercies! The Lord's mercy, that is so abundant, the pardon that is ever theirs who come back to him!" (Ecclus. [Sir.] 17:27–28).

"The permanent value attaching to the sacrament of penance is naturally to be judged on its effect upon our life after confession. Unless the reception of this sacrament is something merely mechanical, each confession should bring us a little higher in the path of perfection.... Many of the saints taught that every daily action should be a thanksgiving after the last Communion and a preparation for the next.... In the same way, during the days following a confession we should be making satisfaction for our sins by supplementing the penance we have already performed with prayers and good works of our own choosing" (J. C. Heenan, *Confession*).

"O Jesus Christ, tender, gentle and faithful Lover of men and kindly Redeemer of sinners, let my soul praise thee, my whole life be a service of thee, my whole being crave for thee. My poor soul has a longing to think of thee; to have yet more knowledge of the wonder that is thyself. Even more do I need an understanding of thy goodness and mercy to sinners lest at any time, despairing of my weakness, I should become estranged from thee. Let me have thoughts of thee that are worthy of thee, a trust in thee who art utterly true" (Anselm of Bury St. Edmunds, twelfth century).

"Well may I rejoice in the Lord, well may this heart triumph in my God. The deliverance he sends is like a garment that wraps me about, his mercy like a cloak enfolding me ... a spring-time of deliverance" (Isa. 61:10–11).

In Forgiveness of Others as We Have Been Forgiven

"Be merciful, then, as your Father is merciful. Judge nobody, and you will not be judged; condemn nobody, and you will not be condemned; forgive, and you will be forgiven" (Luke 6:36–37).

"O God of charity, Giver of the grace of true harmony, thou gavest us, through thy only-begotten Son, but one counsel of perfection, the new commandment, to love one another even as thou dost love us, unworthy and so often faithless as we are. Grant that we may have minds in which injuries do not rankle and hearts that are ever loyal to our brethren" (Liturgy of St. Cyril).

For the Work of the Church,
Christ's Body, Hindered by Our Sins

"My sin has offended God and has injured me: it is a violation of the love that I owe to my Creator, of the proper love that I owe to my Creator and of the proper love that I should bear towards myself as a child of God. But it has also aimed a blow at the Church, the mystical body. 'Every soul which raises itself raises the world.' Every Christian who falls impedes the perfection of the Christian community. The most hidden of sins causes an injury to the tree of which I am a branch. When I cut myself off completely from the tree by mortal sin or merely separate myself from it a little, the whole tree suffers. My spiritual vitality is entirely dependent on the Church, for God, for my benefit, has entrusted his graces to the Church, the body of Christ" (Henri Charles Chéry, O.P., *Frequent Confession*).

"Hear us, O Lord, and come with haste to help us. Give us strength to do all that we know it is our duty to do, and even all that we long to do. So it will come to pass that, whilst thou dost accomplish thy will in and through us, all will redound to thy praise" (Gothic Breviary, seventh century).

Preparation 9

God and the Sinner

"So he took ship across the sea, and came to his own city. And now they brought before him a man who was palsied and bed-ridden; whereupon Jesus, seeing their faith, said to the palsied man, Son, take courage, thy sins are forgiven. And at this, some of the scribes said to themselves, He is talking blasphemously. Jesus read their minds, and said, Why do you cherish wicked thoughts in your hearts? Tell me, which command is more lightly given, to say to a man, Thy sins are forgiven, or to say, Rise up and walk? And now, to convince you that the Son of Man has authority to forgive sins while he is on earth (here he spoke to the palsied man), Rise up, take thy bed with thee, and go home. And he rose up, and went back to his house, so that the multitudes were filled with awe at seeing it, and praised God for giving such powers to men" (Matt. 9:1–8).

The Value of the Sacrament

"Trust in him and he will lift thee to thy feet again; go straight on thy way, and fix in him thy hope" (Ecclus. [Sir.] 2:6).

"Jesus, when he first said: 'Thy sins are forgiven thee,' introduced his forgiveness with the words: 'Be of good heart, son.' It was as if he would say: 'Don't be down-hearted because of sin. Don't give up because of sin. Bad as sin is, it is never so bad but that it can be forgiven. Desperate as may be the state of the sinner, it is never so desperate but, if he will let me, I can still call him son.' The words themselves are proof enough that Jesus Christ our Lord has the sinner more in mind than the sin or sins which he has committed. He has come into the world, not to judge the world, but that the world may be saved through him; and he comes to the sinner, not to judge the sinner, no matter who he may be, but that through him the sinner may be saved. He asks him only to be of good heart; he asks him to come to him; he asks him to look up, not to lose courage, to be faithful against all odds, and in the end all will be right. Though of ourselves we can do nothing, we can do all things in him who strengthens us; if we will be faithful to him, by clinging to him whatever may happen, he will be faithful to us.

"'Be of good heart, son.' It may seem hard at times to give God all that he asks of us. It may seem hard to keep his commandments. Our own human nature may be against us; passion may rage in such a way as to seem irresistible. Our circumstances and our surroundings may be such as to draw us all the other way, and we may think ourselves unable to fight against them.... Nevertheless, in spite of all this, in spite of everything, the words of Jesus continue to ring out: 'Son, be of good heart.' No matter who we are, or what we have done, or what we fear we may do, he continues to cry: 'Come to me, all you that are burthened, and I will refresh you.'

"If the life of Jesus means anything, it surely means this. His name was called Jesus because he would save his people from their sins. He was sent, not so much for the just, but rather to call sinners to repentance. He was sent for the lost sheep of the house of Israel, and he accepted no title more willingly than that of being the 'friend of publicans and sinners.' If we would but recognise this more, then we would have more courage, both to fight the evil that drags us down, and to be faithful to him who is the best friend we

Devotions for Confession

have or shall ever have. No matter what may come, no matter what we have against ourselves, we can always, if we will, hear his encouragement and receive his friendly help: 'Be of good heart, son, thy sins are forgiven thee' " (Abp. Goodier, S.J., *The Life That Is Light*).

In Humility

"He achieves great things who will accept reproof" (Prov. 13:18).

"We think more, yes, far more, if not entirely, of what we have then to take to our Lord, and of what it may cost us to do it, than of what our Lord has to do, and longs to do, for us. It costs us some pain to go at all, and we prepare what we have to show very unwillingly, very imperfectly. There is a want of humility and truth in the examination of what is amiss; and we are restless, perhaps, at times, even resentful, in the disclosure that is needed. We have faith, but it is not the warmth of faith, of love, not the faith of *desire* that 'Christ may live in us,' that his hand may not only restore us, but also bless and fashion us, that his lips may not only speak our forgiveness, but also guide us with words of warning and encouragement.

"The beautiful side of confession is not only the return of the wounded, wandering sheep, but its treatment by the good Shepherd. This forms a great part of the joy of the angels upon one sinner doing penance" (R. Eaton, *The Ministry of Reconciliation*).

"It is good for me, Lord, that thou hast humbled me, that I may learn thy justifications and that I may cast away all pride of heart and presumption. It is profitable for me that shame has covered my face, that I may seek my consolation from thee rather than from men.... I return thee thanks that thou hast not spared my evil ways, but hast bruised me with bitter stripes, inflicting anguish and sending trials, both within and without. There is none else under heaven that can comfort me but thou, O Lord my God, the heavenly Physician of souls, who woundest and healest" (Thomas à Kempis, *The Imitation of Christ*, bk. 3, 50).

"To the Lord betake you, while he may yet be found; cry out while he is close at hand to hear. Leave rebel his ill-doing, sinner his guilty thoughts, and come back to the Lord, sure of his mercy, our God so rich in pardon" (Isa. 55:6–7).

For Confidence

"I am gentle and humble of heart; and you shall find rest for your souls" (Matt. 11:29).

"God is good; he is good to you and means well to you; make, then, a 'return in kind' — briefly: love him because he first loves you. Somehow thus we must paraphrase the simple words. We wish, then, a deep realisation of the goodness of God, with its consequences, gratitude and trust, to anticipate any sense and instinct of abashment, humiliation, even sorrow, let alone terror, to fly before his face.... This does not mean that we forget our sins. On the contrary, God's incredible goodness is manifested 'most chiefly,' says the liturgy, 'in sparing and showing pity.' Indeed, we might hardly dare to contemplate our sins until we were well established in the conviction that God loves us 'with an everlasting love.' He loves us in spite of our sins and even while we were committing them — if he did not, why should he seek so earnestly to bring us to repentance and have redeemed us at the cost of the death of his own Son? Moreover, if we are clear beyond any shadow of doubting that God loves us, we shall reach without any difficulty the supreme motive for being sorry, which is precisely the love of God. Not even the Hebrew trod exclusively, or even chiefly, the road of fear: it is a precarious one, and leads to despondency almost as easily as to contrition, and beats the soul down rather than encourages it; and the motive of fear has anyhow to be corrected afterwards by that of love, whereas if we love aright, we shall not need to use the motive of fear at all, for 'perfect love casteth out fear'" (C. C. Martindale, S.J., *The Sweet Singer of Israel*).

"Most merciful Lord Jesus Christ, truly all my hope; the more the memory of my sins disheartens me, the more the thought of thy boundless kindness and the infinite merits of thy sacred passion encourages and uplifts me, for whatever wrong I have done thy bitter death has cancelled. I know that thy holy Incarnation and thy sufferings make up for all my faults, whatever they may be. Do thou, kind Jesus, in whom all my hope is set, give me some experience of the warmth of thy Fatherly regard" (attributed to John Tauler).

"This, as always, is God's doing; it is he who, through Christ, has reconciled us to himself. . . . Christ never knew sin, and God made him into sin for us, so that in him we might be turned into the holiness of God" (2 Cor. 5:18–21).

For Self-Knowledge

"The man whose life is true comes to the light, so that his deeds may be seen for what they are" (John 3:21).

"God is he who sees. But his seeing is an act of love. With his seeing he embraces his creatures, affirms them and encourages them, since he hates nothing that he has created. When he had created the world he saw that 'everything was very good.' He sees men's possibilities and calls them to use them. He sees the evil in the world and judges it; he sees human sin and passes sentence on it. His judgment penetrates to the roots and nothing can be hidden from him — but he himself has told us that he is loving and merciful and forgiving and redeeming. . . . His seeing is not the kind that merely looks at something; it is creative love, it is the power that enables things to be themselves and rescues them from degeneration and decay.

"God turns his face to men and thereby gives himself to man. By looking at me he enables me to be myself. The soul lives on the loving gaze of God: this is an infinitely deep and blessed mystery.

"God is he who sees with the eyes of love, by whose seeing things are enabled to be themselves, by whose seeing I am enabled to be myself" (R. Guardini, *The Living God*).

"Grant me, O Lord, to know what I ought to know, to love what I ought to love, to praise what is most pleasing to thee, to esteem what appears precious to thee, to abominate what is foul in thy sight. Suffer me not to judge according to the sight of the outward eyes, nor to give sentence according to the hearing of the ears of ignorant men; but to determine matters both visible and spiritual with true judgment; and above all things, ever to seek thy good will and pleasure" (Thomas à Kempis, *The Imitation of Christ*, bk. 3, 50).

"If thy actions are good, canst thou doubt they will be rewarded? If not, canst thou doubt that guilt, thenceforward, will lie at thy door?" (Gen. 4:7).

For Greater Sorrow

"For the time being all correction is painful rather than pleasant; but afterwards, when it has done its work of discipline, it yields a harvest of good dispositions, to our great peace" (Heb. 12:11).

Devotions for Confession

"An act of contrition should not be conceived as something so difficult to make as to be the monopoly of mystics. A Christian can elicit an act of perfect contrition, with the help of God's grace, by the very proper consideration that sin is an unfriendly act, that all creation is for the greater honour and glory of God and that sin has robbed God of that glory which is his due. A great help to contrition is to see sin through the eyes of Christ our Lord. To conquer sin, to rob death of its sting, Christ offered himself as a Victim on the cross. The prospect of the chalice of his suffering filled him with such a human fear as to cause his sweat to become as drops of blood. Though he was so weakened as to beg his eternal Father, if it were possible that this chalice might pass from him, Christ endured his agony and passion to teach us the enormity of sin. Upon him was laid the burden of us all" (J. C. Heenan, *Confession*).

"Thou, O my God, hast a claim on me, and I am wholly thine! Thou art the almighty Creator, and I am thy workmanship. I am the work of thy hands, and thou art my owner.... O my God, I confess that before now I have utterly forgotten this, and that I am continually forgetting it! I have acted many a time as if I were my own master, and turned away from thee rebelliously. I have acted according to my own pleasure, not according to thine. And so far have I hardened myself as not to feel as I ought how evil this is. I do not understand how dreadful sin is — and I do not hate it, and fear it, as I ought. I have no horror of it, or loathing. I do not turn from it with indignation, as being an insult to thee, but I trifle with it, even if I do not commit great sins, I have no great reluctance to do small ones. O my God, what a great and awful difference there is between what I am and what I ought to be" (Newman, *Meditations and Devotions*).

"What if my transgressions should go, all unobserved, from bad to worse, if I should grow hardened in wrongdoing, and add fault to fault? What humiliation were this!…Do not leave me, Lord, at the mercy of a shameless, an unprofitable mind!" (Ecclus. [Sir.] 23:3–6).

Resolution

"This above all the Lord demands of thee, right thou shouldst do…and carry thyself humbly in the presence of thy God" (Mic. 6:8).

"We should all make a resolution to be most determined to give our Lord what he wants now.… It is no good saying you have started before. You can start again and again. Every fresh start is bringing you closer to him. Your good start will never be forgotten, and each good start helps the next to have greater perseverance, and you never know what great graces God will give you, especially if you desire to serve him and realise that of yourself you cannot do it. Tell him how utterly dependent you are on him, and you will find that he will give you graces out of all proportion: personal charity, powers of self-restraint, and the grace to use yourself body and soul for the service of God" (F. Devas, S.J., *What Law and Letter Kill*).

"Do thou thy will in my will, O Lord, as thou dost on earth, with the same power and to the same profit. Long have I prayed and desired this almighty grace by which thou dost lead our hearts to the doing of thy will. Do not leave my heart to emptiness and uselessness, for it is the work of thy hands" (St. Augustine, *Soliloquies*).

"As he sees me dutiful, the Lord will requite me, as he sees me guiltless in act, he will make return" (Ps. 17:21).

Thanksgiving 9

A Thought Before Saying One's Penance

"My sacramental penance, however slight it be, by its very slightness in fact, should enable me to rely above all on Christ crucified and the communion of saints for the offering of adequate satisfaction to God. In saying my *Our Father*, or three *Hail Maries*, I call upon Christ's own act of redemption and on the Church of the Saints, those on earth as well as those in heaven, since it is through my communion with them that I have just received God's forgiveness. I know that all the good I do and all the afflictions I endure will avail as satisfaction for my own sins and those of my brethren. I do not look upon my debt as wholly paid, and quite apart from my sacramental penance, I try to discharge my debt of satisfaction" (Community of St. Sévérin, *Confession*).

For Perseverance

"God's patience is his patience with me. And I to some extent am able to judge what that means because I know how difficult it is to be patient with myself.... If God's attitude to us is the same as our own attitude to ourselves, then the outlook is black indeed. If God takes as poor a view of me as I do of myself, if God does not bear with my bungling, my dishonesty, my constant failures with greater patience than I do myself, I am bound to give up in despair. But

God is love. And in him my nature is truer than in myself. In me it is corrupt; in him it is pure. In his most holy patience he holds in his love my nature which I myself disfigure so terribly and squander so thoughtlessly. From this loving patience he sees and bears me. He has infinite confidence in me. He believes that I am capable of making progress" (R. Guardini, *The Living God*).

"My God, can I sin when thou art intimately with me? Can I forget who is with me, who is in me? Can I expel a divine Inhabitant by that which he abhors more than anything else, which is the one thing in the world which is offensive to him, the only thing which is not his?... My God, I have a double security against sinning; first the dread of such a profanation of all thou art to me in thy very presence; and next because I do trust that that presence will preserve me from sin. My God, thou wilt go from me if I sin; and I shall be left to my own miserable self. God forbid! I will use what thou hast given me; I will call on thee when tried and tempted. I will guard against the sloth and carelessness into which I am continually falling. Through thee I will never forsake thee" (Newman, *Meditations and Devotions*).

"For ever and for evermore true to thy charge thou shalt find me. Freely shall my feet tread, if thy will is all my quest.... Flung wide my arms to greet thy law, ever in my thoughts thy bidding" (Ps. 118:44–47).

In Gratitude

"Praise the Lord, the Lord is gracious; his mercy endures for ever" (1 Par. [1 Chron.] 16:34).

"God does well in giving the grace of consolation; but man does ill in not returning all again to God with thanksgiving.

Devotions for Confession

"And this is the reason why the gifts of grace cannot flow in us: that we are ungrateful to the Giver and do not return all to the Source.

"For grace will always be given to him that duly returns thanks" (Thomas à Kempis, *The Imitation of Christ*, bk. 2, 10).

"O divine Liberator ... when I fell into sin, thou didst with generosity correct me; when sadness overwhelmed me, thou didst take the bitterness from it; when I was utterly without hope, thou didst give me fresh courage and trust; when I fell, thy hand was held out to me; when I walked justly, thou didst encourage me, and, keeping to thy paths, thou didst bear me company; when I dared to draw near to thee, kindly and with tenderness thou didst welcome me" (St. Augustine, *Soliloquies*).

"How rich God is in mercy; with what an excess of love he loved us! Our sins made dead men of us, and he, in giving life to Christ, gave life to us too; it is his grace that has saved you.... He would have all future ages see, in that clemency which he shewed us in Christ Jesus, the surpassing riches of his grace" (Eph. 2:4–7).

In Forgiveness of Others, as We Have Been Forgiven

"The measure you award to others is the measure that will be awarded to you" (Luke 6:38).

"Most kindly Lord Jesus Christ, thou hast bidden us love our enemies and those who speak evil to us, to pray earnestly for those who offend us, or injure us, as thou thyself prayed from the cross for those who hounded thee to death. Increase in us, I beseech thee, the spirit of gentleness and toleration that we may easily overlook any offences and, by the help of thy grace, have peace with our enemies, so rising above the malice and injustice that is in man. We beseech thee, then, give true peace and charity to our enemies that they may find pardon for their faults … and help us by our good works to conquer the evil that is in ourselves" (St. Peter Canisius, *Manuale Catholicorum*).

For the Work of the Church, Christ's Body, Hindered by Our Sins

"It is just and reasonable that, when we know who God is and what he has done for us, we should feel shame and regret for having offended him, whether we have done this by deliberate ingratitude or by weakness. The same habit of mind will make us sensitive to the wrongs done to God by those who belong to us as members of the same family, or nationality, or religion, or race; and it will cause us to make reparation in our own person for their misdeeds. Hence, Jesus Christ, as being of one blood with mankind, suffered shame for what his brethren had done, and was impelled, even by human sentiments, to offer an atonement that was not due from him personally. You owe satisfaction for your individual wrong-doings and for those of the race with which you form a corporate personality. It is your duty to make atonement out of the spirit of penance, as did Jesus Christ" (J. Bellord, *Meditations on Christian Dogma*).

"Grant, O most kindly Father, to thy servants full opportunity, intelligence and strength that, according to thy will, we may do thee loyal service, and let thy inspiration guide us in the right way. Give courage to those who are beginners in the way of holiness, understanding to the young, help to the willing, earnestness to the half-hearted and repentance to the weak, that all may reap the full harvest of their labours. Let our lips speak thy praise, and each and all our days have thy blessing" (Gallican Sacramentary, sixth century).

Preparation 10

God and the Sinner

"It happened that he was standing by the lake of Genesareth, at a time when the multitude was pressing close about him to hear the word of God; and he saw two boats moored at the edge of the lake; the fishermen had gone ashore, and were washing their nets. And he went on board one of the boats, which belonged to Simon, and asked him to stand off a little from the land; and so, sitting down, he began to teach the multitudes from the boat. When he had finished speaking, he said to Simon, Stand out in the deep water, and let down your nets for a catch. Simon answered him, Master, we have toiled all the night, and caught nothing; but at thy word I will let down the net. And when they had done this, they took a great quantity of fish, so that the net was near breaking, and they must needs beckon to their partners who were in the other boat to come and help them. When these came, they filled both boats, so that they were ready to sink. At seeing this, Simon Peter fell down and caught Jesus by the knees; leave me to myself, Lord, he said; I am a sinner. Such amazement had overcome both him and all his crew, at the catch of fish they had made; so it was, too, with James and John, the sons of Zebedee, who were Simon's partners. But Jesus said to Simon, Do not be afraid" (Luke 5:1–10).

Preparation 10

The Value of the Sacrament

"Blessed evermore is the timorous conscience; it is hardened hearts that fall to their ruin" (Prov. 28:14).

"Man should be able not only to acknowledge that he is a sinner, but also able to face the idea — not in a spirit of defiance and self-assertiveness, but with sincerity and goodwill; not in a spirit of self-abasement and mortification, but honourably and responsibly. In short, man must reconcile himself to the idea that he is a sinner and must learn to bear the stigma; this will open the way to self-renewal....

"True forgiveness, the forgiveness which we are seeking and which alone avails us, is a great mystery; it implies, not only that God decides to overlook what has happened and turns lovingly towards the sinner; this would not be sufficient. God's forgiveness is creative, it makes him who has become guilty, free of all guilt. God gathers him into his holiness, makes him partake of it and gives him a new beginning. It is to this mystery that man appeals when he acknowledges his sins, repents of them and seeks forgiveness.

"This is the first of those two motives of prayer which come into being before God's holiness. The other begins with the recognition that despite our resistance to God we cannot be without him. The first expresses what Peter said to Christ when he felt his mysterious powers by the lake of Genesareth: 'Depart from me, for I am a sinful man, O Lord.' The other finds its expression once again in the words of Peter at Capharnaum, when our Lord promised the Eucharist: 'Lord, to whom shall we go? Thou hast the words of eternal life. And we have believed and have known that thou art the Christ, the Son of God.'

"If the knowledge of our sinfulness leads us either to arrogance or dejection, the link between God and man breaks and we turn away from him. But if it leads us to humility and truth, then we may say: 'It is true that by my sins I have forfeited the right of being in the presence of God, but where else shall I be if I cannot be with him?'

"The same holiness which turns man away also recalls him, for holiness is love. It rejects man so that he may find true humility and the new way. When he has done this — however insufficiently — it calls him anew" (R. Guardini, *Prayer in Practice*).

In Humility

"He that humbles himself shall be exalted" (Luke 14:11).

"The great penitents in Holy Scripture are shown to us sorrowing and detesting their sins as a necessary prelude to the resolution of leading a new life and of making satisfaction. 'I know my iniquity, and my sin is always before me ... a contrite and humble heart, O God, thou wilt not despise.' (*Ps. 1*). 'The soul that is sorrowful for the greatness of the evil she hath done ... giveth glory and justice to thee.' (*Baruch 2*). 'I am confounded and ashamed because I have borne the reproach of my youth.' (*Jerem. 31*). In the New Testament, the tears of Peter and of Mary Magdalen, and the grief of the Prodigal son are familiar examples of true repentance" (E. J. Mahoney, *Sin and Repentance*).

"O almighty God, who hast special regard for lowly things, grant us the grace of humility which is so pleasing to thee. Let there be in us no trace of the pride which in its beginning thou dost mark, and in the end dost destroy. By thy mercy, let all arrogance in our sinning be banished from our minds and an ennobling sorrow possess our hearts" (Gothic Breviary, seventh century).

"A heart ready to serve thee, O God, a heart ready to serve thee!" (Ps. 107:2).

For Confidence

"Jesus our Lord, who gives us all our confidence, bids us come forward emboldened by our faith in him. Let there be no discouragement" (Eph. 3:12–13).

"Since the interior man is more present to God's sight than to his own, it may happen that where he himself believes he should accuse and condemn, God will find excuses and will deal leniently. God's estimation is less severe because more justly founded.... He has a minute knowledge of those secret influences which tend to impose our desires upon us, and we may rest assured that he takes them into account in determining the exact degree of our responsibility. He knows of what clay we are fashioned; he has a nice appreciation of the difficulty, the moral impossibility even, of our resisting for any length of time and on several fronts at once without being surprised and outflanked on one side or another. Consequently he owes it in some way to himself and to the nature he has given us to allow a certain margin, and to grant that, within certain limits, our will may run counter to his own without offending him grievously" (Galtier, *Sin and Penance*).

"Trustfully waiting upon thee, O Lord, we beg thee to save us whose confidence is all in thee. As thou hast promised, bring full comfort to us, redeemed at the cost of thy precious blood. Thus shall our sorrow be eased and our doubts laid to rest. Inward peace and joy will be ours once more, and the promise of eternal happiness to come" (Gothic Breviary, seventh century).

"It is my God that brings me aid, and gives me confidence; he is my shield, my weapon of deliverance, my protector, my stronghold. It is he that preserves me from wrong. Praised be the Lord! When I invoke him I am secure" (2 Kings 22:3–4).

For Self-Knowledge

"Fear God, and keep his commandments; this is the whole meaning of man. No act of thine but God will bring it under his scrutiny, deep beyond all thy knowing, and pronounce it good or evil" (Eccles. 12:13–14).

"To take oneself seriously means to see oneself as a child of God; to try to fulfil the tasks he gives us from day to day; to strive towards perfection; to place the centre of the gravity of existence not in the brief 'now' of the present life, but in eternity. It means not only taking *this* life seriously, but also death and the life that follows death. More than anything else, it means taking God himself seriously, as the judge before whom we are responsible, as the Father who is ready, again and again, to welcome home the lost son into the peace and security of his house" (Von Gagern, *Difficulties in Life*).

"O God, who mercifully heard the blind men by the wayside, pleading for the gift of sight, and didst give light to their eyes, give the like merciful hearing to our prayers and open our eyes also to the appreciation of spiritual things. So, with enlightened hearts, we shall learn to hold earthly things at their true worth and look more easily to those of heaven" (Pontifical of Magdalen, eleventh century).

"Where your treasure-house is, there your heart is too" (Matt. 6:21).

Preparation 10

For Greater Sorrow

"Happy the man whom God chastens for his faults! The correction he sends thee never, on thy life, refuse. Wounds he, it is but to heal; the same hand that smote shall medicine thee" (Job 5:17–18).

"Our preparation should largely consist in an effort to arouse in ourselves deep and true sorrow. In our examination of conscience we should avoid excessive introspection; if we frequent the sacraments regularly, serious sin will come to our mind easily, and if we have to search with notable diligence, it is reasonably certain that the deliberation in our acts was so slight as to deprive them of all gravity. But having found our sins, we should dwell almost fiercely on the motives for sorrow: on the goodness of God, on the vileness of even the slightest venial sin, on its ingratitude to God, who gave us the very powers we use in sinning and who keeps us in existence while we sin, and above all on the passion of our Lord, endured because of sin. This should be the chief part of our preparation if we are to receive the full benefit of this sacrament. Our very resolution against sin is rendered far stronger if we have, though only for a time, felt real sorrow for our sins and a genuine detestation of them" (H. Harrington, *The Sacrament of Penance*).

"What a revelation, O Christ the Son of God, is that immense joy and enduring happiness granted to thy saints, in all its sweetness, once their bitter conflict with sin was over! Grant to us, who have not known such grief at the thought of evil, the sorrow that comforts, that we, who by our sins have so often strayed from thee, may have fellowship with the saints and know their lasting joy" (Gothic Breviary, seventh century).

"He who trusts in the Lord finds nothing but mercy all around him" (Ps. 31:10).

Resolution

"If you have really listened to him. If true knowledge is to be found in Jesus, you will have learned in his school that you must be quit now of the old self whose way of life you remember, the old self that wasted its aim on false dreams. There must be a renewal in the inner life" (Eph. 4:21–23).

" 'It costs me a good deal to go to confession at all: it involves both thought and labour, and I try to do all as well as I can, but I do not feel much the better for it.' This may be explained in many ways. Many in their confessions are very perfunctory and casual; others again are intent on the reception of forgiveness, forgetting all which that forgiveness implies.... As a consequence, forgiveness is often regarded as a matter of course, and is received without gratitude and recognition; no pains are taken to realise the greatness of the boon, of the change effected, of the work accomplished. 'Does not the benignity of God lead us to penance?' (Rom. 2:4).... When we asked our Lord to repair that broken twisted link of gold, did we promise nothing? Did we undertake nothing? Should we express no desire, no determination, that never again would the link be twisted and broken; or at least, not so frequently, nor so heartlessly? Certainly our Lord looked for us to do so, if not in words, at least in thought and desire. Otherwise *much* is left undone and the forgiveness so gladly given will not ennoble and strengthen the future as it ought to do" (R. Eaton, *The Ministry of Reconciliation*).

"To thee, O Lord, by whom our frail being is ever supported, we look to be filled with the desire of spiritual realities, that so we may cease to delude ourselves with mere worldly pleasures. It is by these, as we well know, that the enemy of our good blinds us to the supernatural blessings towards which the inspiration of thy grace steadily draws us. Do thou, Almighty God, give us an unerring appreciation of the good, that all our desires may be inspired by truth and not by pretence" (Gothic Breviary, seventh century).

"Nay, Lord, accept these vows of mine; teach me to do thy bidding.... Now and ever thy covenant is my prize, is my heart's comfort. Now and ever to do thy will, to earn thy favour, is my heart's aim" (Ps. 118:108–112).

Thanksgiving 10

"In the sacrament of penance, temporal punishment is scarcely ever remitted in its entirety. Sacramental penance therefore is a convenient means of reducing such punishment.... This is an important point in favour of confessions of devotion; the reduction of temporal punishment obtained through the sacramental penance is reason enough to receive this sacrament as often as possible" (R. Graef, *The Sacrament of Peace*).

For Perseverance

"Vigilantly preserve innocence, and keep the right before thy eyes" (Ps. 36:37).

"The future is before us and we are bound to handle it then and there! We should expect this from a child of tenderest years to whom we forgave a trivial fault: and our heavenly Father expects the same from his children to whom so many times he forgives faults, not trivial, but very grievous, and often accompanied by scandal. The future is before us as we leave the sacred tribunal, and our satisfaction claims immediate attention. Precautions must be taken to avoid the occasions of sin.... Practical resolutions concerning our falls must be made and fixed firmly in the will, for we go forth from our

Saviour's feet with his blessing, refreshed and encouraged indeed, but yet in reality the *self-same* men that we were when we drew near to him with our tale of failure. The outside world and its snares have not changed, nor have we changed radically either. Hence the need of this firm purpose, of this entreaty for perseverance in grace and in the pursuit of good. 'Behold, thou art made whole: sin no more, lest some *worse* thing happen to thee' " (R. Eaton, *The Ministry of Reconciliation*).

"As long as I have any strength left, or a breath of life, I will not cease serving thee, O divine Master! If I am well, I will serve thee in health; if ill, I will serve thee in sickness. O good Jesus, thou knowest that of myself I can do nothing, but what thou dost for me will always be perfect. I will take care never to forsake thy service, and, come what may, I will ever seek to please thee and remain faithful to thee. My desire is to be in thy sight such as thou desirest to see me" (Lanspergius, sixteenth century).

"Blithely as one that has found great possessions, I will follow thy decrees" (Ps. 118:14).

In Gratitude

"For mysteries unfathomable, praise God" (Prov. 25:2).

"Each person must follow the line of thought which is most suitable in leading him to perfect contrition. The fear of God is the beginning of all wisdom, and the thought of eternal separation from God would usually be the starting-point. A further step would be to think of the pain of loss as being inflicted by one who loves us with infinite love. Sin is an offence and an insult against God, for whom we should have nothing but gratitude in return for all his favours, both spiritual and temporal, and above all for his unspeakable gift of grace by which we are made his adopted sons in Christ. 'How hath he not also with him given us all things?' Have we made any return for these gifts, or are all our prayers invariably petitions for further favours? God has been good to us, but why? Not because there is anything beautiful or loveable about us apart from our union with Christ, for whose sake God loves us. No matter how we look at it, there is nothing in us that we have not received from God.... Why, then, is God good to us? For no other reason than because he is good in himself" (E. J. Mahoney, *Sin and Repentance*).

"Thou art a refuge to raise up and direct thy children. We will not go back upon thee who hast so delivered us from all our evils and filled us with good things of thy own. Even now thou givest us these blessings, and how gently thou dealest with us lest we be wearied on the way. Thou dost correct us, chastise us, even punish us, and guide us that we may not stray from the path. So, whether thou dealest gently with us, that we weary not in the way, or dost chastise us lest we leave it, thou art still, O Lord, our refuge" (St. Augustine, *Sermons*).

"In love and pity he ransomed them, lifted them in his arms and raised them up" (Isa. 63:9).

In Forgiveness of Others, as We Have Been Forgiven

"No, it is your enemies you must love, and do them good.... Then your reward will be a rich one, and you will be true sons of the most High, generous like him towards the thankless and the unjust" (Luke 6:35).

"O God, mighty and eternal, filled with a heaven-sent peace so that the angel hosts gave thee praise, singing: Glory be to God in the highest, and on earth peace to men of good will, fill our hearts with the good will that comes from thy gift of peace. Free us, not only from all stain of sin, but from all insincerity and from the soul-destroying nursing of resentment" (Liturgy of St. Basil).

For the Work of the Church, Christ's Body, Hindered by Our Sins

"The theology of the sacrament of penance would be an incomprehensible tangle of conflicting elements but for this fundamental assumption, that through the sacrament Christ enables his own members to make good the harm done by their sins to the supernatural order. So this sacrament is not defined primarily in terms of sorrow, but in terms of powers and deeds. Its efficacy rests on the one hand on the power of the keys, and on the other on the acts of the Christian, of which one only is sorrow or contrition, the others being of the executive order, confession and satisfaction. Though the injuries done to the divine order of Christ's life by sin be very grievous, the sacrament of penance is more powerful than sin. The Christian is a penitent in the true sense, then, only when he enters into that sin-destroying dispensation which Christ has left to his Church for the exclusive benefit of his people. Sorrow external to that dispensation would not meet the needs of the case.... A whole range of divine realities has been disturbed by the sin of the Christian; he cannot make matters right except through the pre-ordained extra mercies of the sacramental re-adjustment. The power of propitiation that is in Christ becomes palpably operative in the sacrament of penance, and the faithful, who are the very people whose sins are in need of propitiation, are called upon to enter effectively into that power of Christ, by doing the works of the sacramental repentance. It is in this fuller sense that the Christian is a penitent" (Vonier, *Christianus*).

"Well knowest thou, my God, that in the midst of all my miseries I have never ceased to recognize thy great power and mercy. May it prove of avail to me that I have not offended thee in this. Restore the time I have lost, my God, by granting me thy grace, both in the present and in the future" (St. Teresa, *Exclamations*).

Preparation 11

God and the Sinner

"So Mary Magdalen brought news to the disciples, of how she had seen the Lord, and he had spoken thus to her. And now it was evening on the same day, the first day of the week; for fear of the Jews, the disciples had locked the doors of the room in which they had assembled; and Jesus came, and stood there in their midst; Peace be upon you, he said. And with that he shewed them his hands and his side. Thus the disciples saw the Lord, and were glad. Once more Jesus said to them, Peace be upon you; I come upon an errand from my Father, and now I am sending you out in my turn. With that, he breathed on them, and said to them, Receive the Holy Spirit; when you forgive men's sins, they are forgiven, when you hold them bound, they are held bound" (John 20:18–23).

The Value of the Sacrament

"This is what the Son of Man is come for, to search out and to save what was lost" (Luke 19:10).

"The Catholic Church shows forth in every act of her life something of Christ's victory; her faith, her prayers, her sacraments, her combats, her whole organization, proclaim that her Head is the one who has overcome all evil and has acquired eternal glory. In order to be a Church of victory she need not be without assaults from outside nor without blemishes in her own children. But one thing is essential to her, she must be able to meet every outside adversary and she must be able to cleanse away every sin that is found in the heart of any of her members; and this the Church has always done, and for this reason we are more than justified in proclaiming her the Church militant, which can only mean the victorious Church.

"It is not without deep significance that the mystery of the resurrection, the mystery of the Spirit and the mystery of the forgiveness of sins are shown as united in the sacred Gospels. When Christ comes back from the dead, when he shows himself to the Apostles, he breathes on them the Spirit and gives them power to remit sins, for the exercise of that power is truly the complete Easter. 'And when he had said this, he shewed them his hands and his side. The disciples therefore were glad, when they saw the Lord. He said therefore to them again: Peace be to you. As the Father hath sent me, I also send you. When he had said this, he breathed on them; and he said to them: Receive ye the Holy Ghost. Whose sins you shall forgive, they are forgiven them: and whose sins you shall retain, they are retained.'

"The power of forgiving sin in the Church is the one great trophy which Christ brought back to his Apostles when he returned from his triumphant battle; he did not bring the grace of complete sinlessness for the Church here below, but he brought the greater grace of the remission of sins in his name, because he had conquered sin. It is as if Christ, in that moment of supreme happiness, was overpowered himself by what he had achieved on the cross and in the tomb and in Limbo, the complete conquest of sin, and so his first words to his disciples are to be these: 'Whose sins you shall forgive, they are forgiven.' They are truly the words of a conqueror. Christ had forgiven sin in his own lifetime, but now he makes a gift of that power to his Church, to the end of time, without any reservation. It is perhaps the unfortunate result of our being familiarized with divine utterances that makes it difficult for us to see the transcending glory of a Gospel passage like this. Had it been left to us to find out which were the first words of Christ to his disciples at so astonishing a moment, would it have occurred to us to put remission of sins in the first rank? But happily we are not asked to speak for God; the Gospels are essentially the dealings of a divine Person and therefore dealings which are mostly unexpected and incomprehensible. Still, does it not sound as if Christ, with infinite graciousness, told his Apostles: 'Here I am once more, and since we have parted I have done what I set out to do: I have destroyed sin. Therefore go forth and forgive sin wherever there is sin to be forgiven'" (Vonier, *The Victory of Christ*).

"But the God-Man, Jesus Christ, who has *the power on earth to forgive sins*, in his bounteous mercy willed to give it to his priests to help men in that need for expiation which troubles every heart. What a consolation to the conscience-stricken and truly repentant sinner to hear the priest in the name of God pronounce the words of absolution: 'I absolve you from your sins!' The fact that these words are spoken by one who must himself seek a like sentence of absolution from another priest should make us think more rather than less of this gift of God's mercy. It is God's hand rather than man's that must be seen bringing about this wonderful event. To quote the words of a distinguished writer ... 'When the priest, overwhelmed at the thought of his own unworthiness and the exalted nature of his office, holds his consecrated hands over our bowed heads; when abashed at finding himself the dispenser of the blood of the New Testament and amazed as often as he pronounces the words that give life, that he, a sinner, has absolved a sinner from his sins, we, the penitents, feel, as we rise from our knees before him, that we have not demeaned ourselves in any way.... We have done it to obtain the priceless status of free men and sons of God'" (Pius XII, *The Catholic Priesthood*).

Devotions for Confession

In Humility

"I will arise and go to my father, and say to him, Father, I have sinned against heaven and before thee" (Luke 15:18).

"The ministry of reconciliation has a large human element attached to it. The powers at work are divine, but they are exercised by human agents, and who can estimate the power of human sympathy that, like oil poured out, reaches the soul in this sacrament of our Lord's love? Men, not angels, are the ministers of the Gospel; and there is no channel of divine aid and strength instituted by our Lord in which the human heart is so much to the front as in this sacrament of mercy.... An angel could not bestow such help as this: but a priest can do so, because he is human and liable himself to err. Our Lord knew this, and arranged his favour accordingly.... Awful though the responsibility be, the heart of every true priest goes out to those who seek his aid in the ministry of reconciliation. Nowhere else does he reap such a harvest for his Lord. He may preach the word in season and out of season, but the kind yet searching words he is privileged to speak in confession — words of truth and encouragement — will bring more consolation, will heal more wounds, will bestow more strength, and effect a greater advance in virtue than the words preached from the house-tops, for they are a message from the Sacred Heart of our Lord direct to his sinful child" (R. Eaton, *The Ministry of Reconciliation*).

"O how humbly and meanly ought I to think of myself! Of how little worth ought I to esteem whatever good I seem to have! O Lord, how profoundly ought I to abase myself under thy unfathomable judgments wherein I find myself to be nothing else but nothing.... Where, then, is there any excuse for pride? Where any room for confidence in my own virtue?" (Thomas à Kempis, *The Imitation of Christ*).

"Out of the depths I cry to thee, O Lord; Master, listen to my voice; let thy ears be attentive to the voice that calls on thee for pardon. If thou, Lord, take heed of our iniquities, Master, who has strength to bear it? Ah, but with thee there is forgiveness; I will wait for thee, Lord, as thou commandest. My soul relies on his promise, my soul waits patiently for the Lord ... the Lord with whom there is mercy, with whom is abundant power to ransom" (Ps. 129:2–8).

"To thee, then, we turn, who art our God, to thee, the great, the strong" (Neh. 9:32).

For Confidence

"God has life waiting for us, if we will but keep faith with him" (Tob. 2:18).

"Distrust ourselves? When did we ever do anything else? We are unequal, no one could be more conscious of it than we are, to so high a vocation as the vocation Christ offers us. But, to proceed from that distrust of self to trust in God, that is a different story. Trust in God is not a mere reasoned calculation, such as any Christian may easily make for himself, that we are all in God's hands all the time, and as we have to depend on him for so much it is only reasonable to recognize that we depend on him altogether. Trust is an overbalancing of our whole weight, into his arms" (R. A. Knox, *A Retreat for Lay People*).

"Reflect and consider, O my soul, lest despair overcome thee. Trust in him of whom thou art fearful. Seek refuge with him from whom thou fleest. Beseech and implore him whom thou hast so lightly offended. Jesus, Jesus, for thy name's sake, deal with me as befits thy name, the name that brings comfort and glad hope to sinners. For what else art thou, my Jesus, except our Saviour? Be to me, for thy name's sake, the Jesus who fashioned me, who redeemed me, that I perish not, that I be not condemned, thou who in goodness created me, that thy work in me be not hindered by my sinfulness" (St. Anselm of Canterbury, twelfth century).

"Such is the merciful kindness of our God, which has bidden him come to us, like a dawning from on high, to give light to those who live in darkness, in the shadow of death, and to guide our feet in the way of peace" (Luke 1:78–79).

For Self-Knowledge

"That abundant kindness of his, which bears with thee and waits for thee? Dost thou not know that God's kindness is inviting thee to repent?" (Rom. 2:4).

"The sacrament of mercy is indeed a reconciliation of friends, but it is also a tribunal; and the effectiveness of the tribunal depends in great measure on the dispositions and work of the penitent. He has his definite part to play. If he merely stands in the dock, as it were, and says in a stoic kind of way: 'I am guilty,' and then demands absolution and reinstatement into many a right and privilege, the reconciliation will be shorn of its warmth and intensity. The mind of our Lord in regard to his channel of favour will not then be realised, and such a confession can bear but scanty fruit, nor any fruit that will endure.... Our Lord would have our ears opened to the voice of conscience and our eyes directed to see aright the picture of our souls as they are seen by God. He would have the will to be moved, and the strings of the heart's love to vibrate afresh; and then, with all hope and humility, with all reverence too, he would that we approach the feet of the Friend of sinners, with longing, with shame, and use the words of the prodigal with all sincerity: 'Father, I have sinned against heaven and before thee'" (R. Eaton, *The Ministry of Reconciliation*).

"Almighty God never despised a creature that asked for forgiveness, for he is so meek and merciful to forgive when the sinner is contrite for his sinful life.... Blessed Lord, give me grace to make recognition and have that as my experience. Thou never despised creature that asked for mercy, because thou art meek and merciful, ready to forgive them that be sorrowful for their offences" (St. John Fisher).

"Give us, O Lord, by the grace of the Holy Spirit, a new outlook on the life of the soul, that our minds may become more receptive of His gifts" (Gregorian Sacramentary, ninth century).

"A mind well-schooled sees the way of life stretching upwards" (Prov. 15:24).

For Greater Sorrow

"Thou wilt turn back to the Lord thy God at last, and listen to his voice. The Lord thy God is a God of mercy; he will not forsake thee" (Deut. 4:30–31).

"The malice of sin lies in that very ingratitude whereby the sinner uses his God-given faculties to defeat the end for which God has created him. The actual offence lies in the frustration of the divine plan. This plan is not vague or general.... It is certain that the infinite wisdom and power of God operates as something individual. Each soul is the result of the personal, creative act of God. Each soul is a plan of God's love. Love is something personal. A mother does not love her children in general. She loves each child in particular. God loves me. Christ 'loved me and delivered himself for me.' Sin on the part of the creature is a deliberate refusal of love, a refusal to co-operate with a plan conceived in order that the will of God might be fulfilled. The will of God is my sanctification, that is, my happiness. If I rebel against his will, I am not holy. I rob myself of the chance of happiness. Incidentally, I rob God of the final success of his plan. But God is self-sufficient. He alone exists of himself and has no need of any other. Sin harms only the sinner" (J. C. Heenan, *Confession*).

"I beg thee, O my dear Saviour, to recover me. Thy grace alone can do it. I cannot save myself. I cannot recover my lost ground. I cannot turn to thee, I cannot please thee, or save my soul without thee. I shall go from bad to worse, I shall fall from thee entirely, I shall quite harden myself against my neglect of duty, if I rely on my own strength. I shall make myself my centre instead of making thee. I shall worship some idol of my own framing instead of thee, the only true God and my Maker, unless thou hinder it by thy grace. O my dear Lord, hear me, I have lived long enough in this undecided, wavering, unsatisfactory state. I wish to be thy good servant. I wish to sin no more. Be gracious to me, and enable me to be what I know I ought to be" (Newman, *Meditations and Devotions*).

"Narrowly our path scan we, and to the Lord return" (Lam. 3:40).

Resolution

"Give yourselves, heart and soul, to the following of the Lord your God" (1 Par. [1 Chron.] 22:19).

"In every kind of contrition a firm purpose of amendment plays a necessary part. Unless it be present, contrition is devoid of value. A resolution of amendment means a firm intention of avoiding sin and its occasions. It does not mean that we shall never offend God again. Conscious of our own weakness, this supposition would make it unlikely that we should ever be able to make a sincere resolve to amend, but it does mean that, here and now, we are serious in our intention to make a strong effort against committing sin in the future. We know that we shall probably be faithless again, but this state of mind is not incompatible with true contrition, 'For charity covereth a multitude of sins.' If our love of God has led us to make a sincere promise to amend, our disposition will be acceptable to God" (J. C. Heenan, *Confession*).

"Grant, O Lord, that I may not lapse into faults unworthy of my belief, rather may I serve it as befits my dignity as a Christian, never demeaning it by any unbecoming act. Let not careless living deny the nobility of the faith I profess. Because I have given myself to a holy purpose, may I seek to be just in all I do, and reject all insincerity both in my thought and words. Give me the grace of reverence for thee and for my faith. Let me also, without pretence, be friendly to all, desiring peace with all, receiving misunderstanding with charity, and giving scandal to no man" (St. Isidore, seventh century).

"Heart whispers, the Lord is my portion; I will trust him yet. In him be thy trust, for him thy heart's longing, gracious thou shalt find him" (Lam. 3:24–25).

Thanksgiving 11

A Thought Before Saying One's Penance

"The Church makes no pretence to weigh up my sins exactly with some instrument of her own, and to balance them with a corresponding weight of penalty. In her view, the penance imposed on me will draw its value to some slight extent from my good dispositions, but mainly from her own holiness and her past fidelity, so costly as it has been, whose value as satisfaction she attaches to my act. Moreover, the priest concludes the formula of absolution with a passage which is often lost on the penitent, but which signifies exactly what we have just said: 'May the passion of our Lord Jesus Christ, the merits of our blessed Lady and all the saints, together with all the good you do, and the ill you suffer, avail you to the remission of your sins, the increase of grace and the reward of eternal life. Amen'" (Community of St. Sévérin, *Confession*).

For Perseverance

"To the task! Never doubting, never daunted; the Lord thy God will be at thy side, never failing thee, never forsaking thee, and see that thou hast strength to do all that must be done" (1 Par. [1 Chron.] 28:20).

"Whether it be a question of passing out of the state of sin, or of perfecting the state of justification already received, it is only personal effort responding to the invitations and assistance received from God that permits the attainment of the desired end. Of course, in this work of deliverance, the initiative does not rest with man; here, it is the person offended who anticipates the offender. But the offender must be on the watch and listen, must see and understand; he must accept such an interior attitude towards his faults as will permit God to pardon them by the restoration of his friendship.

"And once possessed of this friendship, the soul must maintain and strengthen that attitude on pain of losing the gift again. As the spirit of penance is indispensable in order to pass out of the state of sin, so also it is indispensable to prevent a relapse. Moreover, this spirit is made more perfect as God obtains a firmer footing in the soul. Now that is an habitual state; its reaction against sin is the more powerful, the more immediately it is inspired by charity. Thus it comes about that the greatest penitents are also the greatest saints; their sorrow for sin and their zeal in combating it, which is the fruit of grace, is measured by their love of God, whose gift it is" (Galtier, *Sin and Penance*).

"To thee, O Lord almighty, we commend the whole of our life. Wherever we may be, do thou keep alive in us the grace of repentance and the firm conviction of the need to order our lives aright, that we may, at all times, earnestly seek to know the will of thy Majesty, and seek and do what pleases thee" (Liturgy of St. John).

"Surely the Lord will requite me; as he sees me dutiful, as he sees me guiltless in act" (2 Kings [2 Sam.] 22:25).

Devotions for Confession

In Gratitude

"How pitying and gracious the Lord is, how patient, how rich in mercy! He will not always be finding fault, his frown does not last for ever; he does not treat us as our sins deserve, does not exact the penalty of our wrong-doing. High as heaven above the earth towers his mercy for the men that fear him; far as east is from west, he clears away our guilt from us" (Ps. 102:8–12).

"When we are sick to death in sin, God's love seems to be fanned to white heat, and he gives us services that at other times of health are not needed. He does not love the lamb more than the ninety-nine, but he seems to love it more; it needs more. They that need less are not loved less. Equal love of souls, in unequal stress, demands unequal service.... When we are before God, with an overwhelming sense of our own weakness, we feel like a poor strayed lamb which has gone into the marshland and hardly knows which way to turn, faintly bleating that someone may hear. In our bleating, what we say is this: 'He whom thou lovest is sick. He whom thou lovest is strayed. I have lost thee, I cannot find thee. Find me. Seek me. I cannot find thee. I have lost my way. Thou art the way. Find me, or I am utterly lost. Thou lovest me, I do not know if I love thee; but I know thou lovest me. I do not plead my love but thine. I do not plead my strength but thine'" (V. McNabb, O.P., *God's Way of Mercy*).

"How true it is that thou dost bear with those who cannot bear thee to be with them! Oh, how good a friend art thou, my Lord! How thou dost comfort us and suffer us and wait, until our nature becomes more like thine, and meanwhile thou dost bear with it as it is! Thou dost remember the times when we love thee, my Lord, and, when for a moment we repent, thou dost forget how we have offended thee" (St. Teresa).

"Thou wilt find it ever the same; the Lord thy God is God almighty, is God ever faithful; if men will love him and keep his commandments, he is true to his word, and shows mercy to them" (Deut. 7:9).

In Forgiveness of Others, as We Have Been Forgiven

"Then Peter came to him and asked, Lord, how often must I see my brother do me wrong, and still forgive him; as much as seven times? Jesus said to him, I tell thee to forgive, not seven wrongs, but seventy times seven" (Matt. 18:21–22).

"O Lord, who alone art powerful, alone merciful, what ever good thou dost inspire me to wish for my enemies that do thou grant to them, and, in return, to myself also. If I should, at any time, in ignorance, weakness or malice, wish them what charity forbids, let it not be so with them, nor with myself, but do thou, who art the true Light, enlighten their darkness, refresh their souls … for, through the beloved disciple, thou didst warn us — he who lovest not his brother is dead. Grant us, then, O Lord, the fullness of charity which is thy command, lest we sin on account of our brethren in thy sight" (St. Anselm of Canterbury, twelfth century).

For the Work of the Church, Christ's Body, Hindered by Our Sins

"Among brethren, where there is but one living soul, that of our Lord and of the one Father, how can some be separated from others? … The body cannot rejoice at the evil inflicted upon one of its members; on the contrary, the whole body should be grieved and should labour in its healing, for when one or two brethren are to be found, there is the Church and the Church is Christ" (Tertullian, *Concerning Penance*).

"Be my salvation, O Lord, King of eternal glory, thou who canst indeed save all. Make me long to work for thee, long to accomplish what is good and pleasing in thy sight. Come to me and help me when I am worried, when I am persecuted and misunderstood. What I have been, forgive; what I am, correct; what I shall be, defend" (Latin Missal, tenth century).

Preparation 12

God and the Sinner

"Zachary was filled with the Holy Ghost, and spoke in prophecy: Blessed be the Lord, the God of Israel: he has visited his people and wrought their salvation. He has raised up a sceptre of salvation for us among the posterity of his servant David, according to the promise which he made by the lips of holy men that have been his prophets from the beginning; salvation from our enemies, and from the hand of all those who hate us. So he would carry out his merciful design towards our fathers by remembering his holy covenant. He had sworn an oath to our father Abraham, that he would enable us to live without fear in his service, delivered from the hand of our enemies, passing all our days in holiness, and approved in his sight. And thou, my child, wilt be known for a prophet of the most High, going before the Lord, to clear his way for him; thou wilt make known to his people the salvation that is to release them from their sins. Such is the merciful kindness of our God, which has bidden him come to us, like a dawning from on high, to give light to those who live in darkness, in the shadow of death, and to guide our feet into the way of peace" (Luke 1:67–79).

The Value of the Sacrament

"Here men may learn the lesson of insight, the dictates of duty, right and honour" (Prov. 1:3).

"Behold, he stands behind 'our wall'; the wall of our corrupt nature, which shuts us off from breathing, as man breathed in the days of his innocency, the airs of heaven; the wall of sense, which cheats us when we try even to imagine eternity; the wall of immortified affection, which shuts us in with creatures and allows them to dominate our desires; the wall of pride, which makes us feel, except when death or tragedy is very close to us, so independent and self-sufficient. Our wall — we raised it against God, not he against us; we raised it, when Adam sinned, and when each of us took up again, by deliberate choice, that legacy of sinfulness in his own life. And through that wall the Incarnation and Passion of Jesus Christ have made a great window; St. Paul tells us so: 'he made both one, breaking down the wall that was a barrier between us,' as the temple veil was torn in two on the day when he suffered. He 'made both one'; made our world of sin and sight and sense one with the spiritual world; made a breach in our citadel, let light into our prison....

"And at the window, behind the wall of partition that is a wall of partition no longer, stands the Beloved himself, calling us out into the open; calling us away from the ointments and the spikenard of Solomon's court, that stupefy and enchain our senses, to the garden and the vineyards, to the fields and the villages, to the pure airs of eternity. Arise (he says), make haste and come. Come away from the blind pursuit of creatures, from all the plans your busy brain evolves for your present and future pleasures, from the frivolous distractions it clings to. Come away from the pettiness and meanness of your everyday life, from the grudges, the jealousies, the unhealed enmities that set your imagination throbbing. Come away from the cares and solicitudes about the morrow that seem so urgent, your heavy anxieties about the world's future and your own, so short either of them and so uncertain. Come ... where my love will follow you and my hand hold you; learn to live, with the innermost part of your soul, with all your secret aspirations, with all the centre of your hopes and cares, in that supernatural world which can be yours now, which must be yours hereafter.

"Not that he calls us, yet, away from the body, from its claims and its necessities; that call will come in its own time. Nor yet that the occupations, and the amusements of this life, his creatures, given us for our use, are to be despised and set aside as something evil. Rather, as a beam of sunlight coming through the window lights up and makes visible the tiny motes of dust that fill the air, so those who live closest to him find, in the creatures about them, a fresh charm and a fresh meaning, which the jaded palate of worldliness was too dull to detect. But he wants our hearts; *ut inter mundanas varietates ibi fixa sint corda ubi vera suntgaudia* — our hearts must there be fixed, where are pure joys, before we can begin to see earth in its right perspective. We must be weaned away from earth first" (R. A. Knox, *The Window in the Wall*).

In Humility

"Quietly, Lord, thy creatures raise their eyes to thee ... ready to open thy hand, and fill with blessing all that lives" (Ps. 144:15).

"If God knows how to draw advantage from the greatest sins, who can suppose that he will fail to turn our daily faults to our sanctification? It is a remark made by the masters of the spiritual life, that God very often leaves in the holiest souls some defects which, notwithstanding all their efforts, they cannot root out. He acts thus in order to make them conscious of their weakness; to show them what they would be without grace, to guard them from vanity because of his favours, to dispose them to receive other benefits with greater humility, to keep a holy self-hatred alive in them, to withdraw them from the snares of self-love, to preserve their fervour and their confidence in him, and to teach them the necessity of having continual recourse to prayer.... The faults into which we fall often give place to great acts of virtue which otherwise we should never have occasion to practise, and God permits our faults to this end. For example, a dash of temper, a brusque reply, a manifest impatience, just fits one for a good act of humility which abundantly repairs the fault and the scandal it has given. The fault is committed by a sudden impulse; the reparation is made with reflection, by a victory over oneself, and with a full and deliberate will. The latter is an act much more pleasing to God than the former, as a fault, was displeasing to him" (St. Francis de Sales).

"I adore thee, O dread Lord, for what thou hast done for my soul. I acknowledge and feel, not only as a matter of faith, but of experience, that I cannot have one good thought or do one good act without thee. I know that if I attempt anything good in my own strength, I shall to a certainty fail. I have bitter experience of this. My God, I am only safe when thou dost breathe on me.... The minute thou dost cease to act in me, I begin to languish, to faint away. Of my good desires, whatever they may be, of my good aims, aspirations, attempts, successes, habits, practices, thou art the sole cause and present continual source. I have nothing but what I have received, and I protest now in thy presence, O sovereign Paraclete, that I have nothing to glory in, and everything to be humbled at" (Newman, *Meditations and Devotions*).

"Take my yoke upon yourselves, and learn from me; I am gentle and humble of heart; and you shall find rest for your souls. For my yoke is easy, and my burden is light" (Matt. 11:28–29).

For Confidence

"To thee, Lord, I look for refuge, never let me be ashamed of my trust; in thy faithful care deliver me. Grant me audience, and make haste to rescue me, my divine protector, my stronghold of defence, to save me from peril. Thou dost strengthen and defend me; thou, for thy own honour, dost guide and nurture me; by thee protected, I shall escape from the snare that lies hidden in my path" (Ps. 30:2–5).

"Let us turn our minds to him who grants forgiveness. How often has he forgiven us, how often rejoiced that reconciliation gave him the chance to remake his work, rejoiced at forgiving, at giving himself anew. So, then, let us simply contemplate the joy of God. It was a greater work, we may say, for God to reconcile the world to himself than to have created it. As St. Augustine said, 'God rested after creating man, and not before, because he had at last created a being whom he would have the joy of forgiving.' We are those whom God has the joy of forgiving. That is God's prodigious secret, as it is that of the Christian, the sinner, the true penitent" (Community of St. Séverin, *Confession*).

"O God, true and everlasting joy, from whom, through whom, and in whom, all find happiness and meaning in life, by whom, through whom, and in whom all have life, there is nothing apart from thee or without thee. It is thou, O God, dost arouse our faith, give us all our hope, and join us to thyself in loving charity. Thou dost bid us seek, but also helpest us to find; and when we knock, thou dost open. Well we know that to stray from thee is surely to stumble, and just as surely we know that to return to thee is an uplifting of heart, and to remain with thee is security. Not to know thee, O God, is death, as knowledge of thee is life. To reject thee is to perish; to serve thee is to reign royally with thee.... Indeed, thou art my God, living and true, my faithful Lord, my mighty King" (attributed to Alcuin, ninth century).

"He who lives under the protection of the most High, under his heavenly care content to abide, can say to the Lord, Thou art my support and my stronghold, my God in whom I trust" (Ps. 90:1–2).

Devotions for Confession

For Self-Knowledge

"Scrutinize me, O God, as thou wilt, and read my heart; put me to the test and watch the steps I take. See if on any false path my heart is set" (Ps. 138:23–24).

"We can do nothing better than place ourselves and all we have in God's sight: 'Behold me!' Let us put away the fear that prevents us. Let us abandon the sloth, the pretence of independence, the pride. 'Look at the good! look at the shortcomings! The ugly, the unjust, the evil, the wicked, everything — look at it, O God!' Sometimes it is impossible to alter something or other. But let him see it at any rate. Sometimes one cannot honestly repent. None of the shortcomings and evil in our lives are fatal so long as they confront his gaze. The very act of placing ourselves in his sight is the very beginning of renewal. Everything is possible so long as we begin with God. But everything is in danger once we refuse to place ourselves and our lives in his sight" (R. Guardini, *The Living God*).

"O my God, I confess that *thou canst* enlighten my darkness. I confess that thou *alone* canst. I *wish* my darkness to be enlightened. I do not know whether thou wilt; but that thou canst and that I wish, are sufficient reasons for me to *ask* what thou at least hast not forbidden my asking. I hereby promise that by thy grace which I am asking, I will embrace whatever at length I feel certain is the truth, if ever I come to be certain. And by thy grace I will guard against all self-deceit which would lead me to take what nature would have, rather than what reason approves" (Newman, *Meditations and Devotions*).

"Thy steps retrace and this path follow, guiding thy steps by the glow of the light that beckons thee" (Bar. 4:2).

Preparation 12

For Greater Sorrow

"Sinner that will leave his sinning, no harm shall he have ... he has but to repent of his sins, do uprightly" (Ezek. 33:12–14).

"Sin is no empty word, no mere bogey. It is the one evil, the real cause of despoiling, of dissensions and of pain. If we are to tear ourselves away and break loose from its embraces, if it is to be destroyed utterly, some effort is necessary: we must make expiation and reparation. If faith did not teach this, conscience would cry it aloud. To rise again and be free, to rediscover God and the joy of belonging to him, it is imperative that we first recover possession of our own selves and retrace our steps, casting aside our unrighteous and criminal affections; in a word, we must surrender ourselves whole-heartedly to him whom we thought to defy.... This conviction is forced upon us, so soon as we understand what God is to us and what we are to him. To one who has a clear idea of the malice of sin, it is no longer a matter of wonder that it must be met by penance.... We shall have understood nothing of his mission, we shall have none of his love, unless like him, and thanks to him, we are determined to condemn and hate sin, and as far as in us lies, to make reparation for it" (Galtier, *Sin and Penance*).

"Blessed be thy name, O God of our fathers, for even when thou art angered, thy mercy is still waiting, and where there is sorrow, there is ready forgiveness for those who call upon thy name. Look upon me, then, O Lord, as I now acknowledge my sins. Thou knowest them because thou knowest all things before they are; thou knowest how, from my baptism onwards, I have often ignored thy precepts, and have not kept thy commandments. It is through carelessness that I have not done the good I could easily have done and worked the evil I might have avoided.... Look upon me as I now confess my sins before thee

173

and have mercy. Grant that in my life I may do worthy penance, and give me thy forgiveness, for it was in kindliness thou didst say that thy desire was not the death of the sinner, but that he should be converted and live. Let me feel the effect of thy generous mercy in the banishing of the sadness of sin. Grant also, what I scarce dare to ask: steady perseverance in all good that, through thy kindly mercy, I may merit to come to thee, in the glory of thy kingdom" (Alcuin, *De Usu Psalmorum*, ninth century).

"Ease me of the reproach my heart dreads, thou whose awards are gracious" (Ps. 118:39).

Resolution

"And you must not fall in with the manners of this world; there must be an inward change, a remaking of your minds, so that you can satisfy yourselves what is God's will, the good thing, the desirable thing, the perfect thing" (Rom. 12:2).

" 'But,' it might be said, 'how am I always to know what is the will of God for me?' God has not left us without guidance. There is the natural law imprinted in the hearts of men; there are his commandments; there are the duties arising out of our relationship with our fellow-men; there is the example of his Son who came on earth to be for us the way, the truth, and the life; there is Holy Church which he instituted to be the expression of his will and our guide towards eternity. But over and above all this, we know that there is a particular providence over every soul of man. God has a will for *me*, a purpose for *me*. And for me, the highest motive is that I should do with my life just what he means me to do with it, that I should fulfil as perfectly as possible the purpose for which he made *me*. ... 'Do what you are doing,' says Père Caussade, 'suffer what you are suffering; there is only one heart to change.' Yes, only the motive, the intention" (S. J. Brown, *From God to God*).

"Grant me, O Lord, a clear knowledge of the uselessness and vanity of the things of the world and give me to understand how much thou deservest my loyalty. To this end, rouse up in my soul a lively sorrow for the ways in which I have displeased thee, and a firm resolve never to offend thee again. Give me the charity which marks thy true followers, the humility without which no prayer may have hearing, that purity which so pleases thee that thou hast declared the Holy Spirit will never rest upon him who lacks it" (J. B. Pagani, *Anima Devota*).

"Stand firm, my beloved brethren, immovable in your resolve" (1 Cor. 15:58).

Thanksgiving 12

A Thought Before Saying One's Penance

"Never forget that each time we receive this sacrament worthily and with devotion, even if there were only venial sins to be confessed, the Blood of Christ is poured abundantly on our souls to revive them, to strengthen them against temptation, to make them generous in the struggle against attachment to sin, and to destroy in them the roots and the effects of sin. The soul finds, in this sacrament, special graces to uproot its vices and purify itself more and more, so that the life of grace may be recovered or increased in it.... God finds his glory in forgiving us, because all forgiveness is granted to us in virtue of the satisfaction made by Jesus Christ, his beloved Son. The precious Blood of Jesus was shed to the last drop for the remission of sin, and the expiation Christ offered to the justice, holiness and majesty of the Father is of infinite value. Now each time God pardons us, each time the priest gives us absolution, it is as if all the sufferings, all the merits, all the love, all the Blood of Jesus were presented to his Father and applied to our souls to restore life to them or to increase it when it is only a case of venial sins" (Marmion, *Christ the Life of the Soul*).

For Perseverance

"Had they but hearts so true that they would always fear me, always keep my commandments! Then it should go well with them" (Deut. 5:29).

"Moreover, not only the past but the future is to be dealt with. Is there no danger to be guarded against? Is the penitent fixed forever in God's favour? Indeed sin has lost none of its attractiveness; the traces of its work in the soul are still most clear, though its guilt has been wiped away. The penitent's passions are still strong, and his will is weak; old temptations press upon him; there is danger of relapse, of losing heart, of going back to the house whence he came out, of his last state becoming worse than the first. Our Lord knew this, and took human nature as he found it. Confession is his remedy for the building up of ruins, for it means sympathy, direction, encouragement, and consequent progress and final perseverance" (R. Eaton, *The Ministry of Reconciliation*).

"O Lord God, the just Judge, strong and patient, who knowest the frailty and depravity of men: be thou my strength and my whole confidence, for my own conscience does not suffice for me. Thou knowest that which I know not; and therefore under every rebuke I ought to humble myself and suffer meekly. Pardon me, therefore, in thy mercy, for not having acted so in the past, and give me in the future the grace of greater endurance" (Thomas à Kempis, *The Imitation of Christ*).

"Endurance must do its work thoroughly, if you are to be men full grown in every part, nothing lacking in you" (James 1:4).

In Gratitude

"But thou, O Lord, art a God of mercy and pity, patient, compassionate, true to thy promise" (Ps. 85:15).

"Deep souls are thankful; they comprehend that the good has to be received with the feeling of gratitude. This too is a great good. Thanksgiving after confession is a great grace and the means of obtaining lasting effects from the sacrament. Our heart feels the immense graciousness of God's forgiveness; it feels that he has lifted the load off it which was more terrible than fetters.... The sweet feeling of peace pervades our soul — the deep sublime peace which God has promised, something of what the prophet speaks of: 'O that thou hadst hearkened to my commandments! Thy peace had been as a river, and thy justice as the waves of the sea (Isaias 48:18). This is what we enjoy, this is what makes our soul enthusiastic and our disposition sweet. This is what we have to give thanks for, sing, and be grateful!" (Prohaszka, *Meditations on the Gospels*).

"My God, I adore thee for taking on thee the charge of sinners; of those who not only cannot profit thee, but who continually grieve and profane thee.... I adore thee for thy incomprehensible condescension in ministering to me. I know and feel, O my God, that thou mightest have left me, as I wished to be left, to go my own way.... Thou mightest have left me in that enmity to thee which is itself death; I should at length have died the second death, and should have had no one to blame for it but myself. But thou, O eternal Father, hast been kinder to me than I am to myself. Thou hast given me, thou hast poured out upon me, thy grace, and thus I live" (Newman, *Meditations and Devotions*).

"And now you have been brought back to him, your Shepherd, who keeps watch over your souls" (1 Pet. 2:25).

In Forgiveness of Others, as We Have Been Forgiven

"Put ye on therefore, as the elect of God, holy and beloved, the soul of mercy" (Col. 3:12).

"O Blessed Jesus, give me stillness of soul in thee. Let thy mighty calmness reign in me. Rule me, O thou King of gentleness, King of peace. Give me control, great power of self-control, over my words, thoughts and actions. From all irritability and want of meekness and gentleness, dear Lord, deliver me. Give me, instead, patience and quiet of soul in thee" (attributed to St. John of the Cross).

For the Work of the Church, Christ's Body, Hindered by Our Sins

"The *Christianus poenitens* is essentially one who has to bewail his lack of fidelity to Christ, to whom he has already sworn fealty in baptism. The sins of Christians are offences against a state, the state of the redeemed. By committing sin, we walk unworthy of our calling, we prove ourselves to be bad children, people who are unmindful of their election. We sin against Christ, we hurt him in his brethren; whether we be conscious or not of these implications, we cannot avoid having that kind of guilt on our souls every time we transgress. In his repentance the Christian has to think of many things. He has to remember his baptismal robe, he has to bear in mind the adoption of children, the seal of the Spirit, the sweetness of the Bread of life, the Blood of the Lamb, all of which mysteries he has more or less trampled under foot every time he has sinned grievously" (Vonier, *Christianus*).

"Thou, O Father of all, art the beginning of all, the Light eternal and the source of all light, who calls man in his weakness from the dust and raises him up from corruption. So hast thou called us, through thy beloved Son, to the liberty and the dignity of children of thy household. Grant us to be saintly children, and that we be not in thy sight at any time unworthy of that title, grant also that we may perfectly fulfil our vocation by the blamelessness of our lives, and may we do that with purity of heart and clean minds" (Liturgy of St. Denis).

Preparation 13

God and the Sinner

"There is a pool in Jerusalem at the Sheep Gate, called in Hebrew Bethsaida, with five porches, under which a multitude of diseased folk used to lie, the blind, the lame, the disabled, waiting for a disturbance of the water. From time to time, an angel of the Lord came down upon the pool, and the water was stirred up; and the first man who stepped into the pool after the stirring of the water, recovered from whatever infirmity it was that oppressed him. There was one man there who had been disabled for thirty-eight years. Jesus saw him lying there, and knew that he had waited a long time; Hast thou a mind, he asked, to recover thy strength? Sir, said the cripple, I have no one to let me down into the pool when the water is stirred; and while I am on my way, somebody else steps down before me. Jesus said to him, Rise, take up thy bed, and walk. And all at once the man recovered his strength, and took up his bed and walked.... But afterwards when Jesus found him in the temple, and said to him, Behold, thou hast recovered thy strength; do not sin any more, for fear that worse should befall thee, the man went back and told the Jews that it was Jesus who had restored his strength" (John 5:2–15).

Devotions for Confession

The Value of the Sacrament

"It is the friendless he rescues in their need, speaks home to them through the afflictions they endure" (Job 36:15).

" 'Hast thou a mind to recover thy strength?' Dost thou wish for all the conditions and consequences of health and for all its duties? Dost thou wish for it with all the work, self-discipline and self-abnegation? Dost thou wish to become healed and to work for a more beautiful, stronger life? This will exists in few people, for just this indolent, weak, lazy, undisciplined frame of mind is the illness of their soul. But how are we to wish for it? In small, in simple, concrete things we have to educate it in ourselves; we must wish to do this and that and we must carry out our purpose. Let us hate irresolution and indecision. Let us rejoice that we are able to wish with pure, straightforward, healthy mind and soul.

" 'Jesus said to him, Rise, take up thy bed and walk.' We cannot complain that we have no man; Jesus is our man. He it is who helps us to rise, who heals us, who gives us creative words, soul and strength. Who wishes to rise shall not wait for future energies, for the welling of mysterious waters.... Jesus is here, and he it is who says: Rise" (Prohaszka, *Meditations on the Gospel*).

In Humility

"Well for thee that thy heart failed thee, and thou didst humble thyself before God" (2 Par. [2 Chron.] 34:27).

"The more the privilege of the divine friendship is appreciated, the more evident it becomes how real is the offence given to God by these lesser sins, and how odious they are; the more pressing, consequently, becomes the need of expressing the sorrow that is felt, and of making reparation to God for them. Thus, not only does the spirit of penance call forth a detestation for these sins and a desire to make expiation for them; it inspires the effort to seek out, if possible, a more secure means of being rid of them and of obtaining their forgiveness; hence the notion that these sins, too, may be submitted to the sacrament of penance" (Galtier, *Sin and Penance*).

"May he who by his ready grace has a warm welcome for every sinner give us the grace of a humble and repentant heart. May he who gave to the Magdalen this great favour, that at the moment of the Resurrection he appeared to her before all others, grant by her intercession and by our humble sorrow, that the good things we have lost by our sinfulness may be restored to us. She, in return for so many sins forgiven, returned him great love. May God give us, of his kindly mercy, the same perfect and joyful reconciliation" (Benedictional of John Longlonde, sixteenth century).

"Well for us that he, at least, is patient; repent we, and with flowing tears ask his pardon! He will not overwhelm us with reproaches, as men do" (Judith 8:14–15).

For Confidence

"I would bring courage to their hearts; I would see them well ordered in love, enriched in every way with fuller understanding" (Col. 2:2).

"You never approach confession alone. He is always by your side, ready and anxious to help; and he will never fail you nor allow you to fail him if you do your honest best. Remember that confession is a sacrament of mercy, and approach it with childlike trust. He wants our trust and is pained when we do not trust him. And, after Calvary, the Mass and the institution of this sacrament of mercy, is it surprising?" (Wilson, *Pardon and Peace*).

"When, all unhappy, I look back upon my past, I am troubled and afraid ... yet thy holy mercy is such that it could bring my soul from the deepest sin, for thou showest mercy whenever it is thy desire; thy help comes to us in all sureness whenever thou dost pity us, so pardoning that thou dost not in vengeance utterly destroy; nor in reproaching overwhelm; neither, when thou dost accuse, is thy love one whit the less. Still am I hesitant and troubled, for though I cannot forget thy goodness, yet neither can I forget my own past ingratitude.... To thee, therefore, my Jesus, I will confess thus: as to my Saviour and my hope" (St. Aelred of Rievaulx, *Pastoral Prayer*, twelfth century).

"For us thou art God; beneficent and truthful, thou, always patient and merciful towards the world thou governest. Sin we, still we are thy worshippers; have we not proof of thy power? ... To know thee as thou art, is the soul's full health" (Wisd. 15:1–2).

For Self-Knowledge

"He it is that will call you to account for your doings with a scrutiny that reads your inmost thoughts" (Wisd. 6:4).

"Often we speak of conscience as of a voice within us, clear but soft, that seeks to guide us, suggesting the good, and warning us from what is evil. Such a description is true to a point, but it is no explanation of its true nature. Conscience is an act of the human intellect.... It is not a power or faculty of the soul, as distinct from the intellect or reason. Conscience is an act, not a habit. The intellect of man acts upon his will; his knowledge supplies the motive for his will, and sets his will in motion, and the result is an act. Wherefore 'conscience is the application of the natural law, by the practical intellect, to an individual act which presents itself as either to be done, or to be left undone'" (R. Eaton, *The Ministry of Reconciliation*).

"We beseech thee, O Lord, Father almighty, that, having graced our lives with the gift of intelligence, so thou wouldst also show us clearly the way of eternal life, that, recognising our way to thee, we may one day be destined to rejoice with thee in thy kingdom" (Gothic Breviary, seventh century).

"His own path man scans, and nothing sees amiss, but the divine balance weighs our thoughts; share with the Lord the burden of all thy doings, if thou wouldst be sincere in thy intent" (Prov. 16:2–3).

For Greater Sorrow

"If they come here repentant, and acknowledging thy power, pray to thee, and plead with thee in this temple of thine, do thou, in heaven, listen to them, and forgive.... Teach them to guide their steps aright" (3 Kings [1 Kings] 8:33–36).

"When you kneel in the confessional, imagine to yourself that what you see in front of you is not the grille of the confessional, but our Lord's own feet, those feet so weary of tramping through the world and finding no rest anywhere, no welcome anywhere. Put the world away from your thoughts, as the poor Magdalen put away from her the thought of all those great people sitting round the dinner-table: you and he are alone together, and you want to tell him that here, at least, there is no false shame, here at least there is no cold, jealous criticism of his dealings with mankind. Tears you have none to shed, but the very dryness of your eyes is a fresh motive for sorrow. You are doing what you can; it is little, it is miserably little, but he knows you too well to be surprised at that. He will not complain about your lack of contrition if he sees that you are wishing you were more contrite than you are.... God will give us credit for it, if we brace our resolution as best we can. Once again, our lives will be the subject of that satisfying epitaph, written by the finger of omniscience: 'Let her alone: she has done what she could'" (R. A. Knox, *A Retreat for Lay People*).

"O Lord God, the Giver of every grace, grant that I may fittingly regret even my smallest sins, those I have now forgotten as well as those of which I am still conscious and that I may do penance for them all, without exception. May my sorrow and my penance be acceptable to thee; may they restore to me my lost graces and procure for me greater and more efficacious means of salvation" (Thomas à Kempis, *True Wisdom*).

"Bring us back to thee, Lord, and let us find our home" (Lam. 5:21).

Resolution

"But thus, to the sinner, God speaks: How is it that thou canst repeat my commandments by rote, and boast of my covenant with thee, and thou, all the while, hast no love for the amendment of thy ways, casting every warning of mine to the wind? ... He honours me truly who offers me a sacrifice of praise; there lies your path, who would see the saving power of God" (Ps. 49:16–23).

"Repentance says *no* to sin and *yes* to good. In repentance man takes sides with God against his own selfishness, which in turn means that he is taking sides with himself — his true self. A repentant man detests the deed he repents of, and wishes it undone. Resolution is closely linked to repentance. It is the resolve to improve and not to sin again. Unless the repentance is real, no resolution develops; and from the resolution one can tell whether or not the rejection of sin is genuine.... The cure 'from without' is effected by Christ, the source and very essence of the new life, and thus the originator of its restoration. When the Christian presents himself to Christ the Saviour, he is offering himself at the same time to Christ the Judge. This he does by explicitly confessing the sins he has committed: for this reason the common name for the sacrament of penance is 'confession,' though the actual confession is only part of the sacrament" (Pieper-Raskop, *What Catholics Believe*).

"May our Lord who looks down from heaven upon us men with kindly eyes, seeing those that are at variance with him, as also those that know him not, nor seek after him, who knoweth those that are loyal to his commands, give us both the will and the power to understand him, and teach us, and help us to seek him with humble mind and noble and holy words, and so to grant our prayer if it be his will" (English Homily, twelfth century).

"Other defence, other stronghold have I none; in thy law I trust. Out of my path, lovers of wrong; I will keep my God's commandments. Only let thy promised aid preserve me; do not disappoint me of the hope I cherish. Only do thou sustain me in safety, looking ever to thy will.... Overcome my whole being with the fear of thee" (Ps. 118:113–120).

Thanksgiving 13

A Thought Before Saying One's Penance

"Penance, in fact, is not privation or mortification, but precisely repentance, that is to say, returning to a love which was despised, neglected, betrayed.... Penance in Scripture is return, reconciliation and entry upon a renewed intimacy" (Community of St. Sévérin, *Confession*).

For Perseverance

"May you live as befits his servants, waiting continually on his good pleasure; may the closer knowledge of God bring you fruitfulness and growth in all good. May you be inspired, as his glorious power can inspire you, with full strength to be patient and to endure; to endure joyfully, thanking God our Father for making us fit to share the light which the saints inherit" (Col. 1:10–12).

"The Christian carries deep within him the fear that he may decline from God's holy will; the anxiety that he may deface the beauty of his will; that he may lose sight of his irretrievable purpose. And so he prays for the patience of God. And yet he tells himself that it is impossible that God's will be lost. Sin appeared to have destroyed God's will for the world, but it was followed by the tremendous fact of Redemption. The Creation which had been destroyed was taken up into the hope of a 'new heaven and a new earth.'

"But the Christian may not deduce safe guarantees from this. In the constant, absorbing care that God's will be done, he must persevere, and watch and work" (R. Guardini, *The Living God*).

"Let our minds be given, almighty God, to the sacred truths from which we shall reap lasting benefits, and especially to this end: that we may always see our obligations clearly and intelligently, and with intelligence and good will fulfil them. Then the setbacks of this life will find us unperturbed, and we ourselves be worthy of thy heavenly company" (Gregorian Sacramentary, ninth century).

"Let me find life in following thy way" (Ps. 118:37).

In Gratitude

"Merciful the Lord is, and just, and full of pity; he cares for simple hearts" (Ps. 114:5).

"We must remember, above all, that this is a sacrament, and an astounding proof of God's great goodness. If it did not exist, we should earnestly desire it. God in his goodness has given it to us" (H. Harrington, *The Sacrament of Penance*).

"Let all my joy and all my confidence be in thee, O Cross. Through thee my sins are wiped out; through thee my soul has quitted its former state, which was really death, and arisen to a new life of well-doing. As thou, O Lord, cleansed me, in baptism, from the sin in which I was conceived, cleanse me yet again from the sins I have committed since my redemption, that through thee I may attain the joys for which man was created by the grace which is thy gift" (St. Anselm of Canterbury, twelfth century).

"Guide me, Lord, thy own way, thy faithful care my escort, make this heart thrill with reverence for thy name. O Lord, my God, with all my heart I will give thee thanks, eternally hold thy name in honour, for the greatness of the mercy thou hast shewed me in rescuing me thus" (Ps. 85:11–13).

In Forgiveness of Others as We Have Been Forgiven

"Patience is better than resentment" (Eccles. 7:9).

"O Sacred Heart of Jesus, with my whole soul I adore the impulses of goodness and mercy towards sinners, the effects of which I have now most singularly experienced. Thy loving kindness is so desirous of mercy that it threatens to show no mercy to him who is not merciful. And what mercy can I exercise towards my neighbour that can be compared to those I have received and every day receive from thee? O Heart of Jesus, living fountain of mercy, teach me to know and worthily imitate thy mercy" (Dom Innocent le Masson, seventeenth century).

For the Work of the Church, Christ's Body, Hindered by Our Sins

"Thanks to the influence Christ exercises over our souls, there is nothing in our lives that cannot be used to make compensation for our offences against God. In order to lead an upright life, even to pray well, we must needs put ourselves to inconvenience and trouble. The material element of satisfaction (for our sins), then, is to be found in every work that we do, and we are constantly meeting opportunities of suffering in our path. It only remains for us to animate our conduct with the intention of making satisfaction" (Galtier, *Sin and Penance*).

"May God, who in the Sacred Scriptures has shown to his faithful people all the ways of right living, grant us the grace loyally to follow them by laying aside our own restless desires. May he help us to avoid the foolish worship of bodily comfort by overcoming our want of confidence and our impatience. Courage in trial will bring us the reward of goodness, and our loyal service will atone for our past unfaithfulness" (Benedictional of John Longlonde, sixteenth century).

Preparation 14

God and the Sinner

"Then he said, There was a certain man who had two sons. And the younger of these said to his father, Father, give me that portion of the estate which falls to me. So he divided his property between them. Not many days afterwards, the younger son put together all that he had, and went on his travels to a far country where he wasted his fortune in riotous living. Then, when all was spent, a great famine arose in that country, and he found himself in want; whereupon he went and attached himself to a citizen of that country, who put him on his farm to feed swine. He would have been glad to fill his belly with husks, such as the swine used to eat; but none was ready to give them to him. Then he came to himself, and said, How many servants there are in my father's house, who have more bread than they can eat, and here I am perishing with hunger! I will arise and go to my father, and say to him, Father, I have sinned against heaven, and before thee; I am not worthy, now, to be called thy son; treat me as one of thy hired servants. And he arose, and went on his way to his father. But, while he was still a long way off, his father saw him, and took pity on him; running up, he threw his arms around his neck and kissed him. And when the son said, Father, I have sinned against heaven and before thee; I am not worthy, now, to be called thy son, the father gave orders to his servants, Bring out the best robe, and clothe him in it; put a ring on his hand, and shoes on his feet. Then bring out the calf that has been fattened, and kill it; let us eat, and make merry; for my son here was dead, and has come to life again, was lost and is found" (Luke 15:11–24).

The Value of the Sacrament

"But do thou, my Lord and Master, take my part, to defend thy own honour; no mercy is so tender as thine" (Ps. 108:21).

"I will arise and go to my father, and will say to him: Father, I have sinned against heaven and before thee; I am not worthy to be called thy son; make me as one of thy hired servants. As a hired servant the soul enters the confessional; as a son it comes forth. The white robe of charity restored, shoes upon our feet to walk the world's ways bravely once again; the ring of absolution that marks us sons in our Father's house, affiances us to God! Oh, mercy not to be measured by any standard of human mercy, for our judgments are at fault, and our indulgence blind, and our forgiveness grudging. Oh, happiness not to be compared with any human happiness, for our satisfaction is but momentary, and our loves grow old, and our delights wither and decay.... There may be scornful eyes that watch us, bitter tongues that complain of so much charity wasted on the ne'er-do-weel, prophesy fresh falls and keep the record of our sins indelible; but it is our Father's forgiveness, not theirs, we come to cry for. Go to other religions and they will promise you sin condoned, sin discounted, sin explained away: only as Christians do we understand, only in the confessional do we experience, that divine contradiction, sin forgiven" (R. A. Knox, *Pastoral Sermons*).

Devotions for Confession

In Humility

"He is like a shepherd who cares for his sheep, guides and controls all alike; welcome thou this merciful discipline of his, run thou eagerly to meet his will, and he will show pity on thee" (Ecclus. [Sir.] 18:13–14).

"But what great matter is it, if a thing of dust and mere nothingness submits himself to man for God's sake, when I, the Almighty and the most High, who created all things out of nothing, did for your sake most humbly subject myself to man? I became the most humble and the most abject of all men, that you might overcome your pride by my humility" (Thomas à Kempis, *The Imitation of Christ*, bk. 3, 13).

"I own, O most tender God, that I am above measure proud, vain, and often arrogant. Indeed it seems that had I any real power in this world, scarce any would bear with my haughtiness. If it should come to pass, as it seldom does, that my poor self achieved anything which in the world's opinion might be called good, then to no small extent do I preen myself, counting those foolish who fail to speak of it to me, or flatter me.... This, my God and my Creator, is the way I act. Come, then, my Maker, to my assistance, my helper in every weakness, strengthen me, and in thy wondrous mercy utterly root out my pride" (Anselm of Bury St. Edmunds, twelfth century).

"Slaves we are that might have ruled; and the reason of it? Because by our sinning we offended the Lord our God, and left his voice unheeded. It was our fault if we would not listen to his warnings, would not follow the divine commandments he set before us" (Bar. 2:5–10).

Preparation 14

For Confidence

"It is not as if our high priest was incapable of feeling for us in our humiliations; he has been through every trial, fashioned as we are, only sinless. Let us come boldly, then, before the throne of grace, to meet with mercy, and win that grace which will help us in our needs" (Heb. 4:15–16).

"Even sin has its redemptive purpose; even our personal sins can be turned to good, and are meant to be turned to good in our lives. The shame and the sorrow increasing the sense of sin, the realisation of the endless patience of God increasing humility and wonder; all this is part of the process of going down to the depths that there we may learn to be poor, to be meek and to mourn, that then we may be comforted and turned into strong and fearless instruments of God's purposes. We may not sin in order to understand — that way the sense of sin would grow weaker and weaker within us instead of stronger — but having sinned we can use our shame in order to understand: it is part of the deepening influence of suffering in general. But we shall not use this thing as we ought, we shall not turn evil to good as we ought, unless we can find peace in the midst of shame, and joy in the midst of sorrow" (G. Vann, O.P., *The Divine Pity*).

"I know, merciful Lord, that none look to thy mercy in vain; that thou comest at once to all who set out to find thee. I know that the fullness of thy compassion will not be wanting for me, for well I know that the same ease with which thy Almighty power made all things, also raised me from nothingness and gave me so many and great blessings. That is why I am certain that, come one word of mercy from thee, all that in me is deformed shall be made whole" (William of Auvergne, thirteenth century).

"Lord God, our king, thou reignest alone; befriend a lonely heart that can find help nowhere but in thee" (Esther 14:3).

For Self-Knowledge

"Good men see a light dawn in darkness; his light, who is ever merciful, kind and faithful" (Ps. 111:4).

"We must be watchful and alert. We must take conscience seriously and attend to its depths. We must live our daily life and be ready for it to reveal a pattern and a providence. We must live our lives with people and things and listen for the gentle tokens of God's presence" (R. Guardini, *The Living God*).

"See the wounds of my soul, O God, for thy living, unhindered gaze sees into all things, cleaving like a sword into the borderland of soul and spirit. Assuredly thou seest in my own soul the marks of the past, my present peril of sin, and even the future causes and occasions of sin. Thou seest them all, O Lord, and would have me see them. Thou knowest, O Searcher of my heart, that I would have nothing in my soul hid from thee, even were it possible for aught to escape thy knowing.... I ask of thee, fount of pity, trusting simply in thy merciful might, and in thy mighty mercy, by the power of thy most sweet name, and thy sacred kindly humanity, to forgive my sins" (St. Aelred of Rievaulx).

"O God, true Light, who, on the first day of this dawning world, made the heavens and the earth, grant that thy people may ever love thee as their Creator and the Giver of every good thing. That they may one day be worthy of their heavenly home, let them, here on earth, be conscious always of thy presence in them. Disdaining the coarse pleasures of this world, let them ever appear to be such in the sight of thy majesty that thou mayest judge them worthy of thy Fatherly care, and deserving, along with all the saints, of the inheritance of heaven. To that end, we beseech thee, O Lord God, to free them from the delusions of evil, these children of thine whom, on the day of thy Resurrection, thy glorious triumph over death, thou didst claim as thy own" (Benedictional of Abp Robert, tenth century).

"No God-fearing man but will pass his own conscience under review" (Ecclus. [Sir.] 21:7).

For Greater Sorrow

"A lover of God will fall to prayer over his sins, and sin no more" (Ecclus. [Sir.] 3:4).

"Our contrition (be it perfect or imperfect) must also be real, it must be definitely willed, it must be without reservations, and with it there must go an acceptance of the truth that mortal sin is the greatest of evils. It is *not*, however, necessary, nor indeed any part of contrition at all, that it should be emotionally expressed or emotionally felt. Contrition is an act of the will and so is itself outside the domain of feeling altogether. The thought of our sinfulness may inflame the imagination and hence the emotions, but such imaginative and emotional disturbance is but the chance accompaniment of contrition, and its presence or absence is no test of the reality or depth of our contrition" (Philip Hughes, *The Faith in Practice*).

"He is not going to forgive you your sins because you are clever at remembering them, or expressing them, or marshalling them, but for one reason only, that you are sorry for them" (D. Considine, S.J., *The Virtues of the Divine Child*).

"O God, the sure hope of mercy for sinners, as also the joy of the upright, grant to thy servant the opportunity of repentance and full pardon. Spare me, truly sorry as I am, temptations in the future, lest to my sorrow I fall again. In thy own joy at my repentance, pardon all my faults, set my feet firmly on the path of well-doing, and give me joy in the company of those who deserve well of thee" (St. Prudentius, ninth century, adapted).

"Do thou, O almighty God, listen to thy servant's humble prayer. Give back to me the joy of those days when I walked humbly before thee. Guide me always that my works may be works of justice, and show me clearly the way that leads to thyself in heaven" (African Collect, fifth century).

"Good Lord, have mercy on us for thy truth. Thou art true and lovest truth above all things. Have in mind the promise thou didst make to every penitent sinner coming unto thee, which is: thou shalt not cast them away; yea, thou shalt refresh them. We come therefore unto thee, good Lord; cast us not away, but refresh us with thy grace and thy mercy" (St. John Fisher).

"For his own worshippers the Lord has a father's pity, does he not know the stuff of which we are made, can he forget that we are only dust?" (Ps. 102:13).

Resolution

"What return, then, ... does the Lord thy God ask of thee? This, that thou shouldst fear the Lord thy God, and follow the path he chooses for thee, and love him, and serve the Lord thy God with all thy heart and soul, and keep these divine commands and observances" (Deut. 10:12–13).

"Every day we ought to renew our purpose and rouse ourselves to fervour, as if that day were the first day of our conversion.

"And we ought to say, Help me, O Lord God, in my good purpose and in thy holy service, and grant that I may this day begin indeed, since what I have hitherto done is nothing.

"As our purpose is, so will our progress be; and he has need of much diligence that wishes to advance much.

"And if he who strongly purposes nevertheless often fails, what will he do that seldom or but weakly resolves?" (Thomas à Kempis, *The Imitation of Christ*, bk. 1, 19).

"Sweet Jesus, I thank thee with all my heart and all my skill for that sweet-sounding prayer and that holy orison thou madest before thy passion on the mountain of Olivet. And, Lord, I thank thee, for there, indeed, thou didst teach us to pray, when thou didst say: Father, not my will but thine be done. Thy prayer then was not for thyself, rather was it for us, to teach us that when our will, as it often is, be found contrary to the will of the Father in heaven, then we are to leave our will, and pray that the will of the Father be done in us. Here and now, sweet Jesus, I beseech thee that I be ever ready at thy will and not at mine; for when my will accords with thine, that is joy to me. Grant me grace ever to seek out thy will and so to come to thee" (Richard Rolle, fourteenth century).

"I beseech thee, Lord, give me strength to abandon my long-standing evil ways, that by thy help the energy lost in sinfulness may henceforward be wholly used in doing thy will. So may my good deeds overwhelm and atone for my evil-doing" (attributed to St. Bernard).

"Be it mine to guide my steps clear of wrong; deliver me in thy mercy. On sure ground my feet are set" (Ps. 25:10–12).

Thanksgiving 14

A Thought Before Saying One's Penance

"Today, as Catholics know, the penances given are slight. Still, as no act of a creature in itself can atone for an offence against the Creator, the expiatory value of the penance imposed is not wholly judged by its severity. All satisfactory acts depend for their value on their union with Christ's atonement.... Nevertheless, as modern penances are so slight, it is desirable that penitents should increase their value by earnestness in their accomplishment, by other works, and by gaining indulgences" (H. Harrington, *The Sacrament of Penance*).

For Perseverance

"And the grain that fell on good soil stands for those who hear the word, and hold by it with a noble and generous heart, and endure, and yield a harvest" (Luke 8:15).

"If we strove like valiant men to stand firm in the battle, surely we should see God's help coming down to us from heaven.

"For he is ready to help them that fight bravely and trust in his grace: and he himself provides us occasions to fight in order that we may conquer.

"It is hard to give up old habits; it is harder still to resist our own will.

"But if you do not overcome little and easy things, how will you surmount greater difficulties?

"Resist your inclination in the beginning, and unlearn habit, lest by little and little it bring you greater trouble.

"O if you did but consider what peace you would procure for yourself, and what joy for others, by bearing yourself well, I think you would be more solicitous for your spiritual progress" (Thomas à Kempis, *The Imitation of Christ*, bk. 1, 11).

"O Lord, how supremely necessary for me is thy grace, so that I may begin what is good, go forward with it, and accomplish it! For without it I can do nothing: but I can do all things in thee when grace strengthens me" (Thomas à Kempis, *The Imitation of Christ*, bk. 3, 55).

"Let us walk continually in the way until we come to the place whither the way leadeth; let us nowhere lag behind in it until it bring us to the place where we may find peace of mind. By seeking we aim and by our finding attain, and by our seeking and finding meet with that which still remains to be sought. So must it be, until there comes an end of seeking, in our rest in that perfect attainment which leaves no more to discover" (St. Augustine).

"Henceforth we will never forsake thee; grant us life, and we will live only to invoke thy name" (Ps. 79:20).

In Gratitude

"Blessed is thy name, O God of our fathers, who, though thy anger be roused, shewest mercy still, who dost pardon the sinner that cries out to thee in time of need! To thee, O Lord, I turn; on thee my eyes are fixed" (Tob. 3:13–14).

"What do we mean when we say that 'God forgives'? We certainly do not mean that he says: 'Never mind. Try to do better in the future.' Or: 'Don't worry, cheer up! I am not going to take it as seriously as all that.' That would be quite unworthy, and the wrong would remain. We mean something far greater. We mean that the sin no longer exists in truth and reality and in the sight of my conscience.... God draws man to himself, with all that he has done, draws him into his ineffable power over being and non-being.... He draws man into the mystery of his power not only to give life to the non-existent, but to call the guilty to new innocence. A new creation takes place. God draws man to himself with all that he has done, he draws him into his ineffable power and man comes forth again renewed and guiltless.... Something has not been merely covered up: I have been born again. I begin again" (R. Guardini, *The Living God*).

"What return shall we make to him for all that he has done for us? Indeed he has been generous, for he has given us good things in return for our evil ones, even when for his gifts we have heaped insults upon him. How can we atone for what he has suffered from us in this way? How repay his blessings? What fitting acknowledgement can there be to him who took our human nature, for the blows, the insults, the scourging he received for us? Let us at least leave our lives in his hands, and return him love as our debt, in the lovingness and the charity of our service of him, for we are lost if we do not love" (St. Paulinus of Nola, fifth century).

"Blessed be the Lord's name, my plea is heard; the Lord is my strength and shield. Trusting in him I found redress, and, with health renewed, right heartily I praise him" (Ps. 27:6).

In Forgiveness of Others, as We Have Been Forgiven

"Keep good watch over yourselves. As for thy brother, if he is in fault, tax him with it, and if he is sorry for it, forgive him; nay, if he does thee wrong seven times in the day, and seven times in the day comes back to thee and says, I am sorry, thou shalt forgive him" (Luke 17:3).

"O Lord, my God of mercy, I forgive all my enemies. And if anything is wanting in this forgiveness, I beseech thee through thy precious Blood, and through the lamentations and sighs of thy loving heart, to give me perfect charity towards all, and especially towards those who are against me or have done me an injury, so that I may be able to pardon them from the bottom of my heart as I wish to do. May I love them sincerely, willingly, cordially, without any bitterness; may I seek to do them good" (Lanspergius, *Ancient Devotions to the Sacred Heart*).

For the Work of the Church, Christ's Body, Hindered by Our Sins

"Our sins are a violation of our relation to our Lord as his friends and disciples, and also of our relation to society (for our sins have done harm to the world) — they may have given scandal, and, at any rate, they have increased unhappiness, whereas we might have done good, and promoted peace" (R. Eaton, *The Ministry of Reconciliation*).

"Man in his human frailty can never win to the nobler gifts of which he might become possessed, unless his first steps be guided by thee, his Master. Do thou, then, O Lord, prepare our minds for the good thou wouldst advance in us and give increase to what thou hast begun; and let us at all times give our thoughts to the progress of thy kingdom" (African Collect, fifth century).

Preparation 15

God and the Sinner

"Then he went out by the sea again; and all the multitude came to him, and he taught them there. And as he passed further on, he saw Levi, the son of Alpheus, sitting at work in the customs-house, and said to him, Follow me; and he rose up and followed him. And afterwards, when he was taking a meal in his house, many publicans and sinners were at table with Jesus and his disciples; for there were many of these who followed him. Thereupon the scribes and Pharisees, seeing him eat with publicans and sinners in his company, asked his disciples, How comes it that your master eats and drinks with publicans and sinners? Jesus heard it, and said to them: It is not those who are in health that have need of the physician, it is those who are sick. I have come to call sinners, not the just" (Mark 2:13–17).

The Value of the Sacrament

"If thou hast a mind to enter into life, keep the commandments" (Matt. 19:17).

"Levi, that is St. Matthew, saw the Lord, and knew who he was; he felt how far he was from him; he saw the Lord in sublime heights and himself in the depths upon the custom-bench. This is where he cheated and extorted money from the people, and they despised and hated him, but Jesus they loved and followed. Jesus did not collect anything from anyone, and still how rich he was; so rich, that he gave to everybody from his riches. How can this mighty, rich Lord look upon him, is what Levi thought. Yes, the Lord looked upon him, with the look of understanding.... He sees his interest, his longing and dissatisfaction. The Lord also calls us by means of duty, recognition, sight, and finally enthusiasm.... In the face of this mighty revelation, every other voice is silenced, the heart becomes light, it moves and starts: 'I run upon the way of thy commandments, if thou enlargest my heart.' This equally is a creative summons; it creates a new man. Do not let us doubt its strength; it can do much if it comes upon a soul.... He gives us his help, that we may follow him with steps which take us from world to world. If we come to a purer, more beautiful world, we go willingly indeed" (Prohaszka, *Meditations on the Gospels*).

In Humility

"Shame, that is the grace and glory of a man" (Ecclus. [Sir.] 4:25).

"Humility is something much more than a lack of conceit and arrogance. It means that we acknowledge God's gifts and admit what poor use we make of them. 'When you shall have done all these things that are commanded you, say: We are unprofitable servants'" (J. C. Heenan, *The People's Priest*).

"What shall become of me as I daily fall away? How shall I perfectly amend my life? When shall I become better? When shall I grow strong? And when shall I overcome the hindrances to my salvation? Dost thou think there is any hope for me to arise from sin, to amend my life, to advance in virtue, and to persevere to the end?... Remember, I beseech thee, thy creature who has fallen; lift him up, for he cannot stand of himself" (Thomas à Kempis, *True Wisdom*).

"Heart-deep my supplication before thee for the mercies thou hast promised" (Ps. 118:58).

For Confidence

"Cast the burden of thy cares upon the Lord, and he will sustain thee; never will he let thee stumble, his servant if thou be" (Ps. 54:23).

"Wherever the light of the Gospel has penetrated, there is to be found a man who acts in the person of Christ … a shepherd, a father, a healer. He is not one who sits immovable in a dim shrine — who wraps himself in his pride — who is the mere mechanical instrument of one greater than himself. He watches the flock committed to him by day and by night; he goes into the deserts after them, or into crowded haunts that are more repellant than the wilderness. He leads them to the altar; he enlightens their ignorance and prepares their hearts; he has comforting and healing words for them; and he brings them by many persuasions within the circle of that power which Christ, his Master, has given him. For the sacramental prerogative is great and wonderful, and the greatest of all is the power of the Eucharistic consecration which truly and really makes Jesus Christ present under sacramental forms. But how its effect upon the souls of men is enhanced and multiplied by that gift which belongs to the priest, of making himself, in love and solicitude, in word and deed, the image of what Jesus was when he trod the ways of this earth of ours! … That ministerial power, combined with that fatherly solicitude — that mystical ritual and that most human watchfulness — the words of aweful dispensation mingled with the voice of pleading and encouragement — these things present the living Jesus" (Hedley, *The Light of the World*).

"For it is a good thing to confess to thee, O Lord, and to say: Have mercy on me, heal my soul, for I have sinned against thee, not with any thought of abusing thy mercy by freedom in sin, but rather to remember the Lord's warning: 'Behold thou art made whole; sin now no more lest some worse thing befall thee'" (St. Augustine, *Confessions*).

"His faithfulness will throw a shield about thee" (Ps. 90:4).

For Self-Knowledge

"Does it come from God, this thought of mine?" (1 Par. [1 Chron.] 13:2).

"One must take oneself seriously, coming to grips with the evil in oneself which is ever seeking to lead one from the true meaning of life. This force must be recognised and encountered. In other words, one must take one's conscience seriously. It must be admitted that there is a general tendency not to face these things. They are uncomfortable and we tend to feel we would rather know nothing about them! We have far too little trust in redemption and salvation.

"But in so far as we do not face these things, our lives are lacking in reality, and hence contrary to the virtue of wisdom. Every sort of sin, as St. Thomas said, is an offence against wisdom" (Von Gagern, *Difficulties in Life*).

"Thou art the all-seeing, all-knowing God. Thy eyes, O Lord, are in every place. Thou art a real spectator of everything which takes place everywhere. Thou art ever with me. Thou art present, and conscious of all I think, say, or do. *Tu Deus qui vidisti me* — 'Thou, God, who hast seen me.' Every deed, every act, however slight; every word, however quick and casual; every thought of my heart, however secret, however momentary, however forgotten, thou seest, O Lord, thou seest" (Newman, *Meditations and Devotions*).

"Firm let thy feet be set on the path the Lord has chosen for thee; be true to thy own thought, and to the knowledge thou hast, and ever let the counsels of peace and justice guide thee on thy way" (Ecclus. [Sir.] 5:12).

For Greater Sorrow

"Have mercy on me. O God, as thou art ever rich in mercy; in the abundance of thy compassion, blot out the record of my misdeeds. Wash me clean, cleaner yet, from my guilt, purge me of my sin, the guilt of which I freely acknowledge" (Ps. 50:3–5).

"Sin repented is itself a form of creative darkness; and we are given the sacrament of repentance and sorrow that this may be so. True, even without the sacrament, repentance and sorrow which are motivated by the love of God will achieve the same effect; but how difficult it is for some of us in our selfishness to be sure that our sorrow is of that sort! We must not indeed exaggerate the difficulty: for the 'profoundly Christian soul,' as has been wisely said, 'perfect contrition is easy, even very easy' — we have to remember that 'an act of perfect contrition' need not be 'a perfect act of contrition,' and that whether one *feels* emotionally contrite is quite irrelevant. Contrition is 'psychologically' the simple yielding to the attraction of God, the simple sorrow provoked by love, a beginning of a childlike self-surrender to the Father one has left or rejected, a reorientation of one's whole being towards God — Truth, Goodness, Beauty, Love" (G. Vann, O.P., *The Paradise Tree*).

"I humbly stand before thee, O Lord, my conscience witness to my guilt, scarce daring to ask what I hardly deserve to win. For thou, Lord, knowest our shame in confessing what we did not hesitate to do. We have been followers of thine in our words, and have denied thee in our hearts, and of the worth of any promise of ours, our actions have, so far, given little proof. Even so, Lord, spare those who humbly confess to thee, pardon those who have sinned against thee, have mercy on those who entreat thee. Since my appreciation of this sacrament is so weak, and the hardness of my heart might forbid the hearing of my prayer, I beseech thee that thou wilt of thyself generously grant me forgiveness" (Book of Cerne, tenth century).

"He has mercy ever at his side, a God merciful as he is great" (Ecclus. [Sir.] 2:23).

Resolution

"And you, too, must think of yourselves as dead to sin, and alive with a life that looks towards God, through Christ Jesus our Lord" (Rom. 6:11).

"Repeated falls into the same sin do not necessarily argue a defective purpose, or a defective sorrow; it may have been a good act of repentance at the time, though subsequent human infirmity, and the force of habit, have induced the will once more to consent to sin. But in a given instance, the lack of purpose in avoiding sin which could easily be put aside, must sooner or later bring the repentant sinner to review his supposed sorrow, and to ask himself whether his alleged detestation of sin is an illusion" (E. J. Mahoney, *Sin and Repentance*).

"Fast bind me to thyself, sweet Jesus, in faith, hope and charity. Bind me to thyself in faith, sweet Jesus, that no delusion or heresy turn me from what I believe; and grant me, sweet Jesus, that my faith be intelligent, not exaggerated in holding what is not to be believed, nor narrow, rejecting what I should hold. Make me, sweet Jesus, to believe in all the sacraments of holy Church, and in all thy commandments, and give me trust in thee, my God, all my salvation. Sweet Jesus, fast bind me to thyself in hope, that all my trust and hope be solely in thee. Let my hope be not feeble, that I fall into despair, nor yet without restraint, lest I grow presumptuous. Grant me the grace, sweet Jesus, to persevere in good works in thy service, and always with discretion that I may wisely hope and trust in thee. Sweet Jesus, fast bind me to thyself in charity, that all my loving be for thee in will and word and work. Let me love nothing but thee or for thy sake. As thou biddest me, let me love friend and enemy, and grant me thy grace that no foolish anger, hatred or envy break the bond of my charity" (Richard Rolle, fourteenth century).

"The man who loves me is the man who keeps the commandments he has from me" (John 14:21).

Thanksgiving 15

A Thought Before Saying One's Penance

"The virtue of penance manifests itself in several operations of the intellect and will. The interior acts are hatred of sin, regret and shame for having offended, readiness to suffer what is due as a compensation to justice, a resolve to sin no more, a desire to render glory to God in reparation, and also joy in our sense of sorrow" (G. Bellord, *Meditations on Christian Dogma*).

For Perseverance

"You must still love the Lord your God, and follow the paths he has chosen, obeying his commandments, keeping close to him, and offering him the service of your hearts and soul" (Josh. 22:5).

"They alone stride towards the goal where God awaits them, who guard against every fault by maintaining in their souls the spirit of penance.... Not content with preaching its necessity, Christianity has wrought a marvellous thing in making it loved and sought after. It attracts the perfect and the saint even more than the sinner, the neophyte or the convert of yesterday. In pure and innocent souls, it is found in a pre-eminent degree; the more remote they are from sin, the more they delight in combatting it. As they become penetrated with the spirit of Christ, there is implanted in them the spirit of penance" (Galtier, *Sin and Penance*).

"Yet, Lord, sweet Jesus, this life is full of temptations and enemies, and there is no succour but in thee. Then, sweet Jesus, take me to thee, within thy governance and shielding, and never let thy handiwork be abandoned. Yea, sweet Jesus, thou art all good, and to thee belongeth all love; then take me to thy heart wholly, that all my love may be in thee, who didst redeem all, so that my heart, in whatever temptation, may never turn from thee, but ever may cleave fast to thee, to love thee, sweet Jesus" (Richard Rolle, fourteenth century).

"Deign now to show me thy will, thou who hast listened when I opened my heart to thee. Direct me in the path thou biddest me follow, and all my musing shall be of thy wonderful deeds.... Deliver me from every false thought; let thy covenant be my comfort. Duty's path my choice, I keep thy bidding ever in remembrance.... Do but open my heart wide, and easy lies the path thou hast decreed" (Ps. 118:26–32).

In Gratitude

"For us thou art God, beneficent and truthful, thou, always patient and merciful towards the world thou governest" (Wisd. 15:1).

"We say: 'I do not feel much the better for going: my confessions are so formal, and, I fear, very superficial; I do not seem to get much good or comfort from them: I just jog on from one week to another....' Is that really true? If it is, we ought to be pleased and encouraged, for to maintain such a state is no slight achievement. More might be done, no doubt, but do not think disparagingly of even this, nor imagine that something is wrong because greater results do not appear. It is always a great thing if we are able to keep the soul 'even' and no sacrament is lost or wasted that has produced this result in us. It is a great

thing not to go back, or to lose fervour, even though our gain be but slight"
(R. Eaton, *The Ministry of Reconciliation*).

"O Jesu, is any obstinacy too great for thy love? Does any number of falls and
relapses vanquish the faithfulness and endurance of thy compassion? Thou
dost forgive not only seven times, but to seventy times seven. Many waters
cannot quench a love like thine. And such thou art all over the earth, even
to the end — forgiving, sparing, forbearing, waiting, though sinners are ever
provoking thee; pitying and taking into account their ignorance, visiting all
men, all thine enemies with the gentle pleadings of thy grace, day after day,
year after year, up to the hour of their death — for he knoweth whereof we
are made" (Newman, *Meditations and Devotions*).

"Blessed art thou, O Lord; teach me to know thy will.... Blithely as one that
has found great possessions, I follow thy decrees" (Ps. 118:12–14).

In Forgiveness of Others, as We Have Been Forgiven

"How then canst thou press thy quarrel home, and no strife come of it?"
(Prov. 30:33).

"Father, Father of all mankind ... when thou forgivest, teach us to forgive
our fellow-men with a generosity which finds its model in thee" (R. A. Knox,
Pastoral Sermons).

For the Work of the Church, Christ's Body, Hindered by Our Sins

"From whatever angle we visualize the Church's conduct in this matter of
dealing with sin — not the sin of the world but the sin of the elect — one

impression is brought home to us most strongly. We are witnessing, not so much a psychological phenomenon as a manifestation of power; the power to redress the balance of sanctity inside God's kingdom. The psychological element of heart-sorrow belongs to this great healing up of the wounds of the Church" (Vonier, *Christianus*).

"O God, whose Fatherly care we measure by the joy in heaven over one repentant sinner, look down upon the company of the faithful, that, freed from all disturbance, these children of thine inheritance may grow in number and devotion" (Gregorian Sacramentary, ninth century).

Preparation 16

God and the Sinner

"And now the scribes and Pharisees brought to him a woman who had been found committing adultery, and made her stand there in full view: Master, they said, this woman has been caught in the act of adultery. Moses in his law prescribed that such person should be stoned to death; what of thee? What is thy sentence? They said this to put him to the test, hoping to find a charge to bring against him. But Jesus bent down, and began writing on the ground with his finger. When he found they continued to question him, he looked up and said to them, Whichever of you is free from sin shall cast the first stone at her. Then he bent down again, and went on writing on the ground. And they began to go out one by one, beginning with the eldest, till Jesus was left alone with the woman, still standing in full view. Then Jesus looked up, and asked her, Woman, where are thy accusers? Has no one condemned thee? No one, Lord, she said. And Jesus said to her, I will not condemn thee either. Go, and do not sin again henceforward" (John 8:3–11).

The Value of the Sacrament

"Deep lies my soul in the dust, restore life to me, as thou hast promised" (Ps. 118:25).

"Jesus wished to deepen the feeling of morality; he wishes that every sinner should first feel his own sin; that with the loathing of sin and the hatred which we feel first towards ourselves we should start out to improve and save others. Blessing only rests upon such a mentality. Let us therefore go into the depths, into ourselves; let us become pure, then we can affect others. This does not mean that sin has not to be punished; this would lead to moral enervation. Jesus does not here adopt a legal attitude, but deals with the souls of the deceitful men who stand before him. He sees through their guile. He sees that they do not serve morality, but want to ensnare him. How good it is to bring such people to the consciousness of that sinfulness which they want to have punished in others. The woman is a sinner, but they are also deceitful. Let us purify the good intention so that base, selfish, ignoble elements do not mingle with it.... 'I do not condemn thee,' says the Lord — I do not crush thy individuality, live and grow better. I loathe sin, but I wish thee good. Make good thy sins, live purely" (Prohaszka, *Meditations on the Gospels*).

In Humility

"Thou knowest well, almighty God ... how little trust I place in my own power, with my flesh so constantly rebelling against my spirit. I so easily become indignant, impatient, apprehensive, and fearful. I am so quickly swayed by my emotions when I meet with and suffer from any injustice, annoyance, temptation or trial. I come therefore to thee, the heavenly Physician, for help. I seek, most of all, that divine remedy, patience, that most powerful relief in the severest trials.... Give me the grace of a calm and controlled mind, sensibly prepared to accept all things, cheerful and sad, as coming from thy Fatherly hands" (St. Peter Canisius, *Manuale Catholicorum*).

"Turn thy eyes away from my sins, blot out the record of my guilt; my God, bring a clean heart to birth within me; breathe new life, true life, into my being. Do not banish me from thy presence, do not take thy holy spirit away from me; give me back the comfort of thy saving power, and strengthen me in generous resolve" (Ps. 50:11–14).

For Confidence

"The Father himself is your friend, since you have become my friends.... I have said this to you that in me you may find peace" (John 16:27–33).

"There is one moment in religious experience ... when the penitent sinner knows himself to be restored to life, to God; the moment of sacramental absolution. The load is lifted, and with it the sense of being lost, the loneliness; but the joy does not annul the sorrow; rather the joy and the sorrow become fused into a single thing, for which we have no name unless perhaps it be love. Inevitably we are reminded of how Christ gently and subtly made plain to Peter the fact that he was forgiven for having thrice denied him by asking him thrice the same question, 'Simon, son of John, lovest thou me?'" (G. Vann, O.P., *The Paradise Tree*).

"We seek thee, O Lord, for the goodness and kindness we are full certain to find in thee because we know thou didst not despise the poor, nor reject the sinner. Thou didst not shun the good thief ... nor the sinful woman who wept tears of repentance, nor the mother from Canaan who brought her prayer to thee, nor even her who was taken in adultery, nor him who sat at the receipt of custom, nor the publican who begged forgiveness, nor the disciple who denied thee, nor even thy very executioners. It is the fragrance of such divine forgiveness that draws us to seek thee" (St. Bernard, *Sermons*).

"Full of misgiving was my heart; but thou hast set me high up on a rock, thou hast escorted me on my way, thou, my only hope.... Eternally I will sing thy praises, day after day, perform my vows" (Ps. 60:3–9).

For Self-Knowledge

"Once you were all darkness; now, in the Lord, you are daylight. You must live as men native to the light; where the light has its effect, all is goodness, and holiness, and truth; your lives must be a manifestation of God's will" (Eph. 5:8–10).

"God's knowledge of our faults is independent of our knowledge or ignorance of them. Whether we know them or not, God knows them always. It is childish to presume that new knowledge on our part implies new knowledge on God's part; yet that is what we often do presume unconsciously. We are prone to imagine that new knowledge of our faults which has made us seem very objectionable to ourselves, has suddenly made us very objectionable to God. Why should it? Those faults have been as clear as daylight all along" (Wilson, *Pardon and Peace*).

"In praise of thee, O Lord, I do confess the things that are unbecoming in me. I beseech thee, give me grace now to recall in my memory the faults of the past, and to offer thee a sacrifice of rejoicing; for what am I to myself without thee, but a guide to my own downfall?" (St. Augustine, *Confessions*).

"I will make my spirit penetrate you, so that you will follow in the paths of my law, remember and carry out my decrees.... Well may you think with loathing of what you were" (Ezek. 36:27–31).

Devotions for Confession

For Greater Sorrow

"O God, our Saviour, help us; deliver us, Lord, for the glory of thy name, and pardon our sins" (Ps. 78:9).

"The more perfect our contrition is in receiving the sacrament, the more pleasing it is to God, and the more grace is received. For a soul already justified by perfect contrition, in receiving the sacrament, receives still more grace, and becomes more deeply rooted and grounded in charity. It should therefore be our constant care to make more and more perfect the motive of our sorrow for sin. It is difficult in the sense that perfect contrition requires perfect detachment from our sins, and careful reflection on divine things, which, in the modern rush of life, is not always easy to secure; it is difficult, too, because it is not easy to break away from selfish and excessive pre-occupation with our own advantage and happiness, even in matters religious. But granted a certain degree of generosity towards God, it should be comparatively easy gradually to purify our motives and arrive almost imperceptibly at perfect contrition" (E. J. Mahoney, *Sin and Repentance*).

"I beseech thee, most tender Jesus, that evil may not undo the work of thy almighty goodness in me. Do thou, all kindly as thou art, approve thy own work. Destroy utterly in me all that is not thine. Jesus, have mercy on me whilst there is still time for thy mercy to work good in me, lest I come to merit thy condemnation. Admit me, Jesus, my heart's real desire, to the number of thy chosen ones, that with them I may praise thee and find my joy in thee" (St. Anselm of Canterbury, twelfth century).

"Lord, have mercy on me, is my prayer; bring healing to a soul that has sinned against thee.... Lord, have mercy on me; give me back life" (Ps. 40:5–11).

Resolution

"To such as repent, he grants the means of acquittal, and makes their fainting hearts strong to endure, for them, too, he has a share in his promised reward" (Ecclus. [Sir.] 17:20).

"Let us ask ourselves, why it is that we so often wish to do right and cannot? Why is it that we are so frail, feeble, languid, wayward, dim-sighted, fluctuating, perverse? Why is it that we cannot 'do the things that we would'? Why is it that, day after day, we remain irresolute, that we serve God so poorly, that we govern ourselves so weakly and so variably, that we cannot command our thoughts, that we are so slothful, so cowardly, so discontented, so sensual, so ignorant? Why is it that we ... who are ruled by no evil masters and bent upon no earthly ends, who are not covetous, or profligate livers, or worldly-minded, or ambitious, or envious, or proud, or unforgiving, or desirous of name — why is it that we, in the very kingdom of grace, surrounded by angels and preceded by saints, nevertheless can do so little, and instead of mounting with wings like eagles, grovel in the dust, and do but sin and confess alternately? Is it that the *power* of God is not within us? Is it literally that we are *not able* to perform God's commandments? God forbid! We are able. We have that given us which makes us able.... What is it we lack? The power? No; the will. What we lack is the real, simple, earnest, sincere inclination and aim to use what God has given us, and what we have in us" (Newman, *Parochial and Plain Sermons*).

"Hail, sweet Jesus, praise to thee and honour and glory, O Christ, who hast set the heavens, the earth and the sea, and all that heavens, earth and sea contain at my disposal, anxious that they should serve my needs, and be my support and comfort. Grant me grace never to misuse these gifts of thine, for all that thou hast made proclaims thy goodness, all compels my admiration, leading me on to the fuller knowledge of thee, and thence to love of thee" (Nakatenus, *Coeleste Palmetum*).

"Can there be healing where there is no love of right?" (Job 34:17).

Thanksgiving 16

A Thought Before Saying One's Penance

"Before declaring in God's name that the sin has been forgiven, the priest must impose a suitable penance. Apart from being a meritorious act of humility, it is a necessary completion of the duties of a contrite sinner. It is some attempt at expiation, not only of the guilt of sin, but of the temporal punishment which remains due to sin after the guilt has been forgiven" (J. C. Heenan, *Confession*).

For Perseverance

"Be true to thy covenant with God; its words to thy own ears repeat; to that, and to thy enjoined duty, inure thyself" (Ecclus. [Sir.] 11:21).

"With this constant falling into sin we are given two ways of accepting our falls. The first and obvious way is the constant struggle to resist the temptation; and the thing that ought to be so consoling to anyone who constantly falls is the knowledge that every effort — the tiniest as well as the biggest — that he has made to resist, is remembered for all eternity, and for every one of those efforts he will be rewarded. When he does give in and commit the sin, as soon as he confesses it, it is forgiven; and not only forgiven, but forgotten, while all that went before the sin, every kind of effort he made to resist, is *never* forgotten. Therefore, a man may sin and sin, and, at the end of it, it is the efforts he has made to overcome that sin, the determination not to give in, which is the crown of his glory. His struggle is incomparably more valuable in the sight of God than the petty struggles of those who have not the same severe temptation. He may feel, 'What is the use of going to confession, when every time it is the same story over again?' But it is that steady accumulation of merit and perseverance that counts" (F. Devas, S.J., *What Law and Letter Kill*).

"Lord, I am nothing, I can do nothing, I have nothing of myself that is good; but in all things do I fail, and do ever tend to nothing. And unless I am assisted and inwardly instructed by thee, I become wholly lukewarm and slack. But thou, O Lord, art always the self-same, and endurest to eternity; ever good, just and holy; doing all things well, justly and holily; and disposing them in wisdom. But I, who am more inclined to go back than forward, do not continue ever in the same state.... Yet it soon becomes better with me when it pleases thee and thou stretchest out thy helping hand; for thou alone, without man's aid, canst so assist and strengthen me that my countenance shall no more be changed, but my heart be converted and find its rest in thee alone.... Thanks be to thee, from whom all proceeds, whenever things go well with me" (Thomas à Kempis, *The Imitation of Christ*, bk. 3, 40).

"It is for you, then, to observe the commands which the Lord has given you ... still treading the path which the Lord your God has marked out for you" (Deut. 5:32–33).

In Gratitude

"I will give thee eternal thanks for all thou hast done, and put my trust in thy name, as they ever love to do that are thy true servants" (Ps. 51:10–11).

"He must be recognized as our Master, Friend, Saviour, Father. But to one who realises how real are these relations of dependence, forgiveness and friendship, nothing would seem more natural and legitimate than this need of making continued protests against the injustices, the ingratitude and the forgetfulness of the past.... As our moral delicacy increases, the more deeply do we loathe anything that reminds us of sin, or threatens to revive it.... It is a question of gratitude, too; how can we restrain our anger at the ill we have done in return for God's gifts? Finally, and especially, it is a question of love; for one who realises that he is loved, the thought that he once slighted, rejected, betrayed that love must of necessity cause him the deepest pain" (Galtier, *Sin and Penance*).

"My God, what hast thou done for me!... I know so entirely and feel so intimately, that to me thou hast been nothing but forbearance and mercy. O how thou dost forget that I have ever rebelled against thee! Again and again thou dost help me. I fall, yet thou dost not cast me off. In spite of all my sins, thou dost still love me, prosper me, comfort me, surround me with blessings, sustain me and further me. I grieve thy good grace, yet thou dost give me more. I insult thee, yet thou never dost take offence, but art as kind as if I had nothing to explain, to repent of, to amend — as if I were thy best, most faithful, most steady and loyal friend. Nay, alas, I am led to presume upon thy love, it is so like easiness and indulgence, though I ought to fear thee.... Every day is but a fresh memorial of thy unwearied, unconquerable love" (Newman, *Meditations and Devotions*).

"Now the Lord takes delight in thee ... gladly the Lord shall greet thee" (Isa. 62:4–5).

In Forgiveness of Others, as We Have Been Forgiven

"If any have a complaint against another; even as the Lord hath forgiven you, so do you also" (Col. 3:13).

"Hail, sweet Jesus, who for my sake suffered many injuries, many sorrows and constant persecution, and, indeed, from those whom thou hadst loaded with benefits. Give me a sincere and straightforward heart that I may be loyal to my enemies, with kindness excusing them, and faithfully returning them good for evil, that by my patience and charity I may please thee" (Nakatenus, *Coeleste Palmetum*).

For the Work of the Church, Christ's Body, Hindered by Our Sins

"It is in the nature of the sacrament of penance that its effect is not confined to the individual penitent, but extends to the community. Sin, whether mortal or venial, injures not only the sinner himself, but all the faithful, indeed the whole world. Sin is the root of all evil, the source of all suffering.... In this respect, confession plays a very important part in our life, and this point is of special significance with regard to confessions of devotion. This is a sacrament, not merely a sacramental. In it every time the redeeming Blood of Christ is made to flow again. Whatever God does is done wholly. If there is in us no grievous sin to be taken away, if we do not require the power of the precious Blood for the remission of sin, it flows, as it were, right over us, right into the mystical body of Christ, right to our brethren and sisters who, as dead members, are a heavy load in the whole community of the Church and who urgently require the grace of penance, as it were, from those without" (R. Graef, *The Sacrament of Peace*).

"What shall I do, my Lord? What shall I do, my God? O how late have my desires become enkindled, and how early, Lord, didst thou go in search of me, calling me to spend myself wholly in thy service.... Now will it become clear, Lord, if my soul, looking upon the time it has lost, is right in its belief that thou, in a moment, canst turn its loss to gain" (St. Teresa, *Exclamations*).

Preparation 17

God and the Sinner

"He himself stood in the midst of them, and said, Peace be upon you; it is myself, do not be afraid. . . . This is what I told you, he said, while I still walked in your company; how all that was written of me in the law of Moses, and in the prophets, and in the psalms, must be fulfilled. Then he enlightened their minds, to make them understand the scriptures; so it was written, he told them, and so it was fitting that Christ should suffer, and should rise again from the dead on the third day; and that repentance and remission of sins should be preached in his name to all nations, beginning at Jerusalem. Of this, you are the witnesses. And behold, I am sending down upon you the gift which was promised by my Father" (Luke 24:36–49).

The Value of the Sacrament

"All will know me, from the highest to the lowest. I will pardon their wrong-doing; I will not remember their sins any more" (Heb. 8:11–12).

"From the early beginnings of his ministry among men, the remission of sins had been announced as the great boon of the Gospel, in the canticle of Zachary and in the words of his blessed son, who had been the first to speak of our Blessed Lord, under the name of the Lamb of God, who taketh away the sin of the world. And when our Lord began his active work among men, it soon became clear that he took to himself the power to forgive sins, which had never been exercised by priest or prophet before him. . . . We can hardly be wrong in thinking that the Apostles must have received full instructions on the great boon which was now at last to be placed in their hands for the endless benefit of the human race. It is not wonderful that the actions of our Saviour in conferring it were marked by a singular solemnity. . . . This is an appropriate finish and crown to the first Easter day, the work which our Saviour selected as the great gift to the Church before the first night fell on the infant Church. Like all great acts of our Lord, it was carried out in a few simple words, but with great solemnity of manner, in accordance with the immense importance of the subject and the universality of the power now bestowed. There are no sins that are left out in this universality, nor any sign of any person who is excluded; the remission is as universal as the merits of the Saviour by whose Blood they are to be cancelled" (Coleridge, *The Life of Our Life*).

In Humility

"If they come here repentant, and acknowledging thy power, pray to thee and plead with thee in this temple of thine, do thou in heaven listen to them" (3 Kings [1 Kings] 8:33–34).

"Was he not called the friend of sinners, and did he ever disdain the name? Where should we be without this fountain of mercy? . . . The bruised reed he does not crush, the smoking flax he does not extinguish. He sits refining his silver, for the material with which he deals is the same as ever it was before he came to seek and to save that which was lost. Passion is still strong, temptation is still subtle and alluring, scandals still occur, sins are still multiplied on every side — where, then, would be the saving work of our Lord if there were no ministry of reconciliation? Is there one that for a mess of pottage has not more than once sold his birthright? ... Our Lord provided. He knew what was in man: he is Jesus Christ, the same yesterday, to-day and forever. 'Be of good heart, son, thy sins are forgiven thee!' are words he will continue to speak to the paralytic to the end of time" (R. Eaton, *The Ministry of Reconciliation*).

"To thee alone, Lord, have we sinned and done evil in thy sight, even thee, from whom not the deepest secrets of our hearts can be hid; and we are ashamed to acknowledge what we still do not hesitate to do. But do thou, O Lord, who never turnest away from the repentant, hear the prayers of those who are now humbled before thee. Forgive our sins, and may thy Holy Spirit, by the grace of the Trinity, teach us to walk in the ways of goodness.... May God the Father govern us, for he did fashion us; may God the Son guard us, for he redeemed us; may the Holy Spirit fill us with his graces, for he created us" (Gothic Breviary, seventh century).

"Listen to my prayer, thou to whom all mankind must look for pardon" (Ps. 64:3).

For Confidence

"To my summons give heed and hearing; so your spirits shall revive" (Isa. 55:3).

"The sacrament of penance is the great Easter gift made by the Lord to his people, the first fruit of his passion. In his great love and mercy, he would gladly have taken upon himself all our guilt, so that this sacrament would operate by itself, as does baptism. However, divine justice did not permit this: this sacrament is concerned with the free and conscious guilt.... Nowhere could we more rightly apply the words of the psalmist: 'Mercy and truth have met each other, justice and peace have kissed.' Still, in his mercy, Christ took upon himself almost everything, leaving to us only as much as is absolutely necessary to satisfy divine justice. Therefore we can be certain, he does not wish us to believe that everything has to be accomplished by us alone, as if everything depended upon our activity and our ability" (R. Graef, *The Sacrament of Peace*).

"See me, sweet Lord, see me. In thy loving kindness, most merciful is my hope. For thou wilt see me as a faithful physician would, anxious to heal or to correct. This, then, I ask of thee, who art the very fount of kindness, trusting simply in thy mighty mercy, and in thy merciful might ... to forgive my sins, to rouse me from my half-heartedness, forgetting my ingratitude and remembering only thy goodness. Then, as for those vices and evil passions which even yet war in me, whether due to long-standing evil habit, or to my negligence, from day to day repeated, or to the deep-seated defects of my frail nature, or even to the scarce-recognised temptings of evil spirits; against all these foes let thy gentle grace give strength and courage" (St. Aelred of Rievaulx, *Pastoral Prayer*).

"We must observe all these laws of his, and go in fear of the Lord our God. Then the prosperity that is ours to-day will be ours all our life long; he will have mercy on us, if he sees us ever faithful to his commandments, ever obedient to his will" (Deut. 6:24–25).

For Self-Knowledge

"May the Lord direct you, where the love of God and the patience of Christ show you the way" (2 Thess. 3:5).

Devotions for Confession

"Perhaps one of the effects of regular confession ... is precisely a heightening or refining of the sense of sin, so that we become aware that episodes in our past life which at the time we regarded as in no way reprehensible, or at least brushed aside as of little importance, were in fact of considerable moral importance: and that realisation is again no cause for discouragement, but on the contrary for gratitude: it means that we are becoming clearer of vision and cleaner of heart. It is much easier to see our sins than our sinfulness; yet in the last resort it is the latter that we are telling God about. Confession may become a more or less unvarying routine, always the same 'wilful distraction at prayer, vanity, unkindness, laziness' or whatever it may be; but these things can be seen as symbols of the deeper sinfulness we cannot apprehend or at least cannot fully appreciate while at the same time we know it is there, that it is that for which we most have to implore God's mercy and help" (G. Vann, O.P., *The Paradise Tree*).

"Do thou, divine Healer, minister to me, now that I have shown thee my weakness and my wounds. Help me, for thine is the strength which alone can help me to rise, the infinite strength which alone can support me. Come to me as the light which alone can enlighten my hesitating mind; shine but for a moment before my eyes, that the sight of thy beauty may give me comfort and courage in the face of the evils and the temptations of this life; and that I may the better do this, stir my intelligence to some appreciation of thy eternal truth" (St. Augustine, *Soliloquies*).

"My hope is in thee; to thee I lift up my heart: shew me the path I must follow" (Ps. 142:7–8).

Preparation 17

For Greater Sorrow

"Hearts that loved to stray, ten times more eagerly retrace your steps, and come back to him! And he in unfading joy will compass your deliverance" (Bar. 4:28–29).

"We are all sons of God who is King of heaven and who has entrusted each of us into the keeping of an angel.... Let us keep him near us with the fragrance of good works, and let us remain in his care. Christ knows, every one of us pays too little honour to so noble a guardian, and shows him too little gratitude for his service. These, along with many others, are reasons why a man should be bitterly sorry for his sins and weep with great sorrow; and it is well for him who can, for weeping is salutary for the soul. Our Lord acts towards us as people do to a bad debtor; he takes less than we owe him and yet he is satisfied. We owe him blood for blood, which he shed for us, and even so, our blood for his blood, which he shed for us, would be a very unequal exchange.... Our Lord accepts our tears from us in exchange for his blood, and is well pleased. He himself wept on the cross, and over Lazarus, and over Jerusalem, for the sins of others. If we then weep for our own, it is no great wonder" (*Ancren Rimle*, ca. fourteenth century).

"Now, sweet Jesus, I beseech thee to take me to thee and to make me all thine; and if I fly to any sin of the world, of the flesh, or of the fiend, sweet Jesus, fetch me soon home again, as a lord doth his bondman, and drive me with tribulation soon to penance. Sweet Jesus, in thee is all sovereign medicine, and I, Lord, am all sick in sins; therefore, sweet Jesus, take me to thee and set me under thy care, and come near me with grace, as did the Samaritan, and pour into my wounds oil of mercy, and bring me to the hostel of charity, and ever hold me under thy care" (Richard Rolle, fourteenth century).

"Turn thy ear, Lord, and listen to me in my helplessness and my need. Protect a life dedicated to thyself; rescue a servant of thine, that puts his trust in thee. Have mercy, O Lord, for mercy I plead continually; comfort thy servant's heart, this heart that aspires, Lord, to thee. Who is so kind and forgiving, Lord, as thou art, who so rich in mercy to all who invoke him? Give hearing then, Lord, to my prayer; listen to my plea when I cry out to thee" (Ps. 85:1–7).

Resolution

"Can God forget to be gracious, can anger move him to withhold his mercy? And now I resolve to begin afresh; it is at such times that the Most High relents in his dealings with men" (Ps. 76:10–11).

"The sinner who begins to turn to God experiences a great deal of that condition of will which the wise man describes — 'he willeth and he willeth not.' At times he would be virtuous, abandon his sin, and turn to God. But he finds it difficult to bring matters to the point. His best thoughts wander; he is like a man in a mist, he has no definite idea where he is. His past life is blurred and blotted, he is tempted to let it pass. And the consequence is that most men, even with good desires, let the past alone, and content themselves with an indefinite idea that they will be better for the future. Now the sacrament of penance makes this impossible. The penitent has to examine his past life, not with foolish or nervous solicitude, but with fair exactness; he has to get a sort of catalogue of his doings before his eye. This not only impresses him with a true idea of his sinfulness, but it shows him what to do for the future, and, what is more than all, it makes him, on a certain day and hour, lay his sins, as in a bundle, at the feet of his Saviour's cross.... Self-examination, definiteness of place and time, the humbling of ourselves before a fellow-man like our confessor — all this makes us earnest. These things rouse resistance too thoroughly in our lower nature not to make us very intense and determined" (Hedley, *Christ and the Sinner*).

"Free our minds and our thoughts, O Lord, from the common and the vulgar which leaves its mark on our souls. Grant us to stand before thee with clean minds. Keep us from all the sordid effects of sin. Increase in us the spirit of reverence and self-control lest now, or at any time in our lives, our minds should seem graceless and unrefined. Let us desire to stand before thee free from all that is unbecoming, which surely would make us strangers to thee. Grant us the gift of a straight conscience. So will our lives give praise and glory to thee" (Liturgy of St. Dioscorus).

"Expound, O Lord, thy whole bidding to me; faithfully will I keep it. Enlighten me, to scan thy law closely, and keep true to it with all my heart. Eagerly I long to be guided in the way of thy obedience. Ever let my choice be set on thy will, not on covetous thoughts. Eyes have I none for vain phantoms; let me find life in following thy way. Establish now the truth of thy promise to one that serves and fears thee.... Each command of thine I embrace lovingly; do thou in thy faithfulness grant me life" (Ps. 118:33–40).

Thanksgiving 17

A Thought Before Saying One's Penance

"More than anything else, that sacramental element which is called satisfaction is an indication of the covenanted nature of Christian penitence. When we submit to the power of the keys in penance, we are made to perform acts which have a value entirely beyond their human and external import" (Vonier, *Christianus*).

For Perseverance

"Our first principle is that temptations are not sins. Our second principle is: Temptations must not be fought directly. Temptation means to lead me to sin, to allure and entice me, to urge me to sin. The stronger the temptation, the greater the allurement. Therefore temptations must not be fought directly, because by such means the adversary becomes stronger than weaker. What is fought against is considered as serious and important. Accidental trifles are overlooked rather than fought. Internal psychical processes, especially of a predominantly emotional nature, are nourished and strengthened by the attention paid to them. The more attention is paid to fear and worry, the greater their power. Temptation rises from the background of consciousness, vague and weak. When we focus our attention on it in order to fight it, taking aim, as it were, it is dragged from the background to the front of the stage into the very limelight. Before the fight has even started, the adversary has thus been made strong and powerful" (R. Graef, *The Sacrament of Peace*).

"Jesus, make me persevere in virtue and a good life, and never give over thy service till thou bringest me to thy kingdom. In all pious customs and holy duties, in my honest and necessary employments, continue and strengthen, O Lord, my soul and body. Is my life anything but a pilgrimage on earth towards the new Jerusalem, to which he that sitteth down, or turneth out of the way, can never arrive? O Jesus, make me always consider thy blessed example; through how much pain and how little pleasure thou didst press on to a bitter death, that being the way to a glorious resurrection. Make me, O Redeemer, seriously weigh those severe words of thine — he only that persevereth to the end shall be saved" (Jesus Psalter).

"Do thou guide thy steps … as in my presence with an undivided heart and steadfastly; do thou fulfil all that I command, hold true to my observances and decrees" (3 Kings [1 Kings] 9:4).

In Gratitude

"Sweet it is to praise the Lord, to sing, most High God, in honour of thy name; to proclaim thy mercy and faithfulness at daybreak and at the fall of night" (Ps. 91:1–9).

"Even after the offence has been pardoned and remitted, it must remain, none the less, an object of regret and detestation, and it will be the one desire of our hearts to make amends to God; for when love is sincere, it is pained at the memory of the slights and outrages it has inflicted in the past. It is pained, too, at the thought of the offences committed by others, and for this reason hastens to make reparation for these also" (Galtier, *Sin and Penance*).

> "To world of worlds without ending,
> Thanked be thou, Jesus, my King.
> All my heart I give it thee;
> Great right it is that so it be.
> With all my will I worship thee,
> Jesu, blessed may thou be"
> (*Lay Folks Mass Book*, fourteenth century).

"Thanks while yet thou livest, thanks while health and strength are still with thee, to praise God, and to take pride in his mercies" (Ecclus. [Sir.] 17:27).

In Forgiveness of Others, as We Have Been Forgiven

"Two things must never leave thee, kindness and loyalty" (Prov. 3:3).

"O Lord Jesus Christ, upon whose good will all things depend, whose will none may safely resist, who didst deign to be born, to die and to rise again, grant to us, through the mystery of thy five wounds, and the shedding of thy precious Blood, all thou seest necessary for us in soul and body; safeguard us from all temptations, and in all our difficulties, which indeed thou knowest, keep us loyal and strengthen us in thy service, even to the end. Grant us amendment of our lives and forgiveness of all our sins. Especially grant us the grace to love our brethren, both enemies and friends, that we may have joy without end among thy saints in heaven" (Roman Missal, fifteenth century).

For the Work of the Church, Christ's Body, Hindered by Our Sins

"*Tibi soli peccavi*, says the psalm, it is against thee alone I have sinned. But then we go on to discover that there are very few sins against God which do not affect our brethren. It is, indeed, difficult to reach God otherwise than through our brethren, and that applies equally to evil acts as to good" (Community of St. Séverin, *Confession*).

"Come, Lord Jesus, and even now take away what offends thee in thy kingdom, that is my soul, that thou mayest reign there as is thy right; for greed is here claiming a throne in me; conceit seeks to rule over me; pride desires to be my master; luxury says: I will reign. Ambition, criticism, envy, irritation, strive in me. Whose shall I be? For my part, I resist them so far as I can, I struggle with them to the best of my power. I call upon my Master, Jesus. I defend myself for his sake, since I know that he has all rights over me. I cling to him as my Lord and God, saying: I have no King but Jesus. Come, then, Lord, scatter them in thy strength, and do thou rule in me, for thou art my Lord and my God" (St. Bernard of Clairvaux).

Preparation 18

God and the Sinner

"And there was then a sinful woman in the city, who, hearing that he was at table in the Pharisee's house, brought a pot of ointment with her, and took her place behind him at his feet, weeping; then she began washing his feet with her tears, and drying them with her hair, kissing his feet, and anointing them with the ointment. His host, the Pharisee, saw it, and thought to himself, If this man were a prophet, he would know who this woman is that is touching him, and what kind of woman, a sinner. But Jesus answered him thus, Simon, I have a word for thy hearing. Tell it me, Master, he said. There was a creditor, who had two debtors; one owed him five hundred pieces of silver, the other fifty; they had no means of paying him, and he gave them both their discharge. And now tell me, which of them loves him the more? I suppose, Simon answered, that it is the one who had the greater debt discharged. And he said, Thou hast judged rightly. Then he turned towards the woman, and said to Simon, Dost thou see this woman? I came into thy house, and thou gavest me no water for my feet; she has washed my feet with her tears, and wiped them with her hair. Thou gavest me no kiss of greeting; she has never ceased to kiss my feet since I entered; thou didst not pour oil on my head; she has anointed my feet, and with ointment. And so, I tell thee, if great sins are forgiven her, she has also greatly loved. He loves little who has little forgiven him. Then he said to her, Thy sins are forgiven. And his

240

fellow guests thereupon thought to themselves, Who is this, that he even forgives sins? But he told the woman, Thy faith has saved thee; go in peace" (Luke 7:37–50).

The Value of the Sacrament

"Well for thee that fear caught at thy heart, and thou didst humble thyself before the Lord" (4 Kings [2 Kings] 22:19).

"However far the wickedness and weakness of man may extend, so far does the divine mercy reach, and the power and the efficacy of the sacramental absolution cover all.... The justified sinner becomes a new and changed being, interiorly sanctified and in very truth a child of God, a pure and holy creature. There is no more any trace, or even question of his sin; it is forgotten and everything is restored to him by his absolution, namely his dignity in the Church by the restoration of his lost rights.... Such is the overflowing of divine mercy! That he may entertain no doubts about what he has gained, the words of absolution are given to him as a visible pledge and assurance. Like Magdalen, he hears these consoling words: 'Go in peace, thy sins are forgiven thee.' The sinner can point out the very day, the hour, when his sins were forgiven him, for, as the pledge of the reality of his sacramental absolution, he has the infallible word of God, as well as the interior peace and consolation which the Holy Ghost infuses into the heart of the justified sinner. In no sacrament does the Holy Ghost pour out his sweet consolations in such full measure as in this sacrament and in the Holy Eucharist. It is as if he wished to remove the sting from penance and let the sinner taste sensibly of the sweetness of the kiss of reconciliation" (Meschler, *The Gift of Pentecost*).

Devotions for Confession

In Humility

"If anyone is to be my servant, he must follow my way; so shall my servant too be where I am. If anyone serves me, my Father will do him honour" (John 12:26).

"It is neither wise nor humble to persuade ourselves that we shall never sin. In the supreme and most sacred hours of life we must reckon with the possibility that we shall sin again. For this possibility always exists; it exists also in regard to mortal sins for those who have long been slaves of vice. If such persons, when making a good resolution, honestly and sincerely admit: 'I shall most likely fall again,' they act more prudently than those who, by a sort of self-deception, persuade themselves that they will never sin again" (Philip Scharsch and F. A. Marks, *Confession as a Means of Spiritual Progress*).

"May God come to us not only in the fullness of his grace, but dwelling in our hearts enlighten our darkness and help our weakness by giving us the shield of his protection. If he is in us, who can lead us astray? Though human, of what are we not capable in him who strengthens us?" (St. Bernard of Clairvaux, *Sermons*).

"Thee only have my sins offended; thou wast the witness of my wrong-doing; thy warnings were deserved.... But thou art ever faithful to thy purpose; and now, in deep parables, thy wisdom has instructed me. Thou wilt sprinkle me with a wand of hyssop, and I shall be clean; washed, I shall be whiter than snow; a message thou wilt send me of good news and rejoicing, and the body that lies in the dust shall thrill with pride" (Ps. 50:6–10).

For Confidence

"Arise, and go on thy way, thy faith has brought thee recovery" (Luke 17:19).

"When, in the fullness of time, God appeared in Christ, reconciling the world to himself, the prophet and priest, the model and King of all men, he had one supreme work to perform which so predominated his sacred life on earth that his name was taken from it: 'Thou shalt call his name JESUS, for he shall save his people from their sins.' We should not even think of sin and its disastrous effects on our own souls without thinking at the same time of Christ, bearing our infirmities, stricken like a leper and afflicted, wounded for our iniquities, bruised for our sins, offering to his Father the fullest possible satisfaction for the sins of the world by dying on the cross" (E. J. Mahoney, *Sin and Repentance*).

"Those very hands, once nailed to the cross, can lift us up to safety if we are but loyal to thy commandments, if only we desire thy saving grace and keep thy law steadily in our thoughts.... Let us but own that we have strayed, and, like the sheep that was lost, he will seek us out and, laying us on his shoulders, he will restore us safe to his flock; for this he promised" (Arnobius Junior, fifth century).

"In thee evermore I find my stronghold; the God who upholds me; the God whose love meets me on the way" (Ps. 58:10).

For Self-Knowledge

"Never shalt thou thrive by keeping sin hidden; confess it and leave it, if thou wouldst find pardon" (Prov. 28:13).

"The very thought of halting in one's course and retracing one's steps back to God, which at a certain moment arises in the heart; the determination to surrender to that reactionary impulse against sin which makes its appearance in the will, we know not how, are all the effect of the goodness and mercy of God. He it is who, by ways and means whose secret is his own, without the necessity of miracles, nor with any resources but the simplest human psychology, has thus aroused in the inveterate or slothful sinner feelings of disquiet and horror at what had hitherto fascinated and captivated him. He it is who has prompted him to repair, or to endeavour to repair, the evil to which hitherto he had been indifferent. From every point of view, in fact, the beginning of conversion is the work of God himself" (Galtier, *Sin and Penance*).

"Thou never failest, O God, to teach rightly the children of thy Church. We beseech thee, therefore, always to help them to know what it is their duty to do, and firmly and confidently grasp the opportunity of doing it" (Gelasian Sacramentary, eighth century).

"Everyone should examine his own conduct; then he will be able to take the measure of his own worth" (Gal. 6:4).

For Greater Sorrow

"Think we the Lord's rod too light a punishment for our sins? Believe we that he is punishing us as his servants, to chasten, not to destroy" (Judith 8:26).

"Sorrow for sin is the one thing which is of absolute necessity in this sacrament. It is, therefore, the part of the confession on which I must most dwell. Sometimes, am I not apt to worry a great deal about my list of sins, taking surprising pains to discover every single fault and the exact number of times that I have fallen, and then hurrying over my actual sorrow as of less importance? Of course, I know perfectly well that the sorrow was really the more necessary of the two, but it does happen that I devote perhaps less time to it than to the other. Here, then, I must see what can be done to set this right.... I think, therefore, of my sins and then try to realize what they cost our Lord. In the house of the Pharisee, he, with the sensitiveness of perfect humanity, numbered up the slights that had been put upon him. What would he say to me? Nay, what is he saying to me? So many times have I been forgiven and so many times has that forgiveness been forgotten: all his love wasted! — the alabaster box filled with the most precious ointment broken across my heart: the fragrance still fills the world with wonder, and I forget. He is my lover, and he is waiting for me at the trysting-place. To confess is surely a little thing compared with what I have done; to confess it is even a satisfaction, it unburdens my soul of its great weight. But beyond confession is the sorrow" (Bede Jarrett, O.P.).

"O Son of God, for whose sake wert thou so humbled and who was the one so ardently loved? Whose was the benefit of such fatherly devotion? What soul was meant to grow in strength under such tender care? Upon whom did thy love fasten? Who knew such compassion? Indeed, I behaved ill, and thou didst pay the penalty for me, though the sin was mine; I was the criminal, and thou didst accept the guilt and the punishment. I walked in pride, and thou wert brought low; mine the vainglory and thine the shame. I was rebellious, and thou, obedient to the Father, paid the price. I yielded to my appetites and thou wert worn with fasting. I revelled in ease and sensuality whilst the very purity of thy love led thee to the cross. See, O King of Glory, see how thy love is made more manifest by my disloyalty, thy holiness by my sinfulness! What return, my King, my God, can I make for all thou hast done for me? Now, Creator of light, for the sake of the incredible sufferings of thy beloved Son, forgive my faults. I beseech thee, instead of my waywardness, grant me some of his loyalty; his obedience for my obstinacy, his modesty for my arrogance, his humility for my pride, his patience for my irritability, his tenderness for my hardness, his subjection for my disobedience, his tranquillity for my restlessness, his charm for my harshness, his gentleness for my resentment" (John of Fecamp, eleventh century).

"Blessed are they who have their faults forgiven, their transgressions buried deep; blessed is the man who is not guilty in the Lord's reckoning, the heart that hides no treason. While I kept my own secret, all day long I cried to thee in vain.... At last I made my transgression known to thee, and hid my sin no longer; I will be my own accuser, I said, and confess my fault to the Lord; and with that, thou didst remit the guilt of my sin. Let every devout soul, then, turn to thee in prayer while it has time to reach thee" (Ps. 31:1–6).

Resolution

"A man's ear once attentive to the discipline that brings life, no company shall be welcome thenceforward but the wise.... Heed reproof and be master of thy soul. It is the fear of the Lord that teaches the lessons of wisdom" (Prov. 15:31–33).

"Nobody becomes evil all at once. It is a slow and gradual process which leads the will eventually to commit mortal sin. Deliberate transgression of the law of God in small matters causes a habit of mind which grows accustomed to deflections from the moral order, and gradually disposes the sinner to depart from it in a serious matter.... 'He that is faithful in that which is least, is faithful also in that which is greater.' It is because we are creatures of habit, and because each deliberate sin paves the way to one slightly graver, that spiritual writers often refer to venial sin in terms which to the unthinking appear exaggerated. There is no need of warning from spiritual writers. Everyone knows from his own experience, and from the experience of others, that the commission of mortal sin is the result of a series of deliberate transgressions in smaller matters" (E. J. Mahoney, *Sin and Repentance*).

"O Lord, thou hast lighted in my soul a light by which I may always see aright, and truly I am oft affrighted at my ways of darkness. Enlighten that darkness, that I may feel my emotions to be under control; that I may rightly appreciate and justly seek what is worthy of my love" (St. Bernard of Clairvaux).

"May he turn our hearts towards himself, ready to follow every path he has shown us, keep every command, observance and decree.... Wholly be our hearts given to the Lord our God, ready (as we are ready this day) to live by his laws, and keep true to his commandments" (3 Kings [1 Kings] 5:58–61).

Thanksgiving 18

A Thought Before Saying One's Penance

"The sinner must not only make his dispositions beforehand, but having once and for all turned his back upon sin through contrition, he must also be prepared to undergo the penalty — some penalty at least. Hence the necessity, in order to receive absolution, of submitting to the expiation imposed by the representative of God.... He thus completes the expression of his sorrow. The meaning, too, of the sacramental rite, of which his acts are an integral part, now becomes more complete" (Galtier, *Sin and Penance*).

For Perseverance

"Aim at right living, faith, and hope, and love, and fellowship with all those who call on the name of the Lord with a pure heart" (2 Tim. 2:22).

"There are some who feel that they are not growing in grace, but there is no possible means of knowing by feeling. If you are doing everything God wants and not missing opportunities, then you are certainly growing, though you have little to show for it. Now, if you are converted after committing a lot of mortal sins and do not commit any more sins, that is progress. But if you have not committed any mortal sins and have reduced your venial sins to small numbers, you think, 'I do not see that I am growing any more; I have nothing to show.' Your growth is like that of a plant: it is your roots that are growing. You have nothing to show outside, but you are growing deeper and deeper into God. You are becoming more like our Lord. Your faith is stronger, although you do not recognise it. You have a deeper knowledge of God, there is real growth.... To ourselves it is an utterly humiliating progress. We get no credit for it: nobody notices it: there is no sudden change. But there is a steady turning towards the love of God, an increasing desire to give ourselves to God, to gain complete control of ourselves. Because this progress is humble, it is hall-marked with divinity, and because it is hidden, it is safe" (F. Devas, S.J., *What Law and Letter Kill*).

"Let my heart be obedient to thee, O Lord, that it may never feel itself to be the slave of any besetting sin, for its full happiness can only be in thee, whom to lose is ruin most bitter. Let me, then, not go after stolen pleasures, nor set my heart on possessions and ease rather than on thee, but let me look always towards thy mercy who rewardest each one according to his deeds" (Spanish Collect, seventh century).

"Not that I have already won the prize, already reached fulfilment. I only press on, in hope of winning the mastery, as Christ Jesus has won the mastery over me.... Forgetting what I have left behind, intent on what lies before, I press on with the goal in view" (Phil. 3:12–13).

In Gratitude

"Blessed be the living Lord, who is my God, praised be the God who rescues me" (2 Kings [2 Sam.] 22:47).

"Penance automatically leads to thanksgiving. Having received abundant graces, we must not forget to give thanks. He noticed that Simon the Pharisee failed to render him the more or less important attentions of politeness. When he had cured ten lepers, only one returned to give thanks. The Lord asked him: 'Were not ten made clean? And where are the nine? There is no one found to return and give glory to God but this stranger.' What we have received in the sacrament of penance is a grace far greater than what had been given to those ten lepers" (R. Graef, *The Sacrament of Peace*).

"There is a tender joy about this cross, for on this tree our God did offer up his life, and on that rood my life hung that my life might be founded in God. What return of living, O Christ, can I make thee for my life save to take the chalice of my salvation, offered at thy hands, for me to drink?... For thou, O Christ, didst pay, not thy own debts but mine. What love can match thine? Thou, my Lord, wert found in bearing like a slave that thy servant might be as thou. Shall I not think all this a wondrous interchange — our eternal salvation for what is passing, to yield but the earthly to have heaven? Than with thy cross, O God, couldst thou have me more dearly bought?" (St. Paulinus of Nola, fifth century).

"In that evil day he came to my side; the Lord upheld me, and brought me out into freedom again; his great love befriended me. And still, as he sees me dutiful, the Lord will requite me; as he sees me guiltless in act, he will make return" (2 Kings [2 Sam.] 22:19–21).

In Forgiveness of Others, as We Have Been Forgiven

"Do not nurse resentment against thy brother; put thyself in the right by confronting him with his fault" (Lev. 19:17).

"O God, the Lover of peace and charity, grant true peace and charity to all our enemies; give them pardon of their sins, and protect us against the harm they would do to us" (Roman Missal).

For the Work of the Church, Christ's Body, Hindered by Our Sins

"The *Christianus poenitens* has remained the same type through all the ages, he has understood with undiminished clearness that not through his own efforts but through the operation of a divine dispensation, through the workings of a sacramental system in which he is only a partner, justice is re-established and the balance of sanctity redressed. There are the sweet tears of personal repentance, there is the most piercing of soul-pains, that of having offended One who is the more lovable for having allowed himself to be insulted by us, there is the anger with our own flesh for having rebelled against eternal Beauty. These graces, for graces they are indeed, may appear at first sight to be only the individual intercourse of the soul with God. But this would be an imperfect understanding of the movements of grace. It is the Spirit that animates the whole mystical Body of Christ which brings forth these unspeakable groanings of the repentant soul. A loss is made good, and the reparation has its repercussion in heaven where the angels rejoice over one sinner doing penance" (Vonier, *Christianus*).

"O Lord Jesus Christ, unspeakable joy of Christians, to whose power and peaceful reign there shall be no end, give us grace to be loyal subjects of our King, that the sweet yoke of thy rule may ever find acceptance in us to our lasting nobility. Free us from all that is not according to thy will; every way make us thine, that nothing in us may hinder what thou wouldst do through us, nor disturb thy rule over us. Do thou, who reignest King of kings, alone possess us now and always" (Gothic Breviary, seventh century).

Preparation 19

God and the Sinner

"Beloved, we are sons of God even now, and what we shall be hereafter, has not been made known as yet. But we know that when he comes we shall be like him; we shall see him, then, as he is. Now, a man who rests these hopes in God lives a life of holiness; God, too, is holy.

"The man who commits sin, violates order; sin of its nature is disorder. You know well enough that when God revealed himself, it was to take away our sins; there is no sinfulness in him, and no one can dwell in him and be a sinner. The sinner must be one who has failed to see him, failed to recognize him. Little children, do not allow anybody to mislead you; the man who lives right is the man who is right with God; God, too, is right in all his dealings. The man who lives sinfully takes his character from the devil; the devil was a sinner from the first. If the Son of God was revealed to us, it was so that he might undo what the devil had done, and if a man is born of God, he does not live sinfully, he is true to his parentage; he cannot be a sinner, if he is born of God.... My little children, let us show our love by the true test of action, not by taking phrases on our lips. That proves to us that we take our character from the truth, and we shall be able to satisfy our consciences before God; if our consciences condemn us, it is because God is above conscience, and nothing is hidden from him. Beloved, if conscience does not condemn us, we can appear boldly before God, and he will grant all our requests, since we are keeping his

252

commandments, and living as he would see us live. What he commands is, that we should have faith in the name of his Son Jesus Christ, and at his command should love one another. When a man keeps his commandments, it means that he is dwelling in God, and God in him. This is our proof that he is really dwelling in us, through the gift of his Spirit" (1 John 3:2–24).

The Value of the Sacrament

"If our heart condemn us, God is greater than our heart, and knoweth all things" (1 John 3:20).

"The saying is inscrutable. . . . The condemnation of the heart comes from far away. The distance from which it comes is beyond measure. It comes from the very roots of life. There is a kind of wrong to which a name can be given, but from this wrong there emerges something it is impossible to put into words. Life itself condemns us. Life reproaches us with having wronged life itself. . . . It has a depth and a grief far greater than any other.

"In the condemnation of the heart it is God himself who condemns. Wrong has been done to *him*. Wrong has been done to the gentle and holy life that he has awakened in the heart, to the holy trust that binds him to his child. How can man's self-defence reach these depths?

"What possible help is there? John says: 'If our heart condemn us, God is greater than our heart.' Do you observe that this answer comes from the same depths as the condemnation itself? The answer is not: You have done right. Your intentions were good. Be of good cheer. No, the answer is: God is greater than thy heart.

"The heart is great. That is the first thing, and it is amazing that it should be said at all. But God is still greater. The weight of the love to which wrong has been done is so great that it must sink. God is the sea of greatness where everything heavy is made light. The wrong that has been done to life is great. God is the Creator, and God is Life and Grace. He is greater than everything. The holiness to which wrong has been done partakes of the dignity of God. His trust has been infringed. That is terrible. But he himself, his magnanimity, his creative love is greater than all this wrong.... God says: Give these things their full weight. Then I will come to you. I am God. And when he comes the creature will become clear to itself" (R. Guardini, *The Living God*).

In Humility

"Judge me no more; pity and comfort thy servant as thou hast promised. Judge me no more; pardon and life for one that loves thy will.... Jealously let my heart observe thy bidding; let me not hope in vain" (Ps. 118:76–80).

"The practising Catholic receives this sacrament so often that he is sometimes apt to forget that it is a sacrament, a momentous event in his life. For those in mortal sin, confession is like a new baptism.... We should therefore remind ourselves of this and strive to make our confessions the notable occurrences they should be. In them we are entering into sacramental union with Christ on the cross.... Since this is so, and since many of the effects of the sacrament are increased by fervour, we should try to be as fervent in its reception as possible. It not merely forgives our sins, it also gives strength for the future. Penitents, however, who are struggling against some habit of sin, often fail to secure the full benefit of their confessions because they do not make effort enough when they receive the sacrament" (H. Harrington, *The Sacrament of Penance*).

"Why was it, O Lord? What good thing didst thou see in me, a sinner? 'What is man, that thou art mindful of him, and the son of man that thou visitest him?' This poor flesh of mine, this weak sinful soul, which has no life except in thy grace, thou didst set thy love upon it. Complete thy work, O Lord, and as thou hast loved me from the beginning, so make me love thee unto the end" (Newman, *Meditations and Devotions*).

"Direct my way, Lord, as thou wilt, teach me thy own paths. Ever let thy truth guide and teach me, O God, my deliverer, my abiding hope. Forget not, Lord, thy pity, thy mercies of long ago. Give heed no more to the sins and follies of my youth, but think mercifully of me, as thou, Lord, art ever gracious. How gracious is the Lord, how faithful; light of the traveller that has missed his path! In his own laws he will train the humble; in his own paths, the obedient he will guide" (Ps. 24:3–9).

For Confidence

"Jesus said to them, it is not those who are in health that have need of the physician, it is those who are sick. I have come to call sinners, not the just" (Mark 2:17).

"The heavenly Father calls us to his Son by the inspiration of his grace. Like the Magi, as soon as the star shines in our hearts, we should instantly leave all: our sins, the occasions of sin, evil habits, infidelities, imperfections, attachment to creatures. Taking no account of criticism, nor the opinion of men, nor the difficulties of the work to be done, we should set out at once to seek Jesus. He wills this, whether we have lost him by mortal sin, or whether, already possessing him by sanctifying grace, he calls us to a closer and more intimate union with himself. *Vidimus stellam:* Lord, I have seen thy star, and I come to thee: What wilt thou have me to do?" (Marmion, *Christ in His Mysteries*).

"We have a very good friend in Christ. We look at him as man; we think of his moments of weakness and times of trial, and he becomes our companion. Once we have made a habit of thinking of him in this way, it becomes very easy to find him at our side" (St. Teresa).

"The Lord will aid and deliver them, and preserve them from the power of wickedness, because they put their trust in him" (Ps. 36:40).

For Self-Knowledge

"There is one who enlightens every soul born into the world" (John 1:9).

"For the sacrament of penance examination of conscience is, of course, a necessity. But for the health of our inner life, it is well not to content ourselves with that, but to make a *habit* of self-examination and to practise it every day of our lives. It is, perhaps, our best way of obeying that first part of that command of our Lord: 'Watch and pray.' Watchfulness, vigilance must be added to prayer. Watchfulness against enemies without and within. This self-examination, moreover, brings many advantages to our inner life. It helps towards self-knowledge, one of the highest aims of the philosophers of old; self-knowledge ought to lead to humility, that virtue so essentially Christian; it aids in the correction of faults and the avoidance of dangers; it reveals to us the motives that underlie our actions; it ought to furnish answers to heart-searching questions: How do I stand in God's sight? Is there anything, any obstacle, between my soul and God? Lastly, it includes contrition and keeps us ever prepared for the sacrament of penance" (S. J. Brown, *From God to God*).

"Come to us, O Lord, thou who knowest the real worth of all in this world.... Permit us not to dwell in it with bemused and uncertain minds, but teach us to look steadily for truth. So we shall lay the foundations of our faith, not on vague feelings, which the slightest setback may trouble, but upon that firm rock whose strength is thyself" (Gothic Breviary, seventh century).

"But see, thy heart once guided aright, thy hands outspread to him in prayer, thou hast but to cleanse thy hands of their wrong-doing.... Then thou mayest lift up thy head again, free from reproach, waver no more, tremble no more" (Job 11:13–15).

For Greater Sorrow

"The Lord's acts are acts of mercy" (Ps. 102:6).

"It is a source of genuine wonder to pious souls outside the Church that many Catholics frequent the confessional with so little apparent spiritual advancement. It has been said, in consequence, that Catholics may commit grievous sin in the comforting knowledge that they can 'make everything right' in a subsequent confession. While this is a libel upon good Catholics, it is clear that scandal is often given. The cause may be a mistaken concentration on confession as apart from contrition in the reception of the sacrament. Let it be said at once, therefore, that the reality of sorrow for sin, which is of paramount importance, can only be gauged by the sincerity and firmness of the purpose of amendment. No one can make an honest confession unless he is prepared by God's grace to forsake the dangerous occasions of sin" (J. C. Heenan, *Confession*).

"O gracious God, O Saviour sweet,
O Jesus, think on me,
And suffer me to kiss thy feet,
Though late I come to thee.

"Behold, dear Lord, I come to thee,
With sorrow and with shame,
For when thy bitter wounds I see,
I know I cause the same.

"Wherefore my soul doth loathe the things
Which gave it once delight,
And unto thee, the King of kings,
Would mount with all her might"
(Ven. Nicholas Postgate, *Lyra Martyrum*).

"Listen to my voice, Lord, when I cry to thee; hear and spare. True to my heart's promise, I have eyes only for thee; I long, Lord, for thy presence. Do not hide thy face, do not turn away from thy servant in anger, but give me still thy aid; do not forsake me, do not neglect me, O God, my defender. Father and mother may neglect me, but the Lord takes me into his care. Lord, show me the way thou hast chosen for me, guide me into the right path.... My faith is, I will yet live to see the Lord's mercies. Wait patiently for the Lord to help thee; be brave, and let thy heart take comfort" (Ps. 26:7–14).

Resolution

"If you have any love for me, you must keep the commandments which I give you; and then I will ask the Father, and he will give you another to befriend you, one who is to dwell continually with you for ever. It is the truth-giving Spirit, for whom the world can find no room, because it cannot see him, cannot recognize him. But you are to recognize him; he will be continually at your side, nay, he will be in you.... The man who loves me is the man who keeps the commandments he has from me; and he who loves me will win my Father's love, and I too will love him, and will reveal myself to him.... If a man has any love for me, he will be true to my word; and then he will win my Father's love, and we will both come to him; whereas the man who has no love for me lets my sayings pass him by.... Peace is my bequest to you, and the peace which I give you is mine to give; I do not give peace as the world gives it. Do not let your heart be distressed, or play the coward" (John 14:15–27).

"There is the struggle against the special defects that may beset and weaken the divine life. In one it is self-love; in another levity of mind; in this one, jealousy or anger; in that one, sensuality or sloth. These defects, if not resisted, are the occasion of a thousand sins and voluntary infidelities that hinder God's action in us. However little these vices may be apparent, our Lord expects of us that we should take the trouble to see them, and that we should labour generously by constant watchfulness over ourselves ... to extirpate them. He expects us to take no respite until the roots of these vices are so weakened that they can no longer spring up and bear fruit. For the more these roots decrease, the more the divine life grows strong within us, because it has great liberty to unfold" (Marmion, *Christ the Life of the Soul*).

"With the aid of his grace, I will create in me a deep hatred and sorrow for my past sins. I will try hard to detest sin, as much as I have ever loved it. Into God's hands I put myself, not by halves, but unreservedly. I promise thee, O Lord, with the help of thy grace, to keep out of the way of temptation, to avoid all occasions of sin, to turn at once from the voice of the evil One, to be regular in my prayers, so as to die to sin, that thou mayest not have died for me on the cross in vain" (Newman, *Meditations and Devotions*).

"Ah, blessed they ... who follow the law of the Lord! Ah, blessed they who study his decrees, make him the whole quest of their lives!... Attentive to all thy commandments, I go my way undismayed. A true heart's worship thou shalt have, thy just awards prompting me. All shall be done as thy laws demand" (Ps. 118:1–8).

Thanksgiving 19

A Thought Before Saying One's Penance

"My love, now renewed, urges me to this, for I cannot love and at the same time just simply resign myself to having not loved. I am not satisfied myself, and so from now on all the powers of a more ardent love will be used to make up for a past without love or with too little. This is what is suggested by sacramental penance and is its real and most moving significance" (Community of St. Sévérin, *Confession*).

For Perseverance

"Draw your strength from the Lord, from that mastery which his power supplies. You must wear all the weapons in God's armoury if you would find strength to resist.... Use every kind of prayer and supplication; pray at all times in the spirit; keep awake to that end with all perseverance" (Eph. 6:10–18).

"It would be unfortunate if those whose confessions are distressingly similar week by week were to deduce ... that such confessions are of no avail. It is obvious that whilst a person is living in the same surroundings and with the same companions, temptations will be more or less similar, and in consequence the falls into sin will be the same. For everyone a certain routine is inevitable. But an honest penitent, one who is in earnest about contrition, will make it his constant endeavour to avoid routine in this sense at least, that he will strive to decrease the number of his sins" (J. C. Heenan, *Confession*).

"O blessed Lord, thou hast overcome me; thou hast utterly bound me by thy grace and manifold benefits to be thy servant. From henceforth I shall never go from thee" (St. John Fisher).

"So, I do not run my course like a man in doubt of his goal; I do not fight my battle like a man who wastes his blows on the air" (1 Cor. 9:26).

In Gratitude

"How true the Lord is to all his promises, how high above us in all his dealings" (Ps. 144:13).

"This is the great mystery of the forgiveness of sins: *I believe in the forgiveness of sins*. It is the mystery of justice and love of God, of a God made man, who, dying on the cross on Calvary for the salvation of the world, paid to his heavenly Father, in his own Blood, the price of pardon for man's sins, and after his resurrection, and before his ascension, left to his Church the keys of heaven to forgive or retain sins.... (It is) the infinite goodness of God, who has designed, by using the secret conversation of priest and penitent, to set up an inviolable tribunal for the reconciliation of man with God and for his forgiveness, no matter how great the burden of sin that weighs on a repentant soul. In bringing straying souls back to good and making them heirs to a life of blessedness enabling them to attain the divine vision, the holy Church is clearly seen as the mother of saints, while she teaches that reconciliation with God and friendship with him constitute the essence of salvation" (Pius XII).

"Thee, adorable Lord and God, we thank, and praise and glorify thy name before all else. We make due thanksgiving, not indeed according to the measure of thy gifts to us, only as much as is in our power to do. So we confess that all we have and hold is thy gift, and that our life, and our every vital movement, is of thee from whom comes all our energy of soul and body; for it was thou who fashioned us in every link of our being. And all that we are thou hast given into the custody of our human will that we might guard this being of ours, even as a man would guard his home to live and move in as he willed. Therefore, let us so place all our actions under the direction of our intelligence that of them we may make whole-hearted offering to thee in heaven, for all is thine" (Liturgy of St. Dioscorus).

"So would thy own nature manifest a father's universal love" (Wisd. 16:21).

In Forgiveness of Others, as We Have Been Forgiven

"My heavenly Father will deal with you, if brother does not forgive brother with all his heart" (Matt. 18:35).

"Let it be thyself, O Lord, who art the true searcher of hearts, who will deliver us from those who do us harm. Grant us thy own divine patience and a firm control of our thoughts, that to our enemies we do not return evil for evil" (Roman Collect, fifth century).

For the Work of the Church, Christ's Body, Hindered by Our Sins

"As happens in every family and in every society, the more valiant and the more courageous members — in this case, the more innocent and the more generous — offer their prayers, their service, their labours, their privations and their sufferings, for the greater advantage of the rest; and these, thanks to that vital union which, in spite of their sinfulness, they preserve with the whole body and with their Head, can draw benefit from the surplus resources thus accumulated.... In this manner the Church collectively assists each one of her members in freeing himself more completely from the remains of sin. Thus are realised the words of St. Paul, 'God hath so tempered the body, that the members might be mutually careful one for another. And if one member suffer anything, all the members suffer with it.... Now you are (together) the body of Christ, and individually his members" (Galtier, *Sin and Penance*).

"We thank thee, O holy Lord, Father almighty, that thou didst will to give us life in thy own image, that so we might strive after thy example in the ways of gentleness and justice. And that ideal we would the more swiftly achieve did we but love thee as our Creator, and generously love each other as thy children" (Leonine Sacramentary, seventh century).

Preparation 20

God and the Sinner

"Peter was in the court without, and one of the maidservants of the high priest came by: she saw Peter warming himself, and said, looking closely at him, Thou too wast with Jesus the Nazarene. Whereupon he denied it; I know nothing of it, I do not understand what thou meanest. Then he went out into the porch and the cock crew. Again the maid looked at him, and said to the bystanders, This is one of them. And again he denied it. Then, a little while afterwards, the bystanders said to Peter, It is certain that thou art one of them; why, thou art a Galilean. And he fell to calling down curses on himself and swearing, I do not know the man you speak of. Then came the second cock-crow; and Peter remembered the word Jesus had said to him, Before the second cock-crow thou wilt thrice deny me. And all at once he burst out weeping" (Mark 14:66–72).

"So Jesus came up and took bread which he gave to them, and fish as well. Thus Jesus appeared to his disciples a third time after his rising from the dead. And when they had eaten, Jesus said to Simon Peter, Simon, son of John, dost thou care for me more than these others? Yes, Lord, he told him, thou knowest well that I love thee. And he said to him, Feed my lambs. And again, a second time, he asked him, Simon, son of John, dost thou care for me? Yes, Lord, thou knowest well that I love thee. He said to him, Tend my shearlings. Then he asked him a third question, Simon, son of John, dost thou love me?

Peter was deeply moved when he was asked a third time, Dost thou love me? and said to him, Lord, thou knowest all things; thou canst tell that I love thee. Jesus said to him, Feed my sheep" (John 21:13–17).

The Value of the Sacrament

"He will not snap the staff that is already crushed, or put out the wick that still smoulders; but at last he will establish right order unfailingly. Not with sternness, not with violence" (Isa. 42:3–4).

"It is a special feature of Jesus that his judgement is never warped and his attitude is never altered by what men may have said or done to him. He does not store up grievances; he is never vindictive; he goes on as if nothing were amiss. Peter had denied him; but on the Resurrection day he appeared to Peter all alone. All had deserted him; but as soon as they were sufficiently prepared he stood in their midst as if nothing had gone wrong. By the Lake of Galilee, as much as he is able, he shows them that he is his old self; it is as such that John recognizes him. Then he re-elects his Vicar; all the past is forgotten and they will begin again. Jesus to his own is very faithful, yes, even when his own are not what they should be, as is witnessed again and again from Judas to myself; having given them a commission he stands by them. I would that I could be equally faithful to him.... I can only hope, and resolve, and pray, and try.

"And all this in spite of my nothingness, my weakness, sinfulness; in spite of my self-indulgence and human frailty; in spite of the many clouds and barriers raised up entirely by myself to keep him out.

"He stands at the door and watches; there is no remissness on his part. He does not turn away because I am a sorry case; no matter what I am or what I do, no matter what I fail to do, he waits and gives, bearing with me, pitying me, pouring himself into me whenever I allow him an entrance.

"Jesus hates sin, but he never ceased to love the sinner; he made a marked distinction between the two. He condemned sin; he condemned still more persistence in sin; he condemned even sinners in general, who would not repent but would insist on dying in their sin; he never condemned a single individual sinner.

"That we may understand his mind, let us ask ourselves what is our own attitude towards one whom we deeply love. Though he may hurt us, though he may do us wrong, though he may wreck his own life, still, if the love remains and is not killed, we easily forgive and forget; we almost feel hurt by too much confession and apology, we try to make things go on as they had been before.

"Jesus Christ is more sensitive and loving than we are, and the Gospels confirm it on every page. 'While he was yet a great way off the father saw him and running to him fell upon his neck and kissed him.' This is the typical attitude; contrition of heart first, not confession; forgiveness before the Prodigal has yet spoken a word, forgiveness so complete that the offence is ignored. The Prodigal has planned his confession, all that he will say; when he does begin to speak he is interrupted, the father will hear no more.

"The offence is forgotten, it is given another name; the offender is taken back, more honoured than ever before; not as an offender on trial, not on conditions, but as a loved one lost and found" (Abp. Goodier, S.J., *The Life That Is Light*).

In Humility

"Kiss the rod; do not brave the Lord's anger, and go astray from the sure path" (Ps. 2:12).

"He alone can say: 'I am who am.' My own finiteness is the veil which hides him from me. But if I am God's veil — and the very idea is breath-taking — he stands on the other side of my finiteness. It may be objected that it is not only the fact that I am finite that separates me from God, not only the fact that I belong to the world that causes him who 'lives in heaven' to withdraw into the 'inaccessible light,' but the fact that I am sinful. My sin makes me not merely the veil that hides me from God but the 'darkness' that 'comprehendeth him not.' That is certainly true. And yet — and yet! I am still his creature and his image in spite of all my sin. Redemption has taken place and his grace holds sway. And the more absolutely I accept my finiteness, the deeper the humility of my heart, the more honestly I repent my sin — the more it may be granted to me to be mysteriously aware of 'the other side' " (R. Guardini, *The Living God*).

"O beloved Father, I am in thy hands; I bow myself down under the rod of thy correction. Strike thou my back and my neck, that I may bend my crookedness to thy will. Make me a true and humble disciple, as thou art well wont to do, so that I may walk according to thy every nod. To thee I commit myself, and all that is mine, for thy correction. It is better to be chastised here than hereafter. Thou knowest all things and each thing singly, and nothing in man's conscience is hidden from thee. Thou knowest things to come before they happen; and thou needest no man to teach or warn thee of what is being done on earth. Thou knowest what is expedient for my progress, and how greatly tribulation serves to scour off the rust of sin. Do with me according to thy desired good pleasure; and despise not my sinful life, which is known to no one better or more clearly than to thyself" (Thomas à Kempis, *The Imitation of Christ*, bk. 3, 50).

"My God, thou readest our hearts, I know it well, and it is the honest heart thou lovest" (1 Par. [1 Chron.] 29:17).

For Confidence

"Blessed is the man who does not lose confidence in me" (Matt. 11:6).

"We have no doubt as to the power and wisdom of God as Maker and ruler of the universe. He knows all and can do all things. But the thought of God's Fatherhood gives us the further assurance that this power and wisdom will be used on our behalf. . . . And feeling this assurance about the present and future, we feel a like assurance about the past. Alas, our past, even that of ordinary good men and women, is such that the thought of it might well fill us with fear as well as with sorrow, were it not for the one thought — God is my Father. That thought fills me with childlike confidence that all has been forgiven and forgotten. Not to be sure of that is to fail in filial trust towards our Father in heaven. Think of the Father of the Prodigal. Can you imagine him on his son's return going into the son's past with minute and judicial care, carefully weighing the amount of contrition expended on each sin, making sure that the prodigal has accused himself of every vice and crime of which he has been guilty and of all their details? Such an idea would be wholly out of keeping with the parable as told by our Lord, absolutely contrary to its obvious spirit.

"Once you have done, or tried your best to do, *what according to your lights at the time* you knew to be required for a good confession, you ought to banish for ever from your mind all anxiety about the past. Your Father has received you back, and it is his will to give you that most precious boon of the spiritual life — peace of conscience. It was to give you this peace that our Lord instituted the sacrament of penance. Listen to him saying to you: 'Peace I leave with you, my peace I give unto you. Let not your heart be troubled nor let it be afraid'" (Stephen J. Brown, S.J., *From God to God*).

"My Lord, my God, my sovereign Saviour, Jesus Christ, I beseech thee heartily that thou take me, a sinner, unto thy great mercy and grace. For indeed I love thee with all my heart and mind, with all my might; nor do I really love anything so much that be on earth or above the earth as I do my sweet Lord Jesus Christ. And so far as I have hitherto failed to love and worship thee above all things as my Lord God, and my Saviour Jesus Christ, I now pray thee meekly and with contrite heart to forgive my long neglect of the great love thou hast shown me when thou didst offer thy all-glorious body, God-man, to be crucified there on the cross.... And, having steadfast remembrance of this in my heart, I doubt not, my Saviour Jesus Christ, that thou wilt be near to me with thy glorious presence comforting me in body and soul, and at the last thou wilt bring me unto thy everlasting joy which shall have no ending" (Processional of the Nuns of Chester, fifteenth century).

"Thou art all-merciful, as befits the almighty, and dost overlook our human slips, in hope of our repentance" (Wisd. 11:24).

For Self-Knowledge

"May your inward eye be enlightened, so that you may understand to what hopes he has called you" (Eph. 1:18).

"If the knowledge we possess, from reason and from revelation, concerning the evil of sin, is to be a living force in regulating our own lives, we must, by continual meditation and reflection, bring it home to our minds. It is one thing to understand the meaning of sin, and view it with abhorrence in general, and say with David, 'As the Lord liveth, the man that has done this thing is a child of death.' It is another thing to hear the accusing voice of the prophet saying to us individually, 'Thou art the man,' and to see our own sins passing before our eyes, each an object of our own creation and belonging to us more intimately than any other of our possessions. The personal realisation of sin is the first preliminary to repentance" (E. J. Mahoney, *Sin and Repentance*).

"I show myself to thee, O great and eternal High priest, as I truly am, saying: 'For my sin is known to me.' I do, indeed, know my sinfulness, but in part only, and not as thou knowest it, nor yet as I myself am known by thee, whose seeing is brighter than the sun, holding in view the ways of men and gazing into the depths of their hearts. This heart of mine, O God, there is evil in it, and so much uncertainty that I scarce know it myself; but thou, Lord, art aware of our human fashioning, and of all things to the very depths of their being. Thou dost know also my heart and its sinfulness. Pardon me, then, my God, pardon me" (attributed to St. Anselm of Canterbury, twelfth century).

"Go and shew thyself to the priest" (Matt. 8:4).

For Greater Sorrow

"It is those I love that I correct and chasten; kindle thy generosity and repent. See where I stand at the door knocking" (Apoc. [Rev.] 3:19–20).

"God has told us that we are sinners, and it is unbelief not to take it seriously. 'If we say that we have no sin, we deceive ourselves and the truth is not in us. If we confess our sins, he is faithful and just to forgive our sins, and to cleanse us from all iniquity. If we say that we have not sinned, we make him a liar, and his word is not in us' (1 John 1:8–10). These words clearly state our condition before God, and point the path to true understanding. It does not follow that we should torment ourselves over our sinful ways. This also would be acting against truth and, moreover, could become a form of self-indulgence, which might have evil consequences. Obsession with the thought of sinfulness has invariably led either the person so obsessed — or a later generation — to some form of rebellion. Christian teaching about sin gives us a new understanding which encourages and enables us to strive for purer righteousness. The acknowledgment of our sins must not make us despondent and discouraged; on the contrary, it ought to call forth in us the desire for spiritual purification and renewal" (R. Guardini, *Prayer in Practice*).

"What dost thou especially require of a guilty and wretched sinner, but that he should be contrite, and humble himself for his sins? True contrition and humility of heart give hope of forgiveness; the troubled conscience is reconciled; lost grace is restored; man is secured from the wrath to come; and God and the penitent soul meet together in a holy kiss. Humble contrition for our sins is an acceptable sacrifice to thee, O Lord, far sweeter before thee than the odour of frankincense. This also is that pleasant ointment which thou didst will should be poured upon thy sacred feet, for a contrite and humbled heart thou hast never despised" (Thomas à Kempis, *The Imitation of Christ*, bk. 3, 52).

"O most tender and gentle Lord Jesus, when will my heart have a portion of thy perfections? When will my hard and stony heart, my unbelieving, my impure heart, my narrow, selfish heart, be melted and conformed to thine? O teach me so to contemplate thee that I may become like thee, and to love thee sincerely and simply as thou hast loved me" (Newman, *Meditations and Devotions*).

"Lord Almighty ... here be troubled hearts that plead with thee! Listen, Lord, and have mercy, none so merciful as thou; pardon the sins that lie open in thy sight" (Bar. 3:1–2).

Resolution

"The grace of God, our Saviour, has dawned on all men alike, schooling us to forgo irreverent thoughts and worldly appetites, and to live in this present world a life of order, of justice, and of holiness" (Titus 2:11).

"In how many ways God has chosen me! I need not even have been born. I am a Christian; I pray — I put myself into vital touch with God. Anyone has his 'special' purpose in life, simply because God cannot act without a purpose: but why should I have these special privileges unless he has some special purpose for me? O God, let me fulfil the whole of that special purpose! I cannot see what it is, or was, until I look back upon it from 'afterwards': but I know by faith that I am his true adopted son, brother of Jesus Christ, and 'son of his handmaiden'" (C. C. Martindale, S.J., *The Sweet Singer of Israel*).

"May God, who by his grace bids us keep in check our evil desires, grant that we obey his commandments. May he teach us to be heedful of his inspirations, and by orderly thinking bring our way of life under the rule of conscience. So doing, we shall look with confidence for the kindly mercy of the Father and the Son, and have here on earth true hope of an unfailing inheritance to come" (Benedictional of John Longlonde, sixteenth century).

"Every command of his, every utterance of his, cherished in my heart" (Job 23:12).

Thanksgiving 20

A Thought Before Saying One's Penance

"After the priest, Christ's minister, has imposed the necessary satisfaction, he repeats these words over us: 'May whatever good thou dost, and evil thou bearest, be to thee for the remission of thy sins, the increase of grace, and the reward of everlasting life.' This prayer is not essential to the sacrament, but as it has been ordained by the Church, besides containing teaching that the Church assuredly desires to see us put into practice, it has the value of a sacramental. By this prayer, the priest gives to our sufferings, to our acts of satisfaction, of expiation, of mortification, of reparation and patience which he thus links and unites with the sacrament, a special efficacy which our faith should not neglect to consider. The Council of Trent teaches on this subject a very consoling truth. It tells us that God is so munificent in his mercy that, not only the works of expiation that the priest imposes on us, or that we ourselves choose, but even all the sufferings inherent to our condition here below, all the temporal adversities which God sends or permits and we patiently support, serve, through Christ's merits, as satisfaction with the eternal Father" (Marmion, *Christ the Life of the Soul*).

For Perseverance

"And God, the giver of all grace ... will himself give you mastery, and steadiness and strength" (1 Pet. 5:10).

"Far from shifting responsibility on to the confessor, confession, it has well been said, makes the whole of life responsible. For each act now must be remembered (if possible), judged and honestly valued. No Catholic may say: 'Ah, I did so and so, but I don't want to remember it. I tried to forget it at once.' Not till you have looked at yourself, judged yourself, and resolved about your future. This very process, moreover, strengthens the will and prepares that better future, especially if a man sees well that confession as such has nothing directly to do with character, but that it is for him to consolidate it day by day" (C. C. Martindale, S.J., *The Faith of the Roman Church*).

"Unless thou, O Lord, dost keep watch and ward over us, our toil and effort will be in vain; for without thee we cannot live, and assuredly, without thee, we cannot find strength to live well. Since, then, all our striving needs thy help, let us never leave thy side, that thy grace may be with us in all we try to do" (Mozarabic Psalter, eleventh century).

"Here is reassurance when a man stumbles, support when he falls; soul uplifted, eyes enlightened, health and life and blessing bestowed" (Ecclus. [Sir.] 34:20).

In Gratitude

"Would he but reveal to thee the secrets of his wisdom, in its ordered variety! Then thou wouldst learn that the penalty he is exacting of thee is less, far less, than thy sins deserve" (Job 11:6).

"Let us often renew our renunciation of sin. You know that the 'character' given in baptism remains indelibly on the soul; and when we repeat the promises made at the hour of our initiation, a new virtue springs from the baptismal grace to strengthen our power of resistance against all that leads to sin: the suggestions of the devil, and the seductions of the world and the senses. It is thus that we can safeguard the life of grace within us. By this likewise we testify our lively gratitude to Christ Jesus for having taken upon himself our iniquities so as to deliver us from them. 'Who loved me,' said St Paul, on recalling this mystery of infinite charity — 'Who loved me, and delivered himself for me.' May I live for him, for his glory, and no longer for myself, no longer to satisfy my covetousness, my pride, my ambition" (Marmion, *Christ in His Mysteries*).

"What return can I make to the Lord for so bringing these faults to my remembrance in such a way that my heart was not thereby affrighted? I will love thee, Lord; I will thank thee and confess to thy name because thou hast forgiven me such great evils" (St. Augustine, *Confessions*, bk. 2).

"I cried out to the Lord my God, and thou didst grant me recovery. So didst thou bring me back, Lord, from the place of shadows.... With pity the Lord heard me; the Lord himself, now, took my part. Thou hast turned my sadness into rejoicing; thou hast undone the sackcloth I wore, and girded me about with gladness. So may this heart never tire of singing praises; O Lord my God, I will give thanks to thee for ever" (Ps. 29:3–13).

In Forgiveness of Others, as We Have Been Forgiven

"Forget, I pray thee, the crime which thy brethren committed" (Gen. 50:17).

"O God of love and Giver of harmony, thou didst give us, through thy only-begotten Son, this counsel for our well-being, indeed a new commandment, that we should love one another even as thou dost love us, unworthy and wavering as we are. Grant to us, thy servants, that all our days, but especially and particularly now, we may have an easy forgetfulness of past injuries, a pure conscience, honest thoughts, and a heart that can sympathize with our neighbours" (St. Cyril of Alexandria).

For the Work of the Church, Christ's Body, Hindered by Our Sins

"Sin is an attack also on the general order of the world. Not only does it inflict suffering upon the immediate family or social group of the sinner or his victim, as happens in certain cases; it affects human society as a whole. In the divine plan, all mankind form one unit, an immense body, of which Christ is the head, and which is ordered entirely to the glory of God and the eternal happiness of every one of its members. Each in his own place and sphere must contribute to the common task; and, as a consequence, no one acts alone. Each forms part of that immense choir which, in heaven and upon earth, sings the glory of the Creator; and his discordant notes not only disturb the general harmony; they affect also each of the performers. In other words, the guilty acts of one person have their inevitable repercussion on the moral life of humanity as a whole. . . . Hence, in respect of each and every one of them, the sinner contracts a real debt" (Galtier, *Sin and Penance*).

"May God almighty grant us his blessing and may he, the source of all that is worthy and honourable, teach us the ways of upright life. So will there be found in us a care for chastity, restraint in all things, the sincerity of just living, the fullness of faith, the harmony of charity, the virtue of continence and above all kindly affection" (Benedictional of Canterbury, eleventh century, adapted).

Appendix: Examination of Conscience according to the Doctrine of the Christian Virtues

In examining our conscience, we are to consider how we have insulted God. We must form an idea of the circumstances in which we committed our sins, because we are obliged to avoid those circumstances as far as possible in future. The absence of an intention to do so means that we lack true contrition. We are also obliged to mention as far as possible the number of our mortal sins, and the circumstances which have increased our guilt or led us into further sin. We are not to conceal the fact of having caused others to sin, or of having given offence in any way by our misdeeds. If we are in doubt whether an action of ours was or was not sinful, we should include it in our confession and humbly ask the priest to help us form our conscience.

The following guide may be found helpful in the examination of conscience.

Faith

Faith in God is the virtue by which we give our full assent to all that God has revealed concerning Himself and Christ's redeeming work. If our faith is to be a true and living faith, it must be inseparably bound up with hope in God, with a firm belief that, God helping us, we shall one day possess that treasure in its entirety. Faith must also be bound up with the love of God.

Sins against faith in God fall under the first of the Ten Commandments. *We sin against this virtue:*

* ❖ when we willfully entertain doubts of God, of revelation, of the divine precepts of Holy Church
* ❖ when we deliberately risk our faith by reading or listening to anything contrary thereto
* ❖ when we behave superstitiously
* ❖ when we seldom or never meditate upon holy things

Hope

Hope in God is the virtue by which we trust that God, like a good Father, will direct all things here and hereafter for our good. It is God's will that the sinner should be converted and come to everlasting life. By the same token, if the sinner is lost, it is through his own fault.

We sin against hope in God:

* ❖ when we despair of God's goodness and of the strength of His peace
* ❖ when we expose ourselves to bodily or spiritual dangers, presuming on God's help

Love

Love of God is the chief of the three theological virtues. It will come to perfection in the glory of Heaven. We love God because He is infinitely preeminent, infinitely worthy to be loved for His own sake; and also because He is Himself our greatest happiness, and one day will be ours for ever in the glory of paradise.

We sin against the love of God:

❖ when we blaspheme, insulting His name with false or useless oaths, or using His name without need, or without respect (*second commandment*)

❖ when we defy Him by committing sacrilege, as by profaning some consecrated article or holy place or person vowed to God; by receiving the sacraments unworthily; by making an incomplete confession, or confessing without penitence

❖ when we show contempt for God, for God's word in holy Scripture, for Holy Church, for the saints; when we fail in Sunday observance (*third commandment*)

❖ when we repudiate God from timidity, or permit our neighbor, from fear of what others may think, to insult His name or the mysteries of revelation

❖ when we willfully neglect His worship, when we are not zealous to find joy in the eternal blessings, which are promised us (the sin of indolence)

❖ when we deny to God the minimum of worship and of penitence enjoined upon us by the Church's laws:
- presence at Mass on Sundays and holy days
- observance of the rules of fasting and abstinence
- yearly confession of mortal sins
- yearly communion at Easter

Love of Neighbor

We cannot love God truly without also loving our neighbor. Christ Himself has declared that the virtue of love for one's neighbor is as important as that of the love of God. We are to love our fellows because they are all without exception children of the same Father, and because Christ was willing to suffer death on the cross for the sake of all. We show this love when we desire our neighbor's eternal happiness and help him to the best of our ability to fall in with God's plan.

Love of our neighbor is also expressed in all its purity by giving him temporal help, by showing him a service even when the virtue of justice does not strictly oblige us to do so. It is an element in all the other virtues that bear on our dealings with our fellow men.

We sin against the love of our neighbor:

- ❖ when through excessive selfishness we fail to take an interest in the spiritual and material needs of others, and to help our neighbor as we ought, especially when circumstances (and therefore the will of God) bring us in contact with him
- ❖ when by word or deed, by carelessness or neglect, we give cause of scandal
- ❖ when we deny to others, and especially to those with whom we are in constant touch, the goodwill and esteem of which we do not wish to be ourselves deprived by others

The virtue of love for one's neighbor and the virtue of justice bid us respect our parents, obey them, and come to their help (*fourth commandment*). We are under a similar obligation to all our superiors and to our country.

Justice

Justice is the virtue by which we give to each his due. Sins against this virtue are in proportion to the harm done. These sins are especially grave when they involve injustice to our inferiors or to those for whose welfare we are responsible.

We sin against justice:

❖ when we kill or wound anyone without absolute necessity (*fifth commandment*); when we insult anyone

❖ when we are guilty of theft, or unlawful profit-making, or extortion, or wasting what should be saved up for our parents or our children, of unfair competition, of unjust suits at law (*seventh commandment*); when we make a bad use of time for which we are paid; when we are jealous of the lawful good of others (*tenth commandment*)

It is a sin crying for vengeance when we deprive a worker of his lawful pay; and again when we are dishonest or even careless in administering what belongs to widows, orphans, and the poor.

The *eighth commandment* also forbids us:

❖ to speak against the truth

❖ to injure our neighbor's reputation by a lie (calumny)

❖ to disclose our neighbor's faults without sufficient reason (detraction)

❖ to judge rashly of anyone

❖ to divulge professional secrets

❖ to encourage or tolerate any of these sins

It is not enough to repent of sins against justice; we must also be firmly resolved to make restitution: that is, to undo as best we may the harm we have done. If direct reparation is no longer possible, we are bound to get rid of the goods we have acquired unjustly. Here we must scrupulously carry out the directions of our confessor.

Temperance and Chastity

On the cardinal virtue of temperance depends, first of all, the virtue of chastity, which regulates the function of sex and thereby brings us to the love of God. In Christian marriage, the love of man and woman, including sexual relations and all other lawful expressions of love, is hallowed by the sign of Christ's love for the Church. That sign is the mystery which raises marriage contracted in presence of the Church to the dignity of a Sacrament. There are some who wish to follow Christ in His entire detachment and voluntarily abstain from sexual delights. In all ages, numbers of Christians have been divinely inspired to vow their whole life to continence.

The *sixth commandment* forbids sexual intercourse outside marriage. In general, it also forbids all manifestations of love between a man and a woman who are not either married or betrothed. Even the betrothed are bound to refrain from any action that might lead, human weakness being what it is, to sexual intercourse. In married life, husbands and wives are bound to show each other the love and mutual respect demanded by their marriage vows and by the sacredness of the marriage tie. They must never act purposely in any fashion that is contrary to the natural objects of married life.

It is a sin to arouse in oneself or in others, outside lawful married life, the pleasures that go with bodily union, whether by words, by action, or otherwise.

The *ninth commandment* forbids all willful desires tending towards actions forbidden by the sixth commandment.

In confessing sins against the sixth and ninth commandments, we must mention clearly, but not in detail, any circumstances that may heighten our guilt: as for example if we have sinned with a married person, with someone entrusted to our care, and the like.

We also sin against this virtue of temperance:

- ❖ when we eat without moderation at meals; when we knowingly drink to excess
- ❖ when we make an immoderate use of stimulants; or when we otherwise endanger our health

Appendix: Examination of Conscience

Fortitude and Humility

On the cardinal virtue of fortitude depends the virtue of humility, which leads us not to take credit to ourselves for qualities we have received by God's free gift and not to credit ourselves with qualities we do not really possess. Needless to say, the virtue of humility does not exclude the virtue of gratitude, which moves us to acknowledge that we have received all our gifts from God and to promise to serve Him by making the best possible use of them.

The sin against the virtue of humility is pride.

Sophia Institute

Sophia Institute is a nonprofit institution that seeks to nurture the spiritual, moral, and cultural life of souls and to spread the Gospel of Christ in conformity with the authentic teachings of the Roman Catholic Church.

Sophia Institute Press fulfills this mission by offering translations, reprints, and new publications that afford readers a rich source of the enduring wisdom of mankind.

Sophia Institute also operates the popular online resource CatholicExchange.com. *Catholic Exchange* provides world news from a Catholic perspective as well as daily devotionals and articles that will help readers to grow in holiness and live a life consistent with the teachings of the Church.

In 2013, Sophia Institute launched Sophia Teachers to renew and rebuild Catholic culture through service to Catholic education. With the goal of nurturing the spiritual, moral, and cultural life of souls, and an abiding respect for the role and work of teachers, we strive to provide materials and programs that are at once enlightening to the mind and ennobling to the heart; faithful and complete, as well as useful and practical.

Sophia Institute gratefully recognizes the Solidarity Association for preserving and encouraging the growth of our apostolate over the course of many years. Without their generous and timely support, this book would not be in your hands.

www.SophiaInstitute.com
www.CatholicExchange.com
www.SophiaTeachers.org

Sophia Institute Press® is a registered trademark of Sophia Institute. Sophia Institute is a tax-exempt institution as defined by the Internal Revenue Code, Section 501(c)(3). Tax ID 22-2548708.